Cantonese
Chinese
phrase book

Berlitz Publishing Company, Inc.

Princeton   Mexico City   Dublin   Eschborn   Singapore

Cover photo: Victor Carnuccio

ISBN 2-8315-6266-X
Second Printing January 1999
Printed in Spain.

Developed and produced for Berlitz Publishing Company by:
G&W Publishing Services, Oxfordshire, U.K.
Cantonese edition: Ms. Annie Mead, Ms. Joanne Wong, and Chen Ji.

Contents

Pronunciation

This section is designed to familiarize you with the sounds of Cantonese using our simplified phonetic transcription. You'll find the pronunciation of the Cantonese sounds explained below, together with their "imitated" equivalents. This system is used throughout the phrase book. When you see a word spelled phonetically, simply read the pronunciation as though it were English, noting any special rules.

The Cantonese dialect

Discounting Mandarin Chinese, the official language of the People's Republic of China (P.R.C.), there are nine other groups of dialects. Around 70 percent of the population speaks Mandarin, but this does not mean that it is their first language.

Cantonese is one of the main dialect groups and is spoken in Hong Kong, Macau, Guangdong, and Guangxi ➤ 223. Although Cantonese speakers read and write Mandarin Chinese, the Cantonese dialect is different in sentence structure, pronunciation, and to a certain extent grammar and vocabulary. This means that Cantonese speakers speak in one way (Cantonese dialect), but write in another way (Mandarin Chinese).

The written language

Chinese is not written using an alphabet, but with characters or ideograms. The system evolved from basic pictograms used by primitive hunter gatherers to record men, animals, and objects. Over thousands of years, however, this representational language has changed beyond recognition and, with the exception of a few characters, it is impossible to see how any particular character came to represent its current meaning.

Following the founding of the People's Republic of China, the government in Beijing set up a committee to reform the Chinese language. Some 2,200 characters were simplified. However, communities outside the P.R.C., notably Hong Kong and Taiwan, continue to use the traditional full-form characters. This factor further confuses the similarities and dissimilarities between Cantonese and Mandarin Chinese.

Today, about 56,000 ideograms exist, but many of these are obsolete. It is generally thought that a well-educated Chinese person today would know between 6,000 and 8,000 characters. To read a Chinese newspaper you will need to know 2,000 to 3,000 characters, but 1,200 to 1,500 would be enough to get the gist.

While the building block of the Chinese language is the single character, words are usually a combination of two or more characters ➤ 9.

Cantonese sounds

Cantonese is composed less of vowels and consonants than of syllables, consisting of a consonant and a vowel. It is also a language with a large number of homonyms (words of different meaning but with identical spelling). In reality, every syllable is pronounced with one of nine tones (e.g. high, rising, falling~rising, falling). It is very difficult for non-natives to even hear these tones, let alone reproduce them – hence the phonetic transliteration system used in this phrase book has been much simplified, and excludes tonal markers.

The phrase book also contains the Chinese script. If, despite your efforts, your listener does not seem to understand you, show him or her the book and indicate what you want to say.

Regional variations

There is some difference between terminology as used in Guangdong Province (mainland China) and Hong Kong/Macau. Where this is the case the phrases and dictionary listings give the Hong Kong usage first and, in parentheses, the usage in Guangdong Province ➤ 70.

Consonants

Letter	Approximate pronunciation	Symbol	Example	Pronunciation
b, ch, d, f, g, h, j, k, l, m, n, p, s, t, w, y	approximately as in English			
gw	like *gw* in *Gw*endoline	*gw*	貴	*gwai*
kw	like *qu* in *qu*ite	*qu*	裙	*qu-un*
mm	pronounce *mm* without opening the mouth	*mm*	唔	*mm*
ng	like *ng* in ly*ing*, but further back in the mouth	*ng*	我	*ngor*

Vowels and diphthongs

There are a large number of diphthongs or vowel sound combinations in Cantonese. Only a few of the more complex are given below. Remember that the phonetic system has been specifically designed so that you can simply read the pronunciation as though it were English.

Letter	Approximate pronunciation	Symbol	Example	Pronunciation
a	like *a* in b*a*th, long *a*	*a*	巴	*ba*
e	like *e* in l*e*t	*e*	啡	*fe*
i	like *ee* in b*ee*	*ee*	市	*see*
o	like *o* in g*o*	*o*	高	*go*
au	like *ow* in n*ow*, said with no emphasis	*au*	收	*sau*
un	like *un* in *un*der, but very short and quick	*un'*	樽	*jun'*
ut	like *ut* in c*ut*, but very short	*ut'*	出	*chut'*
ooi	like *oo* in z*oo* + *ee*	*oo-ee*	每	*moo-ee*

Basic Chinese characters

The chart gives some basic Chinese characters which still demonstrate the characters' origin in pictograms, e.g., the character for *mountain* looks very much like a mountain or hill. In addition, you will see how two characters can be combined to form another word that still has an obvious meaning when its two constituent parts are known, e.g., *fire* and *mountain* together give you the word *volcano*. You will also notice that some combinations have both a straightforward "concrete" meaning and an additional "abstract" or poetic meaning. However, this is at the simplest level only. There are many more cases of character combinations in which the meaning is not obvious even if the individual characters are known. In this case a student of the language would have to refer to the dictionary. Beyond two character combinations there are also three and multiple combinations. To add to the growing complexity, there are also single characters made up of parts of other characters. As you can see, written Chinese it is not as simple as it might first appear!

Some basic Chinese characters

山	mountain/hill	*saan*
火	fire	*for*
火山	volcano	*for saan*
水	water	*sur-ee*
山水	landscape, natural scenery	*saan sur-ee*
日	the sun, day	*yut*
月	the moon, month	*yu-eet*
日月	time (*poetic*)	*yut yu-eet*
上	upper, up, upward, previous	*surng*
下	under, down, downward, forthcoming	*ha*
風	wind	*f-owng*
雨	rain	*yu-ee*
風雨	the elements, trials and hardships	*f-owng yu-ee*
大	big	*daai*
小	small	*seeu*
大小	size	*daai seeu*
人	human being, person	*yun*
大人	grown-up	*daai yun*
小人	vile person, villain	*seeu yun*

Basic Expressions

ESSENTIAL

Yes.	是	*hai*
No.	不是	*mm hai*
Okay.	好	*ho*
Please.	請	*cheng/mm goy*
Thank you.	謝謝	*dor je/mm goy*
Thank you very much.	非常感謝	*dor je saai/mm goy saai*

Greetings/Apologies 問候和道歉

Hello./Hi!	你好！	*nay ho*
Good morning/afternoon.	早晨 / 你好。	*jo sun/nay ho*
Good evening.	你好。	*nay ho*
Good night.	晚安。	*jo tau*
Good-bye.	再見。	*joy g-in*
Excuse me! (getting attention)	請問！	*cheng mun/mm goy*
Excuse me. (May I get past?)	請讓一下。	*mm goy je je*
Excuse me!/Sorry!	對不起！	*dur-ee mm ju-ee*
Don't mention it.	不用客氣。	*mm sai haak hay*
Never mind.	不要緊。	*mm gun yeeu*

INTRODUCTIONS ➤ 118

Communication difficulties

溝通困難

Do you speak English?	你會說英語嗎？ *nay sick mm sick gong ying mun a*
Does anyone here speak English?	這裡有誰會說英語嗎？ *nay do yau mo yun sick gong ying mun a*
I don't speak (much) Cantonese.	我不（大）會說中文。 *ngor mm (hai gay) sick gong j-owng mun*
Could you speak more slowly?	請說慢點。 *mm goy gong maan dee*
Could you repeat that?	請再說一遍。 *cheng joy gong yut chee*
Excuse me? [Pardon?]	請再說一遍。 *cheng joy gong yut chee*
Please write it down.	請寫下來。 *mm goy se dai*
Can you translate this for me?	請替我翻譯一下。 *mm goy bong ngor faan yick yut ha*
What does this/that mean?	這／那是什麼意思？ *gum hai mut ye yee see a*
Please point to the phrase in the book.	請在這本書裡指出這個詞句。 *cheng hai nay boon su-ee do jee nay gur-ee chut' lay*
I understand.	我明白。 *ngor ming*
I don't understand.	我不明白。 *ngor mm ming*
Do you understand?	你明白嗎？ *nay ming mm ming a*
Here you are.	給你。 *hai do*

– *saam sup ng mun.*
– *ngor mm ming.*
– *saam sap ng mun.*
– mm goy se dai … orr, "thirty-five dollars"
… na, hai do.

Questions 詢問

Cantonese nouns have no articles (a, an, the) and no plural forms. Whether the noun is singular or plural is judged from the context, or by a number modifying the noun.

Ngor yeeu <u>yut</u> jurng hur-ee gau l-owng ge fay.
I'd like a (<u>one</u>) ticket to Kowloon.
Ngor yeeu <u>saam</u> jurng hur-ee gau l-owng ge fay.
I'd like <u>three</u> tickets to Kowloon.

Where? 哪裡？

Where is it?	在哪裡？	*hai bin do*
Where are you going?	你去哪裡？	*nay hur-ee bin do a*
at the meeting place [point]	在集合地點	*hai jaap hup day dim*
away from me	和我相距 …	*t-owng ngor surng gaak …*
downstairs	樓下	*lau ha*
from the U.S.	從美國	*yau may gwock*
here (to here)	這裡（到這裡）	*nay do (do nay do)*
in the car	在車裡	*hai che do*
in Hong Kong	在香港	*hai hurng gong*
inside	裡面	*lur-ee bin*
near the bank	在銀行附近	*hai ngun hong foo gun*
next to the post office	在郵局旁邊	*hai yau guk pong bin*
opposite the market	在市場對面	*hai see churng dur-ee min*
on the left/right	在左邊 / 右邊	*hai jor bin/yau bin*
there (to there)	那裡（到那裡）	*gor do (do gor do)*
to the hotel	到酒店	*do jau dim*
towards Wanchai	向著灣仔那邊	*hurng ju-ee waan jai gor bin*
outside the cafe	咖啡室外面	*ga fe sut chut' bin*
up to the traffic lights	一直到交通燈	*yut jick do gau t-owng dung*
upstairs	樓上	*lau surng*

When? 什麼時候？

When does the museum open?	博物館幾點開門？ *bock mut goon gay dim hoy moon a*
When does the train arrive?	火車幾點到？ *for che gay dim do a*
10 minutes ago	十分鐘之前 *sup fun j-owng jee chin*
after lunch	午飯後 *sick yu-een aan jee hau*
always	總是 *seng yut*
around midnight	半夜十二點左右 *boon ye sup yee dim jor yau*
at 7 o'clock	七點 *chut dim*
before Friday	星期五之前 *sing kay ng jee chin*
by tomorrow	明天 *ting yut*
early	早 *jo*
every week	每星期 *moo-ee sing kay*
for 2 hours	兩小時 *lurng gor j-owng tau*
from 9 a.m. to 6 p.m.	由上午九點至下午六點 *yau surng jau gau dim jee ha jau luk dim*
immediately	立刻 *jick huck*
in 20 minutes	二十分鐘後 *yee sup fun j-owng hau*
never	從來沒有 *ch-owng loy mo*
not yet	還沒有 *j-owng may*
now	現在 *yee ga*
often	時常 *see surng*
on March 8	在三月八號 *hai saam yu-eet baat ho*
on weekdays	週日 *jau yut*
sometimes	有時 *yau see*
soon	很快 *ho faai*
then	然後 *yin hau*
within 2 days	兩日之內 *lurng yut jee noy*

What sort of ...? 什麼樣子的 .... ?

I'd like	我想要 ...
something ...	*ngor surng yeeu ...*
It's ...	這個 ... *nay gor ...*
beautiful/ugly	漂亮 / 難看 *leng/chau gwaai*
better/worse	好些 / 更不好 *ho dee/j-ownng mm ho*
big/small	大 / 小 *daai/sai*
cheap/expensive	便宜 / 貴 *peng/gwai*
clean/dirty	乾淨 / 骯髒 *gon jeng/woo jo*
dark/light (color)	深色 / 淺色 *sum sick/chin sick*
delicious/revolting	好吃 / 難吃 *ho sick/ho naan sick*
easy/difficult	容易 / 難 *y-owng yee/naan*
empty/full	空 / 滿 *h-owng/moon*
good/bad	好 / 不好 *ho/mm ho*
heavy/light	重 / 輕 *ch-owng/heng*
hot/warm/cold	熱 / 暖 / 冷 *yit/nu-een/d-owng*
modern/old-fashioned	新款 / 舊款 *sun foon/gau foon*
narrow/wide	窄 / 闊 *jaak/foot*
old/new	舊 / 新 *gau/sun*
open/shut	開 / 關 *hoy/saan*
pleasant, nice/unpleasant	很好 / 不好 *ho ho/mm ho*
quick/slow	快 / 慢 *faai/maan*
quiet/noisy	清靜 / 嘈吵 *ching jing/cho*
right/wrong	對 / 不對 *ngaam/mm ngaam*
tall/small	高 / 矮 *go/ai*
vacant/occupied	有人 / 無人 *yau yun/mo yun*
young/old	年輕 / 年老 *nin heng/nin lo*

Why? 爲什麼 ?

Why is that?/Why not?	爲什麼？/ 爲什麼不能？ *dim gaai/dim gaai mm duck*
It's because of the weather.	是因爲天氣的關係。 *hai yun wai tin hay ge gwaan hai*
It's because I'm in a hurry.	因爲我趕時間 *yun wai ngor gon see gaan*
I don't know why.	我不知爲什麼 *ngor mm jee dim gaai*

Word order in Cantonese is usually *subject – verb – object*, which is also the usual order in English sentences.

Adjectives and other modifying phrases are usually placed in front of nouns.

Ngor yeeu yut gaan ho ge jau dim.   I want a good hotel.

(**ho ge** = good/**jau dim** = hotel)

To form a simple question in Cantonese, use the following order: *subject + verb positive + verb negative + object*.

Nay yau mo see gaan?   Do you have time?

(= you + have + not have + time; **mo** = not have)

Nay sick mm sick kur-ee?   Do you know her?

(= you + know + not know + her)

How much/many? 多少？

How much is that?	那個多少錢？ *gor gor gay dor chin a*
How many are there?	那裡有多少個？ *gor do yau gay dor gor*
1/2/3	一／二／三 *yut/yee/saam*
4/5	四／五 *say/ng*
none	一個也沒有 *yut gor do mo*
about 100 dollars	一百元左右 *yut baak mun jor yau*
a little	少許 *seeu seeu*
a lot of milk	很多牛奶 *ho do ngau naai*
enough	夠了 *gau la*
few/a few of them	很少／有幾個 *ho seeu/yau gay gor*
more than that	多些 *dor dee*
less than that	少些 *seeu dee*
much more	多很多 *dor ho dor*
nothing else	沒有其他的了 *mo kay ta ye la'*
too much	太多 *taai dor*

Who?/Which? 誰？/ 哪個？

Who's there?	是誰呀？ *bin gor a*
It's me!	是我！ *hai ngor a*
It's us!	是我們！ *hai ngor day a*
someone/no one	有人／無人 *yau yun/mo yun*
Which one do you want?	你要哪個？ *nay yeeu bin gor*
this one/that one	這個／那個 *nay gor/gor gor*
one like that	像那個一樣的 *ho chee gor gor gum yurng ge*
not that one	不是那個 *mm hai gor gor*
something	一樣東西 *yau yurng ye*
nothing	沒有東西 *mo ye*
none	一個都沒有 *yut gor do mo*

Whose? 誰的？

Whose is that?	那是誰的？ *hai bin gor ge*
It's …	是 … *hai …*
mine/ours/yours/yours (pl)	我的／我們的／你的／你們的 *ngor ge/ngor day ge/nay ge/nay day ge*
his/hers/theirs	他的／她的／他們的 *kur-ee ge/kur-ee ge/kur-ee day ge*
It's … turn.	輪到 … 了 *lun do … la*
my/our/your/your (pl)	我／我們／你／你們 *ngor/ngor day/nay/nay day*
his/her/their	他／她／他們 *kur-ee/kur-ee/kur-ee day*

GRAMMAR

Negatives: **mm** (no/not) is added in front of the verb to indicate negation.

Ngor yeeu daan yun fong.	I want a single room.
Ngor mm yeeu daan yun fong.	I don't want a single room.

Yes/No: The approximate equivalent for *yes* is **hai** (meaning *right*), and for *no* it's **mm hai** (meaning *not right*). You can use these to affirm or negate something, or you can simply repeat the verb which was used in the question.

Nay yum mm yum cha a?　　Would you like (to drink) some tea?
(= you + drink + not drink + tea)

Yum, mm goy. Yes, I would.　　**Mm yum, mm goy.** No, thank you.
(= drink, thank you)　　　　　　(= not drink, thank you)

16

How? 怎樣？

How would you like to pay?	你想怎樣付款？	*nay surng dim yurng bay chin*
by credit card	用信用卡	*y-owng sun' y-owng kaat*
with cash	現金	*yin gum*
How are you getting here?	你打算怎樣來這裡？	*nay da su-een dim yurng lay nay do a*
by car/by bus/by train	坐汽車／坐巴士／坐火車	*chor hay che/chor ba see/chor for che*
on foot	步行	*haang lo*
quickly	快點	*faai dee*
slowly	慢點	*maan dee*
too fast	太快	*taai faai*
very	很	*ho*
with a friend	和朋友一起	*t-owng pung yau yut chai*
without a passport	沒有護照	*mo woo jeeu*

Is it …?/Are there …? 是不是 … ？／有沒有 … ？

Is it …?	是不是 … ？	*hai mm hai …*
Is it free?	是不是免費的？	*hai mm hai min fai ga*
It isn't ready.	還沒準備好。	*j-owng may duck*
Is/Are there …?	有沒有 …. ？	*yau mo …*
Is there a shower in the room?	房間裡有沒有花洒？	*fong do yau mo fa sa*
Are there buses into town?	有沒有去市區的巴士？	*yau mo ba see hur-ee see kur-ee a*
There is a good restaurant near here.	這附近有家很好的餐廳。	*nay do foo gun yau gaan gay ho ge chaan teng*
There aren't any towels in my room.	我房間裡沒有毛巾。	*ngor fong do mo mo gun*
Here it is/they are.	在這裡。	*hai nay do*
There it is/they are.	在那裡。	*hai gor do*

Can/May? 可以嗎？

Can I have ...?	可以給我 ... 嗎？
	hor mm hor yee bay ... ngor
May we have ...?	可以給我們 ... 嗎？
	hor mm hor yee bay ... ngor day
May I speak to ...?	我可以見見 ... 嗎？
	ngor hor mm hor yee g-in g-in ...
Can you tell me ...?	請問 ...？ *cheng mun ...*
Can you help me?	你可以幫助我嗎？
	nay mm hor yee boṅg ha ngor
Can you direct me to ...?	請問怎樣去 ...？
	cheng mun dim yurng hur-ee ...
I can't help you.	我不幫了你。
	ngor bong mm do nay

What do you want? 你要什麼？

I'd like ...	我想要 ... *ngor surng yeeu ...*
Could I have ...?	請給我 ... *mm goy bay ...*
We'd like ...	我們想要 ... *ngor day surng yeeu ...*
Give me ...	給我 ... *bay ngor ...*
I'm looking for ...	我想找 ... *ngor surng wun ...*
I need to ...	我需要 ... *ngor sur-ee yeeu ...*
go to ...	去... *hur-ee ...*
find ...	找... *wun ...*
see ...	見... *g-in ...*
speak to ...	和 ... 談一談 *t-owng ... king ha*

– mm goy.
– *mut ye see a?*
– nay hor mm hor yee bong ha ngor?
– *dong yin hor yee.*
- ngor hor mm hor yee g-in g-in chun sin saang a?
– *cheng dung yut jun.*

Other useful words 其他應用詞彙

fortunately	幸運地 *ho choy*
hopefully	希望 *hay mong*
of course	當然 *dong yin*
perhaps/possibly	或許 / 可能 *waak je/hor nung*
probably	很可能 *ho hor nung*
unfortunately	可惜 *hor sick*

Exclamations 感嘆詞

At last!	終於 … 了！ *j-owng yu-ee … la*
Go on.	說下去。 *gong maai lock hur-ee*
I don't mind.	我不介意。 *ngor mm gaai yee*
No way!	不可能！ *mm duck*
Really?	真的？ *jun ge*
Nonsense!	胡說。 *lu-een gong*
That's enough.	夠了。 *gau la*
That's true.	真的。 *jun ga*
How are things?	近來怎樣？ *gun lay dim a*
Fine, thank you.	很好，謝謝。 *gay ho, yau sum*
It's …	這個 … *nay gor*
terrific	好極了 *ho do gick*
great	非常好 *fay surng ho*
fine	很好 *gay ho*
not bad	不錯 *mm chor*
okay	過得去 *gwor duck hur-ee*
not good	不好 *mm ho*
terrible	很糟 *ho cha*

GRAMMAR

Cantonese verb forms are even more invariable than English ones, with no differences between the singular and plural forms.

Personal pronouns (I/me, you, he/him, she/her, etc.) all have the same form whether they are the subject or the object.

Ngor bay jor jurng fay kur-ee. I gave the ticket to him.

Kur-ee bay jor jurng fay **ngor**. He gave the ticket to me.

Accommodations

Hong Kong

Here you will find some of the most luxurious hotels in the world offering excellent business services and conferencing facilities. It is advisable to reserve a room in advance. The *Hong Kong Reservation Centre* at the International Airport can also help with reservations, and it is open from 7 a.m. to midnight. Slightly cheaper hotels and guesthouses can be found in **Kowloon**.

Macau

Macau is cheaper than Hong Kong. However, hotel prices double and even the ferries charge more on weekends. If you are looking for a hotel room in the middle to upper price range, you will get a discount of around 20% by booking through a Hong Kong travel agent. You will find numerous travel agencies at the *Shun Tak Center* (the Macau Ferry Pier) at Sheung Wan in Hong Kong.

Guangdong

Major tourist hotels can be found in the capital, **Guangzhou**, and the Special Economic Zones (SEZs) of **Shenzhen** and **Zhuhai**, but they are not cheap. It can often be difficult to find budget accommodation as these rooms are usually taken up by Chinese people.

酒店　*jau dim*
Western-style hotels. Some major hotel chains have properties in Hong Kong, Macau, and the large cities in Guangdong. The advantage of staying at on of the upscale Western-style hotels is that English is spoken.

友誼賓館　*yau yee bun goon*
Friendship hotels. These are often enormous government-run complexes with many wings in spacious grounds. Set up in the 1950s for traveling government officials and foreign dignitaries, many of these hotels have been renovated and now provide mid-range accommodation.

招待所　*jeeu doy sor*
Guesthouses. The standard varies, and it is best to have a look at the rooms and facilities before making a reservation.

青年旅社　*ching nin lur-ee se*
Youth hostels. In Hong Kong these are usually situated far away from the hustle and bustle, in the New Territories. In Guangdong there is a youth hostel in the center of Guangzhou.

Reservations 預訂房間

In advance 事前

Can you recommend a
hotel in …?

你可以介紹一家在 …
的酒店嗎？ *nay hor mm hor
yee gaai seeu yut gaan hai …
ge jau dim a*

Is it near the center of town?

近市中心嗎？
kun mm kun see j-owng sum a

How much is it per night?

多少錢一晚？ *gay dor chin yut maan a*

Do you have a cheaper room?

有沒有便宜些的？ *yau mo peng dee ge*

Could you reserve [book]
me a room there, please?

請替我在那裡訂個房間。
*cheng bong ngor hai gor do deng
gaan fong*

How do I get there?

我怎樣去那裡？
ngor dim yurng hur-ee gor do a

At the hotel 在酒店

Do you have a room?

有空房嗎？ *yau mo fong a*

Is there another hotel nearby?

附近有沒有其他酒店？
foo gun yau mo kay ta jau dim a

I'd like a single/double room.

我想要一個單人／雙人房間。 *ngor surng
yeeu yut gaan daan yun/surng yun fong*

Can I see the room, please?

可以看看房間嗎？
hor mm hor yee tai ha gaan fong a

I'd like a room with …

我想要一個有 …. 的房間
ngor surng yeeu yut gaan yau … ge fong

twin beds

兩張床 *lurng jurng chong*

a double bed

雙人床 *surng yun chong*

a bath/shower

浴缸／花洒 *ch-owng lurng gong/fa sa*

– yau mo fong a?
ngor surng yeeu yut gaan lurng gor yun ge fong.
– dur-ee mm ju-ee, mo saai fong la.
– or. foo gun yau mo kay ta jau dim a.
– yau, baak lock jau dim ho kun nay do.

Reception 接待

I have a reservation.	我訂了房間。 ngor deng jor fong
My name is ...	我叫 ... ngor geeu ...
We reserved a double and a single room.	我們訂了一個雙人和一個單人房間。 ngor day deng jor yut gaan surng yun fong t-owng yut gaan daan yun fong
I confirmed my reservation by mail.	我寫信來確定預訂的。 ngor se sun' lay kock ding yu-ee deng ge
Could we have adjoining rooms?	可以要兩個相連的房間嗎？ hor mm hor yee yeeu lurng gaan chee maai ge fong

Amenities and facilities 設施

Is there (a/an) ... in the room?	房間裡有沒有 ...？ fong do yau mo ...
air conditioning	空調 laang hay
TV/telephone	電視 / 電話 din see/din wa
Does the hotel have (a/an) ...?	酒店有沒有 ...？ jau dim yau mo ...
cable TV	有線電視 yau sin din see
laundry service	洗衣服務 sai yee fuk mo
solarium	日光浴室 yut gwong yuk sut
swimming pool	游泳池 yau wing chee
Could you put ... in the room?	可以在房間裡加 ... 嗎？ hor mm hor yee hai fong do ga ...
an extra bed	多一張床 dor yut jurng chong
a crib [a child's cot]	一張小兒床 yut jurng sai lo gor chong
Do you have facilities for children/the disabled?	你們這裡有沒有給兒童 / 傷殘人士用的設施？ nay day nay do yau mo bay sai lo gor/surng chaan yun see y-owng ge chit see a

How long …? 多長時間？

My name is …	我叫 …。 *ngor geeu …*
We'll be staying …	我們打算住 … *ngor day da su-een ju-ee*
one night only	一晚 *yut maan*
a few days	幾天 *gay yut*
a week (at least)	(至少) 一個星期 *(jee seeu) yut gor sing kay*
I don't know yet.	還不知道。 *j-owng may jee do*
I'd like to stay an extra night.	我想多住一晚。 *ngor surng ju-ee dor yut maan*
What does this mean?	這是什麼意思？ *gum hai mut ye yee see a*

– nay ho. ngor geeu John Newton.
– a, Newton sin saang, nay ho.
– ngor surng ju-ee lurng maan.
– mo mun tai. mm goy tin se nay jurng (dung gay) beeu.

可以看看你的護照嗎？	May I see your passport, please?
請填寫這張登記表。	Please fill out this form.
你的車牌幾號？	What is your car registration number?

房間 … 元	room only … dollars
包括早餐	breakfast included
餐食供應	meals available
姓 / 名	last name/first name
住址 / 街道 / 門牌	home address/street/number
國籍 / 職業	nationality/profession
出生日期 / 出生地點	date/place of birth
護照號碼	passport number
車牌號碼	car registration number
地點 / 日期	place/date
簽名	signature

Price 價錢

How much is it ...?	... 多少錢？	...gay dor chin a
per night/week	一晚／一個星期	yut maam/yut gor sing kay
for bed and breakfast	房間連早餐	fong lin maai jo chaan
excluding meals	不包括膳食	mm bau sick
for full board (American Plan [A.P.])	包食宿	bau sick suk
for half board (Modified American Plan [M.A.P.])	半食宿	boon sick suk
Does the price include ...?	價錢包括 ... 嗎？	ga chin bau mm bau maai ...
breakfast	早餐	jo chaan
sales tax [VAT]	增值稅	jung jick sur-ee
Do I have to pay a deposit?	需要付按金嗎？	sai mm sai bay on gum a
Is there a discount for children?	兒童有折扣嗎？	sai lo gor yau mo jit kau a

Decision 決定

May I see the room?	可以看看房間嗎？	hor mm hor yee tai ha gaan fong a
That's fine. I'll take it.	很好。就要這間。	gay ho. jau yeeu nay gaan
It's too ...	這間太...	nay gaan taai ...
dark/small	暗／小	um /sai
noisy	嘈吵	cho
Do you have anything ...?	有沒有 ... 的？	yau mo ... ge
bigger/cheaper	大些／便宜些	daai dee/peng dee
quieter/lighter	清靜些／光亮些	ching jing dee/gwong maang dee
No, I won't take it.	我不要這間。	ngor mm yeeu nay gaan

24

Problems 問題

The ... doesn't work.	... 壞了。 ...waai jor
air conditioning	空調 laang hay
fan	風扇 f-owng sin
heating	暖氣 nu-een hay
light	電燈 din dung
I can't turn the heat [heating] on/off.	暖氣打不開／關不上。 ngor hoy mm do/saan mm do nu-een hay
There is no hot water/ toilet paper.	沒有熱水／廁紙。 mo yit sur-ee/chee jee
The faucet [tap] is dripping.	水喉滴水。 sur-ee hau dick sur-ee
The sink/toilet is blocked.	洗臉盆／廁所塞了。 sai min poon/chee sor suck jor
The window/door is jammed.	窗／門打不開。 gor churng/moon hoy mm do
My room has not been made up.	我的房間還未整理好。 ngor gaan fong j-owng may jup ho
The ... is/are broken.	... 壞了。 ... waai jor
blinds	百葉窗 baak yip churng
lamp	燈 dung
light switch	燈掣 dung jai
lock	鎖 sor
There are insects in our room.	我們的房間有蟲。 ngor day gaan fong yau ch-owng

Action 行動

Could you have that seen to?	請派人修理。 mm goy paai yun sau lay
I'd like to move to another room.	我想換個房間。 ngor surng woon gwor gaan fong
I'd like to speak to the manager.	我想見經理。 ngor surng g-in ging lay

Requirements 一般要求

Standard voltage is 200/220-volt, 50-cycle AC, but plugs can vary greatly (there are at least four different types). However, conversion plugs are available in major cities.

About the hotel 酒店

Where's the …?	… 在哪裡 ？ *… hai bin do*
bar	酒吧 *jau ba*
bathroom	浴室 *ch-owng lurng fong*
dining room	餐廳 *chaan teng*
elevator [lift]	電梯 *din tai*
parking lot [car park]	停車場 *ting che churng*
sauna	桑拿浴室 *song na yuk sut*
shower	花洒 *fa sa*
swimming pool	游泳池 *yau wing chee*
tour operator's bulletin board	旅行團佈告板 *lur-ee hung tu-een bo go baan*
Where is the bathroom [toilet]?	洗手間在那裡 ？ *sai sau gaan hai bin do a*
What time is the front door locked?	這裡幾點鎖門 ？ *nay do gay dim sor moon a*
What time is breakfast served?	早餐幾點供應 ？ *jo chaan gay dim g-owng ying a*
Is there room service?	有沒有客房送餐服務 ？ *yau mo haak fong s-owng chaan fuk mo*

電鬚刨插座	razors [shavers] only
緊急出口（太平門）	emergency exit
防火門	fire door
請勿打擾	do not disturb
外線請撥 …	dial … for an outside line

Personal needs 個人需要

Public toilets are not always easy to find except in the main tourist areas. Most are not well maintained, so those located in hotels or Western fast-food restaurants may be a better bet. Carry tissues with you when using public toilets.

The key to room ..., please.	請給 … 號房間的鑰匙。 *mm goy bay ... ho fong ge sor see*
I've lost my key.	我丟了鑰匙。 *ngor mm g-in jor sor see*
I've locked myself out of my room.	我把鑰匙鎖在房間裡了。 *ngor ge sor see sor jor hai fong do*
Could you wake me at ...?	請 … 叫醒我。 *mm goy ... geeu seng ngor*
I'd like breakfast in my room.	我想在房間裡吃早餐。 *ngor surng hai fong do sick jo chaan*
Can I leave this in the safe?	可以把這些東西寄存在保險箱裡嗎？ *nay dee ye hor mm hor yee baai hai bo him surng do*
Could I have my things from the safe?	我想取回我寄存在保險箱裡的東西。 *ngor surng lor faan ngor baai hai bo him surng do ge ye*
Where is our tour guide?	我們的旅行團導遊在哪裡？ *ngor day ge lur-ee hung tu-een do yau hai bin do a*
May I have an extra ...?	可以多要 … 嗎？ *hor mm hor yee yeeu dor ...*
bath towel/blanket	一條毛巾 / 一張毛氈 *yut teeu mo gun/yut jurng mo jin*
hanger/pillow	一個衣架 / 一個枕頭 *yut gor yee ga/yut gor jum tau*
soap	一塊肥皂 *yut gau faan gaan*
Is there any mail for me?	有沒有我的信？ *yau mo ngor ge sun'*
Are there any messages for me?	有沒有留給我的口信？ *yau mo yun lau dai hau sun' bay ngor*

BREAKFAST ➤ 43; CHANGING MONEY ➤ 138

Renting 租房

We reserved an apartment/cottage in the name of ...	我們訂了一間公寓 / 別墅，是用 ... 名義訂的。 ngor day deng jor gaan g-owng yu-ee/bit sur-ee, hai y-owng ... ming yee deng ge
Where do we pick up the keys?	到哪裡拿鑰匙？ hur-ee bin do lor sor see a
Where is the...?	... 在哪裡？ ...hai bin do a
electricity meter	電錶 din beeu
fuse box	灰士箱（保險絲盒） foo-ee see surng (bo him see haap)
valve [stopcock]	水掣 sur-ee jai
water heater	熱水爐 yit sur-ee lo
Are there any spare ...?	有沒有備用...？ yau mo bay y-owng...
fuses	灰士（保險絲） foo-ee see (bo him see)
gas bottles	煤氣罐 moo-ee hay goon
sheets	床單 chong daan
Which day does the maid come?	清潔工人哪一天來？ ching git g-owng yun bin yut la y a
Where/When do I put out the trash [rubbish]?	垃圾要放在哪裡 / 什麼時候拿出來？ laap saap yeeu baai hai bin do/gay see ling chut' lay a

Problems? 有問題？

Where can I contact you?	我怎樣聯絡你？ ngor dim yurng lu-een lock nay a
How does the stove [cooker]/ water heater work?	煮食爐 / 熱水爐怎麼開？ ju-ee sick lo/ yit sur-ee lo dim yurng hoy a
The ... is/are dirty.	... 很髒。 ... woo jo
The ... has broken down.	... 壞了。 ... waai jor
We accidentally broke/ lost ...	我們不小心弄壞了 / 丟失了... ngor day mm seeu sum jing laan jor/mm g-in jor...
That was already damaged when we arrived.	我們來到的時候，那已經損壞了。 ngor day lay do gor jun, gor yurng ye yee ging waai jor la

HOUSEHOLD ARTICLES ➤ 148

Useful terms 應用詞彙

boiler	熱水爐	*yit sur-ee lo*
crockery	碗碟	*woon dip*
cutlery	刀叉	*do cha*
frying pan	煎鍋	*jin wock*
kettle	水煲	*sur-ee bo*
lamp	燈	*dung*
refrigerator/freezer	雪櫃 / 冰櫃	*su-eet gwai/bing gwai*
saucepan	煲	*bo*
stove [cooker]	煮食爐	*ju-ee sick lo*
toilet paper	廁紙	*chee jee*
washing machine	洗衣機	*sai yee gay*

Rooms 房間

balcony	露台	*lo toy*
bathroom	浴室	*ch-owng lurng fong*
bedroom	睡房	*sur-ee fong*
dining room	餐廳	*chaan teng*
kitchen	廚房	*chu-ee fong*
living room	客廳	*haak teng*
toilet	廁所	*chee sor*

Youth hostel 青年旅社

Do you have any places left for tonight?	今晚還有空位嗎？	*gum maan j-owng yau mo wai jing a*
Do you rent [hire] out bedding?	有床鋪出租嗎？	*yau mo chong po chut' jo a*
What time are the doors locked?	幾點鎖門？	*gay dim sor moon a*
I have an International Student Card.	我有國際學生證。	*ngor yau gwock jai hock saang jing*

REQUIREMENTS ➤ 26; CAMPING ➤ 30

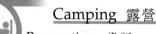

Camping 露營

Reservations 登記

Is there a campsite near here?
這附近有沒有營地？
nay do foo gun yau mo ying day a

Do you have space for a tent/ trailer [caravan]?
有沒有搭帳幕／泊旅行拖車的空位？
yau mo daap jurng mock/paak lur-ee hung to che ge wai a

What is the charge ...?
... 要多少錢？
... yeeu gay dor chin a

per day/week
一天／一個星期
yut yut/yut gor sing kay

for a tent/car
帳幕／汽車
jurng mock/hay che

for a trailer [caravan]
旅行拖車
lur-ee hung to che

Facilities 設施

Are there cooking facilities on site?
營地有沒有煮食設備？
ying day yau mo ju-ee sick chit bay

Are there any electrical outlets [power points]?
有沒有電插座？
yau mo din chaap jor

Where is/are the ...?
... 在哪裡？
... hai bin do

drinking water
飲用水 *yum y-owng sur-ee*

trash cans [dustbins]
垃圾桶 *laap saap t-owng*

laundry facilities
洗衣設備 *sai yee chit bay*

showers
花洒 *fa sa*

Where can I get some butane gas?
在哪裡可以買到罐裝煤氣？ *hai bin do hor yee maai do goon jong moo-ee hay a*

---

①	飲用水	drinking water
	禁止露營	no camping
②	禁止生火／燒烤	no fires/barbecues

Complaints 投訴

It's too sunny/shady/
crowded here.

這裡太晒 / 陰暗 / 擠擁。
*nay do taai saai/yum um/
jai bick*

The ground's too hard/
uneven.

地面太硬 / 凹凸不平。
day min taai ngaang/nup dut

Is there a more level spot?

有沒有平坦些的位置？
yau mo ping dee ge wai jee a

You can't camp here.

不能在這裡露營。
mm hor yee hai nay do lo ying

Camping equipment 露營用具

butane gas	罐裝煤氣	*goon jong moo-ee hay*
campbed	摺床	*jip chong*
charcoal	炭	*taan*
flashlight [torch]	電筒	*din t-owng*
groundcloth [groundsheet]	鋪地防水布	*po day fong sur-ee bo*
guy rope	支索	*laai sing*
hammer	鐵鎚	*tit chur-ee*
kerosene [primus] stove	氣化煤油爐	*hay fa for sur-ee lo*
knapsack	背囊	*boo-ee nong*
mallet	木槌	*muk chur-ee*
matches	火柴	*for chaai*
(air) mattress	（充氣）床褥	*(bum hay) chong yuk*
paraffin	煤油	*for sur-ee*
penknife	袖珍摺刀	*jau jun jip do*
sleeping bag	睡袋	*sur-ee doy*
tent	帳幕	*jurng mock*
tent pegs	帳幕釘	*jurng mock deng*
tent pole	帳幕支柱	*jurng mock jee chu-ee*

Checking out 退房

What time do we have to check out by?	我們幾點要退房？	*ngor day gay dim yeeu tur-ee fong a*
Could we leave our baggage [luggage] here until ... p.m.?	可以把行李留在這裡到下午 ... 點嗎？	*hor mm hor yee lau dai dee hung lay hai nay do, do ha jau ... dim*
I'm leaving now.	我現在要走了。	*ngor yee ga yeeu jau la*
Could you order me a taxi, please?	請替我叫輛的士。	*mm goy bong ngor geeu ga dick see*
We had a very enjoyable stay.	這次住得很愉快。	*nay chee ju-ee duck ho yu-ee faai*

Paying 付帳

A service charge of 10% – 15% (sometimes more in Guangdong) is normally added to the hotel bill. In Hong Kong, tip when you have received exceptionally good service. Suggested rates: hotel porter, HK$3 – 5 per bag; maid, HK$60 per week; lavatory attendant, HK$2 – 5. On mainland China tipping is not expected, but there are times when tips are offered in advance to ensure good service.

May I have my bill, please?	請結帳。	*mm goy git so*
I think there's a mistake in this bill.	這帳單好像有錯。	*nay jurng daan ho chee yau do chor jor*
I've made ... telephone calls.	我打了 ... 個電話。	*ngor da jor ... gor din wa*
I've taken ... from the mini-bar.	我從小酒吧拿了 ...	*ngor hai jau ba jai lor jo ...*
Can I have an itemized bill?	可以開張收費清單嗎？	*hor mm hor yee hoy jurng sau fai ching daan a*
Could I have a receipt, please?	請開張收條。	*mm goy hoy jurng sau teeu*

Eating Out

In a country as big as China, regional styles of cooking were bound to develop. In Hong Kong restaurants, every major school of Chinese cooking is represented, as the former colony has inherited recipes and chefs from all parts of China, but the regional style is mainly Cantonese.

Cantonese cuisine is probably very familiar to Western visitors as many Cantonese have emigrated and opened restaurants in the West. A vast range of ingredients is used and either stir-fried, boiled, or steamed to capture the natural flavor as well as the color and vitamins. One of the most famous specialties is **dim sum** (點心), small snacks usually steamed in small bamboo baskets and served for breakfast and lunch. Choose whatever looks interesting, from spring rolls, dumplings, spareribs, and so on. Cantonese cuisine is also known for its sweet and sour dishes. The Chinese usually have soup towards the end of a meal but, in Hong Kong, local people tend to begin with it. Steamed white rice is normally served with a Cantonese meal, although you can order fried rice instead.

In **Macau** you will find a colorful mixture of Portuguese and Cantonese cuisine. Not all Portuguese restaurants have English menus, so it is useful to look out for **carne de vaca** (beef), **peixe** (fish), **galinha** (chicken), **borrego** (lamb), **carne de porco** (pork), **cozido** (boiled), **assado** (roasted), **frito** (fried), **grelhado** (grilled), and **no forno** (baked). Portuguese specialties include **bacalhao** (dried cod), **linguado** (Macau sole), and **feijoada** (stewed black beans, potatoes, sausages, bacon, and pork).

Chopsticks 筷子

In Western and upscale Chinese restaurants you may be able to get cutlery, but usually you will be given chopsticks and a spoon. When eating rice with chopsticks, bring the bowl up to your lips and shovel the rice into your mouth. Take care not to place the chopsticks across the rice bowl, but let them rest either on the holder provided or against a plate.

Table manners 用餐禮節

Toasts regularly punctuate a formal Chinese dinner or banquet, and it is considered bad form to drink before the host has first proposed a toast to his guests' health. The guest of honor is expected to either reply straight away or when the next dish is served. When using toothpicks, the mouth should be covered with one hand.

Where to eat 餐廳

Hong Kong, Macau, and large cities in Guangdong offer a variety of restaurants in every price range and various culinary styles.

Dim sum restaurant 茶樓 *cha lau*

Noodle bar 麵店 *min dim*

Meal times 一日三餐

Breakfast 早餐 *jo chaan*

Hotels serve American, British, or Continental breakfast from about 7 a.m. to 10 a.m. A traditional Chinese breakfast consists of **juk** (粥), a rice gruel or porridge, to which almost anything may be added, from fried batter to salted fish. You'll also see early risers digging into noodle soup with vegetables and hunks of pork.

Lunch 午餐 *ng chaan/an*

In hotels, lunch is generally served from 1 p.m. to 3 p.m, but restaurants are more flexible, often starting as early as 10:30 a.m.

Dinner 晚餐 *maan chaan*

In hotels, dinner is generally served from 6:30 p.m. to 9:30 p.m. Restaurant times vary more widely. In some areas restaurants may start serving at 4:30 p.m. and finish at 8 p.m., so check on closing times when you decide where to eat or you may be disappointed.

To get a table in a well-known restaurant, it is best to call ahead.

A table for ..., please.	請安排一張 ... 的桌子。
	mm goy bay jurng ... ge toy
1/2/3/4	一 / 二 / 三 / 四個人
	yut/yee/saam/say gor yun
Thank you.	謝謝。 *mm goy*
I'd like to pay.	我要付賬。 *mm goy maai daan*

Finding a place to eat 找地方吃飯

Can you recommend a good restaurant?	你可以介紹一家好的餐館嗎？ *nay hor mm hor yee gaai seeu yut gaan ho ge chaan goon a*
Is there a ... near here?	這附近有沒有 ... ？ *nay do foo gun yau mo ...*
traditional local restaurant	傳統式地方風味的餐廳 *chu-een t-owng boon day f-owng may ge chaan teng*
Chinese restaurant	中式酒樓 *j-owng sick jau lau*
fish restaurant	海鮮酒家 *hoy sin jau ga*
Italian restaurant	意大利餐廳 *yee daai lay chaan teng*
inexpensive restaurant	價錢不貴的餐館 *ga chin mm gwai ge chaan goon*
Japanese restaurant	日本料理 *yut boon leeu lay*
vegetarian restaurant	素菜館 *jai choy goon*
Where can I find a(n) ...?	請問哪裡有 ... ？ *cheng mun bin do yau ...*
burger stand	漢堡飽檔 *hon bo bau dong*
café	咖啡室 *ga fe sut*
restaurant	餐廳 *chaan teng*
fast-food restaurant	快餐店 *faai chaan dim*
ice-cream parlor	雪糕店 *su-eet go dim*
pizzeria	意大利薄餅店 *yee daai lay bock beng dim*
steak house	牛扒餐廳 *ngau pa chaan teng*

DIRECTIONS ➤ 94

Reserving a table 訂座

I'd like to reserve a table for two.	我想訂一張兩個人的桌子。 *ngor surng deng jurng lurng gor yun ge toy*
For this evening/ tomorrow at …	今晚／明晚 … *gum maan/ting maan …*
We'll come at 8:00.	我們八點來。 *ngor day baat dim lay*
A table for two, please.	兩位，謝謝。 *lurng wai, mm goy*
We have a reservation.	我們訂了座位的。 *ngor day deng jor toy ge la*

請問貴姓？	What's the name, please?
對不起，我們這裡滿座了。	I'm sorry. We're very busy/full up.
… 分鐘後會有座位。	We'll have a free table in … minutes.
請 … 分鐘後回來。	Please come back in … minutes.

Where to sit 座位

Could we sit …?	我們可以坐在 … 嗎？ *ngor day hor mm hor yee chor … a*
over there	那邊 *gor bin*
outside	外面 *chut' bin*
in a non-smoking area	非吸煙區 *fay kup yin kur-ee*
by the window	靠窗口的座位 *gun churng hau ge wai*
Smoking or non-smoking?	吸煙還是不吸煙？ *sick mm sick yin ga*

– *ngor surng deng yut jurng gum maan ge toy.*
  – *gay dor yun?*
  – *say gor.*
– *nay day gay dim lay a?*
– *ngor day baat dim lay.*
– *cheng mun gwai sing?*
  – Smith.
  – *ho, do see g-in.*

Ordering 點菜

Waiter!/Waitress!	伙記！／小姐！ *for gay/seeu je*
May I see the wine list, please?	可以看看酒單嗎？ *hor mm* *hor yee lor gor jau paai tai ha*
Do you have a set menu?	有沒有套餐？ *yau mo to chaan a*
Can you recommend some typical local dishes?	你可以介紹一些地道的菜式嗎？ *nay hor mm hor yee gaai seeu yut dee* *day do ge choy sick a*
Could you tell me what … is?	請問 … 是什麼？ *cheng mun … hai mut ye a*
What's in it?	裡面有些什麼？ *lur-ee bin yau dee mut ye*
What kind of … do you have?	有些什麼 …？ *yau dee mut ye …*
I'd like …	我想要 … *ngor surng yeeu …*
I'll have …	我要 … *ngor yeeu …*
a bottle/glass/carafe of …	一瓶／一杯／一瓶散裝 … *yut jun'/yut boo-ee/yut jun' saan jong …*

可以點菜了嗎？	Are you ready to order?
想要些什麼？	What would you like?
要不要先叫點飲品？	Would you like to order drinks first?
我介紹 …	I recommend …
我們沒有 …	We don't have …
那個要等 … 分鐘。	That will take … minutes.
慢慢吃。	Enjoy your meal.

– hor yee dim s-owng may a?
– nay hor mm hor yee gaai seeu yut dee
   day do ge choy sick a?
– hor yee, ngor gaai seeu …
– ho, jau yeeu nay gor, t-owng maai sa lut'?
– ho. surng yum dee mut ye a.
– yut jun' saan jong h-owng jau, mm goy.
– ho

Side dishes/Accompaniments 配菜

Could I have … without the …?	… 可以不要 …嗎？ *hor mm hor yee mm yeeu …*
With a side order of …	另加一個 … *ling ga yut gor …*
Could I have salad instead of vegetables, please?	請把蔬菜改為沙律。 *mm goy jurng sor choy goy jo sa lut'*
Does the meal come with vegetables/potatoes?	這個餐有蔬菜 / 薯仔嗎？ *nay gor chaan* *yau mo sor choy/su-ee jai a*
Do you have any sauces?	有沒有醬？ *yau mo jurng a*
Would you like … with that?	要不要 … ? *yeeu mm yeeu … a*
vegetables/salad	蔬菜 / 沙律 *sor choy/sa lut'*
potatoes/fries	薯仔 / 炸薯條 *su-ee jai/ja su-ee teeu*
rice	白飯 *baak faan*
sauce	醬 *jurng*
ice	冰 *bing*
May I have some …?	可以給我一些 … 嗎？ *hor mm hor yee bay dee …*
bread	麵飽 *min bau*
butter	牛油 *ngau yau*
lemon	檸檬 *ning m-owng*
mustard	芥醬 *gaai laat*
pepper	胡椒粉 *woo jeeu fun*
salt	鹽 *yim*
seasoning	調味品 *teeu may bun*
soy sauce	醬油 *see yau*
sugar	糖 *tong*
artificial sweetener	人造糖 *yun jo tong*
vinaigrette [French dressing]	醋油沙律汁 / 法國式沙律汁 *cho yau sa lut' jup/faat gwock sick* *sa lut' jup*

General questions 一般詢問

Could I/we have a(n) (clean) ..., please?　請給我 / 我們 …
mm goy bay …

cup/glass　一個 (乾淨的) 杯 / 水杯
yut gor (gon jeng ge) boo-ee/ sur-ee boo-ee

fork/knife　一支叉 / 張刀 *yut jee cha/jurng do*

plate/spoon　一個碟 / 只匙羹 *yut gor dip/je chee gung*

serviette [napkin]　一條餐巾 *yut teeu chaan gun*

ashtray　一個煙灰缸 *yut gor yin foo-ee gong*

I'd like some more ..., please.　我想要多些 … *ngor surng yeeu dor dee …*

Nothing more, thanks.　夠了，謝謝。 *gau la, mm goy*

Where are the bathrooms [toilets]?　廁所在哪裡？
chee sor hai bin do a

Special requirements 特別要求

I mustn't eat food containing ...　我不能吃含有 … 的食物。
ngor mm sick duck yau … ge ye

flour/fat　麵粉 / 脂肪 *min fun/jee fong*

salt/sugar　鹽 / 糖 *yim/tong*

Do you have meals/drinks for diabetics?　有沒有給糖尿病人吃的餐 / 喝的飲品？
yau mo bay tong neeu beng yun sick ge chaan/yum ge ye a

Do you have vegetarian dishes?　有沒有素菜？ *yau mo jaai choy a*

For the children ... 有關兒童的要求

Do you have children's portions?　有沒有兒童餐？
yau mo yee t-owng chaan a

Could we have a child's seat, please?　請拿張兒童坐椅。
mm goy lor jurng sai lo gor dung

Where can I feed the baby?　我可以在哪裡給嬰兒餵奶？
ngor hor yee hai bin do wai B B jai a

Where can I change the baby?　我可以在哪裡給嬰兒換尿片？
ngor hor yee hai bin do bong B B jai woon neeu pin a

CHILDREN ➤ 113

Fast food/Café 快餐店 / 咖啡室

Something to drink 飲品

In towns and cities you will see a large variety of fast-food outlets, many of which are internationally known. These serve the usual burgers and fries, hot dogs, pizzas, etc.

I'd like a cup of ...	我想要一杯 ... *ngor surng yeeu yut boo-ee ...*
tea/coffee	茶 / 咖啡 *cha/ga fe*
black/with milk	不要奶 / 要奶 *mm yeeu naai/yeeu naai*
I'd like a ... of red/white wine.	我想要 ... 紅酒/白酒。 *ngor surng yeeu ... h-owng jau/baak jau*
glass/carafe/bottle	一杯 / 一瓶散裝 / 一瓶 *yut boo-ee/yut jun' saan jong/yut jun'*
Do you have beer?	有沒有啤酒？ *yau mo be jau a*
bottled/draft [draught]	瓶裝 / 生啤 *jun' jong/saang be*

And to eat ... 食品

A piece of ..., please.	要一塊 ... *mm goy, yut faai ...*
I'd like two of those.	我要兩個那種的。 *ngor yeeu lurng gor gor j-owng ge*
I'd like a(n)/some ...	我想要 ... *ngor surng yeeu ...*
burger	漢堡飽 *hon bo bau*
fries	炸薯條 *ja su-ee teeu*
omelet	奄列 *um lit*
cake	蛋糕 *daan go*
sandwich	三文治 *saam mun jee*
ice cream	雪糕 *su-eet go*
vanilla	香草 *wun nay na*
chocolate	朱古力 *ju-ee goo lick*
strawberry	士多啤梨 *see dor be lay*
mango	芒果 *mong gwor*

– cheng mun yeeu dee mut ye?
– lurng boo-ee ga fe, mm goy.
– yeeu mm yeeu naai?
– yeeu naai.
– yeeu mm yeeu sick dee mut ye?
– mm yeeu la, mm goy.

Complaints 投訴

I don't have a/any …	我沒有 … *ngor mo …*
knife/fork/spoon	刀 / 叉 / 匙羹 *do/cha/chee gung*
chopsticks	筷子 *faai jee*
There must be some mistake.	一定是搞錯了。 *yut ding hai gau chor jor la*
That's not what I ordered.	這不是我叫的。 *nay gor mm hai ngor geeu ge*
I asked for …	我要的是 … *ngor yeeu ge hai …*
I can't eat this.	我不能吃這個。 *ngor sick mm lock nay yurng ye*
The meat is …	這肉 … *dee yuk …*
overdone/underdone	煮得太老 / 不夠熟 *ju-ee duck taai lo/mm gau suk*
too tough	太韌 *taai ngun*
This is too …	這個太 … *nay gor taai …*
bitter/sour	苦 / 酸 *foo/su-een*
The food is cold.	這個菜冷冷了。 *nay dip ye d-owng jor*
This isn't fresh/clean.	這個不新鮮 / 不乾淨。 *nay gor mm sun sin/mm gon jeng*
How much longer will our food be?	還要等多久才上菜？ *j-owng yeeu dung gay loy jee surng choy a*
We can't wait any longer. We're leaving.	我們不能再等了。我們要走了。 *ngor day mm joy dung la. ngor day jau la*
I'd like to speak to the head waiter/manager.	我要見部長 / 經理。 *ngor yeeu g-in bo jurng/ging lay*

Paying 付款

In general, tipping in Hong Kong is not expected. And in mainland China it has been officially discouraged, although it is becoming more common in some areas. However, a service charge of 10% or more is commonly added to the bill in upscale establishments.

I'd like to pay.	我想付帳。 *ngor surng jau so*
The bill, please.	請結帳。 *mm goy maai daan*
We'd like to pay separately.	我們各付各的 *ngor day gock bay gock ge*
It's all together.	請全部一起算。 *mm goy chu-een bo yut chai gai*
I think there's a mistake in this bill.	我覺得這帳單有錯。 *ngor gock duck nay jurng daan yau do chor jor*
What's this amount for?	這個數目是付什麼的錢？ *nay gor so muk hai bay mut ye ge chin*
I didn't have that. I had …	我沒有吃那個。我吃的是 … *ngor mo sick gor yurng. ngor sick ge hai …*
Is service included?	包括服務費在內嗎？ *bau mm bau maai fuk mo fai ga*
Can I pay with this credit card?	可以用這張信用卡付款嗎？ *hor mm hor yee y-owng nay jurng sun' y-owng kaat bay chin*
I've forgotten my wallet.	我忘了帶錢包。 *ngor mm gay duck daai ngun bau*
I don't have enough money.	我沒有足夠的錢。 *ngor mm gau chin*
Could I have a receipt, please?	請開張收條。 *mm goy họy jurng sau teeu*
That was a very good meal.	這頓飯很好吃。 *nay chaan faan ho ho sick*

– for gay. mm goy maai daan.
– *ho. daan hai do.*
– bau mm bau maai fuk mo fai ga?
– *bau maai.*
– hor mm hor yee y-owng nay jurng sun'
y-owng kaat bay chin a?
– *dong yin.*
– nay chaan faan ho ho sick.

Course by course 各道菜

Breakfast 早餐

In almost every hotel in China, Western tourists are automatically served a European/American-style breakfast. This consists of eggs, toast, butter, jam, and coffee or tea. If you want to try a Chinese breakfast – porridge, buns, and perhaps noodles and cold appetizers – you will have to make it clear to the waiter/waitress.

I'd like ...	我想要 ...	*ngor surng yeeu*
bread/butter	麵飽 / 牛油	*min bau/ngau yau*
a boiled egg	一只煮蛋	*yut je saap daan*
fried eggs/scrambled eggs	煎蛋 / 炒蛋	*jin daan/chau daan*
fruit juice	果汁	*gwor jup*
orange/grapefruit	橙 / 西柚	*chaang/sai yau*
honey/jam	蜜糖 / 果醬	*mut tong/gwor jurng*
milk	牛奶	*ngau naai*
rolls	餐飽	*chaan bau*
toast	多士	*dor see*

Appetizers/Starters 頭盤

拼盤 *ping poon*
Combination platter, an assortment of different varieties of cold meat.

燒味拼盤 *seeu may ping poon*
Roast meat combination platter. Served cold.

龍蝦沙律 *l-owng ha sa lut'*
Lobster salad.

大蝦沙律 *daai ha sa lut'*
Shrimp [prawn] salad.

點心 *dim sum*

Dim sum is traditionally eaten as breakfast or lunch and not as in the West where it is served as lunch, or even as an evening meal.

Servers wander from table to table chanting names of the foods contained in bamboo steamers on their trays or carts. The waiter will compute the bill on the basis of empty dishes on the table. Many restaurants only serve this speciality from morning to mid-afternoon. Dozens of different delicacies are available, for example: **seeu maai** (燒賣), pork and shrimp dumplings; **ha gaau** (蝦餃), delicate steamed shrimp dumplings; **cha seeu baau** (叉燒飽), barbecued pork buns; **dau sa go** (豆沙糕), sweet bean-filled pastry; and **gai tong wun tun** (雞湯餛飩), chicken soup with vegetable dumplings.

Soups 湯類

At banquets or set meals, soup is often served towards the end of a meal to aid digestion. An exception is shark's fin soup which comes at the middle of a meal because it is so special.

菜肉清湯	*choy yuk ching tong*	meat and vegetable broth
雪利酒雞湯	*su-eet lay jau gai tong*	chicken broth with sherry
大蒜湯	*daai su-een tong*	garlic soup
洋蔥湯	*yurng ch-owng tong*	onion soup
湯麵	*tong min*	noodle soup
海鮮湯	*hoy sin tong*	seafood soup
水魚湯	*sur-ee yu-ee tong*	turtle soup
雜菜湯	*jaap choy tong*	vegetable soup

蟹肉粟米湯 *haai yuk suk mai tong*
Crabmeat and corn soup.

魚翅湯 *yu-ee chee tong*
Shark's fin soup. This thick soup may contain mushrooms, chicken, and bacon or ham, as well as shark's fin.

鮑魚湯 *bau yu-ee tong*
Abalone, mushrooms, and pork.

燉白鴿 *dun baak gup*
Broth with pigeon, winter melon, and mushrooms.

Poultry 雞鴨類

Chicken, duck, and pigeon are used in a great variety of forms, either as main dishes or for flavoring.

鴨	*aap*	duck
火雞	*for gai*	turkey
雞	*gai*	chicken
鵝	*ngor*	goose
鵪鶉	*um chun'*	quail
白鴿	*baak gup*	pigeon

燒雞 *seeu gai* Roast or grilled chicken.

甜酸雞肝 *tim su-een gai gon* Sweet and sour chicken liver.

燒鴨 *seeu aap* Roast duck.

菠蘿鴨 *bor lor aap* Pineapple duck.

Fish and seafood 魚和海鮮

Cantonese cuisine is renowned for its imaginative use of fish and seafood.

鯇魚	*waan yu-ee*	grass carp
大頭魚	*daai tau yu-ee*	catfish
鱸魚	*lo yu-ee*	sea bass
白鱗魚	*baak lun' yu-ee*	herring
撻沙	*taat sa*	sole
魚翅	*yu-ee chee*	shark's fin
紅魚	*h-owng yu-ee*	red snapper
金槍魚	*gum churng yu-ee (tun' na yu-ee)*	tuna
鱈魚	*su-eet yu-ee*	cod
銀魚	*ngun yu-ee*	whitebait
蠔	*ho*	oysters
蜆	*hin*	clams
鮑魚	*bo yu-ee*	abalone
帶子	*daai jee*	scallops
魷魚	*yau yu-ee jai*	baby squid
蝦	*ha*	shrimp
大蝦	*daai ha*	large shrimp [prawns]
龍蝦	*l-owng ha*	lobster
青口	*cheng hau*	mussels
章魚	*jurng yu-ee*	octopus
鱒魚	*jun' yu-ee*	trout

炒蝦碌 *chaau ha luk'*
Shrimp coated in a light batter and fried in ginger and garlic.

蠔油鮑魚片 *ho yau bau yu-ee pin*
Abalone braised with oyster sauce.

炒魚 *chaau yu-ee*
Whole fish braised with soy sauce and sherry, with sping onions and ginger.

甜酸魚 *tim su-een yu-ee*
Sweet and sour fish.

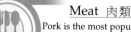

Meat 肉類

Pork is the most popular meat served in southern China, and every part of it is eaten (skin, feet, ears, etc.). Although beef and lamb are available, these meats are used more often in northern Chinese cooking.

牛肉	*ngau yuk*	beef
羊肉	*yurng yuk*	lamb
豬肉	*ju-ee yuk*	pork
火腿	*for tur-ee*	ham
煙肉	*yin yuk*	bacon
牛仔肉	*ngau jai yuk*	veal
兔肉	*to yuk*	rabbit
乳鴿	*yu-ee gup*	spring pigeon
牛扒	*ngau pa*	steak
肝 / 潤	*gon/yun'*	liver
腎 / 腰	*sun/yeeu*	kidneys
香腸	*hurng churng*	sausages

Meat cuts 肉類切段

牛柳	*ngau lau*	fillet steak
西冷牛扒	*sai laang ngau pa*	sirloin steak
牛臀肉	*ngau tu-een yuk*	rump steak
T-骨牛扒	*T gwut ngau pa*	T-bone steak
肉扒	*yuk pa*	chops
肉排	*yuk pai*	cutlet

甜酸排骨 *tim su-een paai gwut* Sweet and sour spareribs.

燒排骨 *seeu paai gwut* Barbecued spareribs.

紅燒豬肉 *h-owng seeu ju-ee yuk*
Casserole of "five-flowered pork": lean and fat pork cooked with sherry, ginger, garlic, and anise and served with spinach.

獅子頭 *see jee tau*
Steamed or simmered meatballs made mainly from pork and served with hearts of Chinese cabbage.

菜遠牛柳 *choy yu-een ngau lau* Beef fillets with green vegetables.

豉椒牛肉 *see jeeu ngau yuk*
Beef in black bean sauce with sweet peppers.

46

Vegetables 蔬菜

Chinese cuisine has a great variety of vegetable-based dishes but many contain small amounts of meat, seafood, or poultry which add flavor but can make it difficult for vegetarians.

椰菜	ye choy	cabbage
洋蔥	yurng ch-owng	onion
青豆	cheng dau	peas
豆角	dau gock	green beans
矮瓜	ai gwa	eggplant [aubergine]
生菜	saang choy	lettuce
薯仔	su-ee jai	potatoes
紅椒	h-owng jeeu	sweet red peppers
蘑菇	mor goo	mushrooms
紅蘿匐	h-owng lor baak	carrots
白菜	baak choy	Chinese cabbage
菜心	choy sum	Chinese flowering cabbage
菠菜	bor choy	spinach
芽菜	nga choy	bean sprouts
豆苗	dau meeu	pea sprouts
西蘭花	sai laan fa	broccoli
西芹	sai kun	celery
青瓜	cheng gwa	cucumber
番茄	faan ke	tomato
露筍	lo sun'	asparagus
竹筍	juk sun'	bamboo shoots
西洋菜	sai yurng choy	watercress
荷蘭豆	ho laan dau	snow peas [mangetout]

羅漢齋 *lor hon jaai*
Buddhist monk's vegetable creation, containing a variety of stir-fried vegetables and bean curd.

開洋白菜 *hoy yurng baak choy*
Stir-fried Chinese white cabbage with dried shrimps.

Salad 沙律

Salad isn't part of traditional Chinese cuisine. However, in Western-style restaurants you can find a variety of salads and dressings.

Eggs 蛋

Eggs are usually stir-fried, as in omelets, or steamed, as in custards. They are often added to meat, vegetable, and rice dishes and to soups.

蒸蛋 *jing daan* Steamed egg custard.

芙蓉蛋 *foo y-owng daan*
Rich egg omelet with vegetables and bits of meat, poultry, or shrimp.

Bean curd 豆腐

Bean curd (**dau foo**) is made from soy bean purée and has the texture of firm custard. It is a great source of protein and has a neutral taste which absorbs the flavor of the food it's cooked in. There are two main types of bean curd: the coarser type more suitable for frying, and the silken type, which is better suited for inclusion in soups.

多菇豆腐 *d-owng goo dau foo*
Stir-fried bean curd with mushrooms, onions, and soy sauce.

麻醬豆腐 *ma jurng dau foo*
Bean curd with sesame or peanut butter sauce.

Rice 飯

Rice is the staple food of China and has various names, depending on the type of grain and the stage of its preparation. Cooked rice is **faan** (飯); glutinous rice is **nor mai** (糯米); and rice porridge, or gruel, is **juk** (粥).

白飯 *baak faan*
White rice.

炒飯 *chaau faan*
Fried rice with eggs, onions, and bits of pork.

豬肉粥 *ju-ee yuk juk*
Hot rice porridge with pork and onions.

Noodles 麵

Noodles (**min**) are made from wheat, rice, or bean flour. They are traditionally seen as a symbol of longevity because of their length.

湯麵 *tong min*
Noodles in a broth with an assortment of vegetables and meat.

炒麵 *chaau min*
Stir-fried noodles with meat, seafood, or vegetables.

燴麵 *woo-ee mien*
Braised or pot-cooked noodles with gravy, served with a garnish.

Dessert 甜品

The Chinese seldom finish their meals with sweets or cakes but often have fruit. Some upscale restaurants have added ice cream (**su-eet go**) to their menu. However, in general, sweet things are eaten as snacks and are seldom available in restaurants, with the exception of those in Western-style hotels.

Fruit 水果

車厘子	*che lay jee*	cherries
李	*lay*	plums
士多啤梨	*see dor be lay*	strawberries
石榴	*sek lau*	pomegranates
蘋果	*ping gwor*	apples
桃	*to*	peaches
橙	*chaang*	oranges
香蕉	*hurng jeeu*	bananas
西柚	*sai yau*	grapefruits
提子	*tai jee*	grapes
蜜瓜	*mut gwa*	honeydew melon
荔枝	*lai jee*	lychees
龍眼	*l-owng ngaan*	longans*
芒果	*mong gwor*	mangoes
雪梨	*su-eet lay*	pears
菠蘿	*bor lor*	pineapple
楊桃	*yurng to*	star fruit
柑	*gum*	tangerines
杏	*hung*	apricots

* small white fruit similar to a lychee

Cheese 芝士

Cheese is not part of traditional Cantonese cuisine. However, you will find it available in Western-style hotels and supermarkets.

Drinks 飲品

You may find that quite a few Chinese like drinking French cognac with their meals, possibly because of a vague belief that it has aphrodisiac qualities. European and Australian table wines are also available, but they can range in price from tolerable to extortionate. Chinese wines have a 4,000-year history, yet few visitors develop a taste for them. Some are too sweet, others too strong.

Beer 啤酒

Beer is the second most popular drink after tea. The locally brewed San Miguel (生力啤 **saang lick be**) is cheap and refreshing. Tsingtao (青島啤酒 **ching do be jau**), the most popular Chinese beer, has a hearty European taste. You'll also find some of the best beers of Asia, Australia, and Europe on better menus.

beer	啤酒	*be jau*
bottled/draft [draught]	瓶裝 / 生啤	*jun' jong/saang be*

Wine 葡萄酒

Each region has its own wine or liqueur, often rather sweet, made from local fruits, flowers, or herbs.
The red wines of Shanghai and the dry white wines of Yantai have drawn praise from connoisseurs. There are also many rice wines. These are usually colorless and often very potent.

red (grape) wine	紅酒	*h-owng jau*
white (grape) wine	白酒	*baak jau*
rice wine	米酒	*mai jau*

Spirits and liqueurs 烈酒和甜酒

Chinese brandies also display regional variations, incorporating flavorings such as bamboo leaves, chrysanthemums, and cloves. The best known, a staple for banquet toasts, is **mau toy**, which is fragrant and mellow but potent.

Chinese brandy	茅台	*mau toy*
whisky	威士忌	*wai see gay*
gin/vodka	氈酒 / 獲特加	*jin jau/wock duck ga*
with water/soda	加水 / 加梳打	*ga sur-ee/ga sor da*
straight [neat]/on the rocks	不加水 / 加冰	*mm ga sur-ee/ga bing*
single/double	一份 / 雙份	*yut fun/surng fun*
glass/bottle	一杯 / 一瓶	*yut boo-ee/yut jun'*

Tea and coffee 茶 / 咖啡

The Chinese virtually revere tea and have been drinking it for many centuries as a thirst-quencher, general reviver, and ceremonial beverage. Jasmine-scented green tea and fermented black tea are the most popular ones and are usually drunk without sugar or milk (except in places where they serve English tea with milk and sugar).

Indian tea is not generally available outside of international supermarkets.

Coffee is not as popular but can be found in snack bars and Western-style restaurants. Instant coffee can be bought in supermarkets.

tea	茶	*cha*
coffee	咖啡	*ga fe*
black / with milk	不要奶 / 要奶	*mm yeeu naai/yeeu naai*
iced coffee	凍咖啡	*d-owng ga fe*
green tea	綠茶	*luk cha*
black tea	紅茶	*h-owng cha*
jasmine tea	香片	*hurng pin*
lychee tea	荔枝紅茶	*lai jee h-owng cha*

Other drinks 其他飲品

Familiar soft drinks, both the genuine and copycat versions, are cheap and widely available. You can also find a wide variety of tropical fruit juices.

Fresh milk is rare as an off-the-shelf item, but you can buy imported UHT milk at Western-style supermarkets.

fruit juice	果汁	*gwor jup*
orange juice	橙汁	*chaang jup*
lemonade	檸檬汽水	*ning m-owng hay sur-ee*
Coca-Cola	可口可樂	*hor hau hor lock*
Seven-Up	七喜	*chut hay*
soda water	梳打水	*sor da sur-ee*
tonic water	湯力水	*tong lick sur-ee*
milkshake	奶昔	*naai sick*

Menu Reader

This Menu Reader gives listings under main food headings. You will see that the Chinese characters are shown in large type. This is to help you to identify, from a menu that has no English, at least the basic ingredients making up a dish.

Meat, fish, and poultry

肉	yuk	meat (general)
牛肉	ngau yuk	beef
豬肉	ju-ee yuk	pork
羊肉	yurng yuk	lamb/mutton
狗肉	gau yuk	dog
雞	gai	chicken
鴨	aap	duck
鵝	ngor	goose
乳鴿	yu-ee gup	young pigeon
魚	yu-ee	fish (general)
海鮮	hoy sin	seafood (general)
鱔	sin	eel
蛇	se	snake
蛋	daan	eggs (general)

Vegetables

蔬菜	*sor choy*	vegetable(s)
露筍	*lo sun'*	asparagus
竹筍	*juk sun'*	bamboo shoots
豆角	*dau gock*	beans
芽菜	*nga choy*	bean sprouts
西蘭花	*sai laan fa*	broccoli
椰菜	*ye choy*	cabbage
西芹	*sai kun*	celery
白菜	*baak choy*	Chinese cabbage
黃芽白	*wong nga baak*	Chinese leaves
青瓜	*cheng gwa*	cucumber
矮瓜	*ai gwa*	eggplant [aubergine]
磨菇	*mor goo*	mushrooms
青椒	*cheng jeeu*	peppers (green)
荷蘭豆	*hor laan dau*	snow peas [mangetout]
菠菜	*bor choy*	spinach
蔥	*ch-owng*	spring onions
番茄	*faan ke*	tomatoes
馬蹄	*ma tai*	water chestnuts

Fruit

生果	*saang gwor*	fruit (general)
蘋果	*ping gwor*	apples
香蕉	*hurng jeeu*	bananas
提子	*tai jee*	grapes
蜜瓜	*mut gwa*	melon
奇異果	*kay yee gwor*	kiwi fruit
龍眼	*l-owng ngaan*	longan *small white fruit similar to a lychee*
荔枝	*lai jee*	lychees
芒果	*mong gwor*	mangoes
橙	*chaang*	oranges
桃	*to*	peaches
雪梨	*su-eet lay*	pears
菠蘿	*bor lor*	pineapple
李	*lay*	plums
士多啤梨	*see dor be lay*	strawberries
西瓜	*sai gwa*	watermelon

Staples: bread, rice, noodles, etc.

麵飽	*min bau*	bread
飯	*faan*	rice
粥	*juk*	rice porridge
點心	*dim sum*	dumplings
豆	*dau*	beans [pulses]
河粉	*hor fun*	rice noodles
麵	*min*	wheat noodles
蛋麵	*daan min*	egg noodles

Basics

鹽	*yim*	salt
胡椒粉	*woo jeeu fun*	pepper
豉油	*see yau*	soy (sauce)
柱侯醬	*chu-ee hau jurng*	soybean paste
蠔油	*ho yau*	oyster sauce
豆豉醬	*dau see jurng*	black bean sauce
海鮮醬	*hoy sin jurng*	hoisin sauce
蘇梅醬	*so moo-ee jurng*	plum sauce

蒸	*jing*	steamed
炒	*chaau*	stir-fried
煎	*jin*	fried
炸	*ja*	deep-fried
干燒	*gon seeu*	dry-fried
滾；煠	*gwun*; saap*	boiled
紅燒	*h-owng seeu*	stewed
扒	*pa*	braised
燒	*seeu*	grilled
焗	*guk*	baked
烤	*hau*	roasted
燒烤	*seeu hau*	barbecued

* Do not use the term **gwun** for *boiled* when referring to eggs (e.g. boiled egg) as it means something impolite! In such cases use the term **saap**.

Classic dishes

菜遠斑球	*choy yu-een baan kau*	fish (garoupa) balls and green vegetables
清蒸鱸魚	*ching jing lo yu-ee*	steamed whole perch
豉汁焗蟹	*see jup guk haai*	baked crab in black bean sauce
酥炸生蠔	*so ja saang ho*	deep-fried oysters in a crispy batter
中式牛柳	*j-owng sick ngau lau*	Chinese fillet steak in a sweet, tangy sauce
咕嚕肉	*goo lo yuk*	sweet and sour pork
炸子雞	*ja jee gai*	deep-fried chicken
叉燒	*cha seeu*	barbecued pork
燒鵝	*seeu ngor*	roast goose
燒肉	*seeu yuk*	roast pork with crispy skin
北京塡鴨	*baak ging tin aap*	Peking duck
煎釀豆腐	*jin yurng dau foo*	fried bean curd stuffed with fish, meat, or shrimp, served in a sauce
豆腐煲	*dau foo bo*	braised bean curd with assorted meat and vegetables

Noodles, rice, breads, etc.

白飯	*baak faan*	cooked white rice
炒飯	*chaau faan*	fried rice
米	*mai*	hulled rice
糯米	*nor mai*	glutinous rice *sticky, short grain rice*
麵	*min*	wheat noodles
粉絲	*fun see*	cellophane noodles
河粉	*hor fun*	rice noodles
米粉	*mai fun*	fine rice noodles
油條	*yau teeu*	fried breadsticks
饅頭	*maan tau*	steamed buns
燒餅	*seeu beng*	clay-oven bread
銀絲卷	*ngun see gu-een*	steamed or fried bread rolls
蝦片	*ha pin*	shrimp toast [prawn crackers]
酥餅	*so beng*	crusty pastry

Drinks

牛奶	*ngau naai*	milk
咖啡	*ga fe*	coffee
凍咖啡	*d-owng ga fe*	iced coffee
綠茶	*luk cha*	green tea
紅茶	*h-owng cha*	black tea *"black" tea is called "red" tea in Chinese*
香片	*hurng pin*	jasmine tea
荔枝紅茶	*lai jee h-owng cha*	lychee tea
紅酒	*h-owng jau*	red (grape) wine
白酒	*baak jau*	white (grape) wine
威士忌	*wai see gay*	whisky
啤酒	*be jau*	beer
生啤	*saang be*	draft beer
米酒	*mai jau*	rice wine
茅台	*mau toy*	Chinese brandy

水	*sur-ee*	water
礦泉水	*kong chu-een sur-ee*	mineral water
滾水	*gwun sur-ee*	hot water for making tea
果汁	*gwor jup*	(fruit) juice
橙汁	*chaang jup*	orange juice
西柚汁	*sai yau jup*	grapefruit juice
檸檬汽水	*ning m-owng hay sur-ee*	lemonade
可口可樂	*hor hau hor lock*	Coca-Cola
七喜	*chut hay*	Seven-Up
梳打水	*sor da sur-ee*	soda water
湯力水	*tong lick sur-ee*	tonic water
奶昔	*naai sick*	milkshake

Snacks

薯條	*su-ee teeu*	French fries [chips]
漢堡飽	*hon bo bau*	hamburger
餅乾	*beng gon*	cookies [biscuits]
蛋糕	*daan go*	cake
三文治	*saam mun jee*	sandwich
薯片	*su-ee pin*	potato chips [crisps]
花生	*fa sung*	peanuts
朱古力	*ju-ee goo lick*	chocolate
熱狗	*yit gau*	hot dog
點心	*dim sum*	boiled dumplings with a variety of fillings
春卷	*chun' gu-een*	spring rolls *pancake rolls filled with pork, shrimp, and vegetables*
叉燒飽	*cha seeu bau*	steamed barbecued pork buns
雞飽	*gai bau*	steamed chicken buns

Soups/soup-based dishes

雞蓉粟米湯	*gai y-owng suk mai tong*	chicken and sweetcorn soup
酸辣湯	*su-een laat tong*	hot and sour soup
冬瓜盅	*d-owng gwa j-owng*	assorted meat soup served in a gourd
魚翅羹	*yu-ee chee gung*	shark's fin soup
燕窩羹	*yin wor gung*	swallow's nest soup
蛇羹	*se gung*	snake soup *shredded snake and chicken meat with vegetables in a thick soup served with bean sprouts, chrysanthemum petals, and tiny crackers*
冬菇雞湯	*d-owng goo gai tong*	chicken and mushroom soup
西洋菜湯	*sai yurng choy tong*	Chinese watercress soup

Dairy products and soy products

芝士	*jee see*	cheese
酸奶	*su-een naai*	yogurt
奶油	*gay lim*	cream
牛油	*ngau yau*	butter
牛奶	*ngau naai*	milk
豆腐	*dau foo*	tofu
豆漿	*dau jurng*	soy milk, usually sweetened
花奶	*fa naai*	evaporated milk
煉奶	*lin naai*	condensed milk
脫脂奶	*tu-eet jee naai*	skimmed milk
奶粉	*naai fun*	powdered milk
人造牛油	*yun jo ngau yau*	margarine
酸奶雪糕	*su-een naai su-eet go*	frozen yogurt

Desserts

雪糕	*su-eet go*	ice cream
鬆糕	*s-owng go*	Chinese sponge cake
芝麻卷	*jee ma gu-een*	sesame seed roll
八寶飯	*baat bo faan*	eight jewel rice *rice pudding with nuts, dates, and candied fruit*
拔絲香蕉	*but see hurng jeeu*	glazed toffee banana
拔絲蘋果	*but see ping gwor*	glazed toffee apple
椰汁西米露	*ye jup sai mai lo*	sago milk with coconut, served cold
芒果布甸	*mong gwor bo din*	mango pudding
西多士	*sai dor see*	French toast
班戟	*baan kick*	pancakes
克戟	*haak kick*	hot cakes
蛋撻	*daan taat*	custard tarts *available at cafés, bakeries, and restaurants serving **dim sum***

Travel

ESSENTIAL

1/2/3 ticket(s) to …	一張 / 兩張 / 三張去 … 的票。 *yut jurng/lurng jurng/saam jurng hur-ee … ge fay*
To …, please.	去 … 的，謝謝。 *hur-ee … ge, mm goy*
one-way [single]	單程 *daan ching*
round-trip [return]	來回 *loy woo-ee*
How much …?	… 多少錢？ *… gay dor chin a*

Hong Kong, Macau, and Guangdong have well-developed public transportation systems encompassing trains, buses, and boats.

Safety 安全

Would you accompany me …?	請陪我 …。 *mm goy poo-ee ngor …*
to the bus stop	去巴士站 *hur-ee ba see jaam*
to my hotel	回酒店 *faan jau dim*
I don't want to … on my own.	我不想自己一個人 …。 *ngor mm surng jee gay yut gor yun …*
stay here	留在這裡 *lau hai nay do*
walk home	走路回家 *haang faan uk kay*
I don't feel safe here.	我覺得在這裡不安全。 *ngor gock duck hai nay do mm on chu-een*

POLICE ➤ 152; EMERGENCY ➤ 224

Arrival 抵境

Hong Kong. Visitors from the U.S. and South Africa can stay for one month without a visa; those from Australia, Canada, Ireland, and New Zealand for three months; and U.K. citizens six months (leisure only).

Macau. Most visitors just need a valid passport to enter Macau and can stay for at least 20 days.

Guangdong. All visitors need valid passports and visas (either single or multiple entry); the standard is 30 days but 60 or 90 days can also be obtained. It is best to get the visa in advance.

Customs. Channels are clearly marked red and green (nothing to declare), and you cannot take more than 6000 yuan into Guangdong, but there is no limit on foreign currency. It is also forbidden to import media that are considered "detrimental to China's politics, economy, culture, and ethics".

Duty Free Into:	Cigarettes	Cigars	Tobacco	Spirits	Wine
Hong Kong	200	50	250g	1L of alcohol	
Guangdong	600 cigarettes or equivalent			2 L of alcohol	
Australia	200 or	250g or	250g	1L or	1L
Canada	200 and	50 and	900g	1L or	1L
S. Africa	400 and	50 and	250g	1L and	2L
U.K.	200 or	50 or	250g	1L and	2L
U.S.	200 and	100 and	*	1L or	1L
* a reasonable amount					

Passport control 護照檢查

We have a joint passport.	我們持共同護照。 *ngor day ja g-owng t-owng woo jeeu*
The children are on this passport.	孩子們都是用這個護照。 *sai lo gor do hai y-owng nay gor woo jeeu*
I'm here on vacation [holiday]/business.	我來這裡度假 / 我因公事來這裡。 *ngor lay nay do do ga/ngor yun wai g-owng see lay nay do ge*
I'm just passing through.	我只是過境。 *ngor jee hai gwor ging*
I'm going to …	我準備去 … *ngor jun' bay hur-ee …*
I'm …	我 … *ngor …*
on my own	自己一個人來的 *jee gay yut gor yun lay ge*
with my family	和家人一同來的 *t-owng ga yun yut chai lay ge*
with a group	隨團來的 *gun tu-een lay ge*

WHO ARE YOU WITH? ➤ 120

Customs 海關

I have only the normal allowances.	我只帶了通常限額的物品。 *ngor daai ge hai t-owng churng haan ngaak ge ye*
It's a gift.	這是禮物。*nay gor hai lai mut*
It's for my personal use.	這是我的私人用品。 *nay gor hai ngor ge see yun y-owng bun*
I would like to declare ...	我想申報 ... *ngor surng bo ...*

你有什麼要申報的嗎？	Do you have anything to declare?
這件東西要納稅。	You must pay duty on this.
這是在那裡買的？	Where did you buy this?
請打開這個袋。	Please open this bag.
你還有其他行李嗎？	Do you have any more luggage?

I don't understand.	我不明白。*ngor mm ming*
Does anyone here speak English?	這裡有誰會說英語嗎？*nay do yau mo yun sick gong ying mun a*

護照檢查	passport control
邊防檢查站	border crossing
海關	customs
無物品報關	nothing to declare
貨物報關	goods to declare
免稅品	duty-free goods

Duty-free shopping 購買免稅品

What currency is this in?	這是用什麼貨幣計算？*nay gor hai y-owng mut ye for bai gai ge*
Can I pay in ...	我可以用 ... 支付嗎？*ngor hor mm hor yee bay ...*
dollars	美元 *may gum*
pounds	英鎊 *ying bong*
renminbi	人民幣 *yun mun bai*

COMMUNICATION DIFFICULTIES ➤ 11

Plane 飛機

There are airports in Hong Kong, Macau, Guangzhou, Shenzhen, Zhanjiang, and Shantou, and the national air carriers are Macau Air, Dragonair (Hong Kong), and CAAC (Civil Aviation Administration of China). There are also various Chinese domestic airlines which connect the area with the rest of China.

Tickets and reservations 機票和預訂

When is the … flight to Shanghai?	… 去上海的班機幾點開？ *hur-ee surng hoy ge baan gay, gay dim hoy a*
first/next/last	第一班 / 下一班 / 最後一班 *dai yut baan/ha yut baan/jur-ee hau yut baan*
I'd like 2 … tickets to Shenyang.	我想要兩張去沈陽的 … 機票。 *ngor surng yeeu lurng jurng hur-ee sum yurng ge … gay peeu*
one-way [single]	單程 *daan ching*
round-trip [return]	來回 *loy woo-ee*
first class	頭等 *tau dung*
business class	商務客位 *surng mo haak wai*
economy class	經濟客位 *ging jai haak wai*
How much is a flight to …?	去 … 的機票多少錢？ *hur-ee … ge gay peeu gay dor chin a*
Are there any supplements/ discounts?	有沒有附加費 / 折扣？ *yau mo foo ga fai/jit kau*
I'd like to … my reservation for flight number 154.	我想 … 我在一五四號班機的預訂。 *ngor surng … ngor hai yut ng say ho baan gay ge yu-ee deng*
cancel/change/confirm	取消 / 更改 / 確認 *chur-ee seeu/gung goy/kock ying*

Inquiries about the flight 班機查詢

What time does the plane leave?	飛機什麼時間起飛？ *fay gay gay see hay fay a*
What time will we arrive?	我們什麼時間到？ *ngor day gay see do a*
What time do I have to check in?	我什麼時間要到機場辦登機手續？ *ngor gay see yeeu do gay churng baan dung gay sau juk a*

Checking in 辦登機手續

Where is the check-in desk for flight …?	… 號班機的登記櫃檯在哪裡？ *… ho baan gay ge dung gay gwai toy hai bin do a*
I have …	我有 … *ngor yau …*
three cases to check in	三個箱入艙 *saam gor gip yup chong*
two pieces of hand luggage	兩件手提行李 *lurng g-in sau tai hung lay*

請出示機票 / 護照。	Your ticket/passport, please.
請問要靠窗口還是靠通道的座位？	Would you like a window or an aisle seat?
吸煙區還是非吸煙區？	Smoking or non-smoking?
請到候機室等候。	Please go through to the departure lounge.
你有多少件行李？	How many pieces of baggage do you have?
你的行李超重。	You have excess baggage.
你需付 … 元附加費。	You'll have to pay a supplement of … dollars.
那件手提行李太重 / 太大了。	That's too heavy/large for hand baggage.
這些行李都是你自己收拾的嗎？	Did you pack these bags yourself?
裡面有沒有尖銳物品或電器？	Do they contain any sharp or electronic items?

抵境（到達）	arrivals
離境（出發）	departures
安全檢查	security check
請時刻注意閣下的行李	Do not leave bags unattended.

LUGGAGE/BAGGAGE ➤ 71

Information 資訊

Is there any delay on flight …?	… 號班機會延遲嗎？	*… ho baan gay woo-ee mm woo-ee yin chee a*
How late will it be?	會延遲多久？	*woo-ee chee gay noy*
Has the flight from … landed?	從 … 來的班機降落了嗎？	*yau … lay ge baan gay gong lock jor may a*
Which gate does flight … leave from?	… 號班機從哪個閘口開出？	*… ho baan gay yau bin gor jaap hau hoy a*

Boarding/In-flight 登機 / 機上

Your boarding card, please.	請出示登機證。	*dung gay jing, mm goy*
Could I have a drink/ something to eat, please?	請給我拿點飲品 / 食品好嗎？	*mm goy, hor mm hor yee lor dee ye yum/sick*
Please wake me for the meal.	用餐時請叫醒我。	*sick chaan ge see hau, mm goy geeu seng ngor*
What time will we arrive?	我們什麼時候到？	*ngor day gay see do a*
An air sickness bag, please.	請給我拿個嘔吐袋。	*mm goy lor gor au to doy*

Arrival 到達

Where is/are (the) …?	… 在哪裡？	*… hai bin do a*
buses	巴士 (公共汽車 *)	*ba see (g-owng g-owng hay che)*
car rental [hire]	租車公司	*jo che g-owng see*
currency exchange	外幣找換店	*ngoy bai jau woon dim*
exit	出口	*chut' hau*
taxis	的士 (出租汽車 *)	*dick see (chut' jo hay che)*
Is there a bus into town?	有沒有去市區的巴士 (公共汽車 *)？	*yau mo ba see (g-owng g-owng hay che) hur-ee see kur-ee a*
How do I get to the … hotel?	我怎樣去… 酒店？	*ngor dim yurng hur-ee … jau dim a*

* The first entry is the name for *bus/taxi* in Hong Kong. The entry in parentheses is that used in Guangdong Province.

LUGGAGE/BAGGAGE► 71; CUSTOMS ► 67

Baggage 行李

It is not obligatory to tip porters, but in practice Hong Kong airport porters expect between HK$3 – 5.50 per bag.

Porter! Excuse me!	麻煩你！ *mm goy nay*
Could you take my luggage to …?	可以幫我把行李搬到 … 上嗎？ *hor mm hor yee bong ngor boon dee hung lay surng …*
a taxi/bus	的士（出租汽車）/ 巴士（公共汽車）*dick see (chut' jo hay che)/ba see (g-owng g-owng hay che)*
Where is/are (the) …?	… 在哪裡？ *… hai bin do a*
baggage carts [trolleys]	行李推車 *hung lay che*
luggage lockers	行李鎖櫃 *hung lay sor gwai*
baggage check [left-luggage office]	行李寄存處 *hung lay gay chu-een chu-ee*
baggage reclaim	領回行李處 *ling woo-ee hung lay chu-ee*
Where is the luggage from flight …?	… 號班機的行李在哪裡？ *… ho baan gay ge hung lay hai bin do a*

Loss, damage, and theft 遺失、損壞及失竊

I've lost my baggage.	我丟失了行李。 *ngor mm g-in jor hung lay*
My baggage has been stolen.	我的行李被人偷了。 *ngor dee hung lay bay yun tau jor*
My suitcase was damaged.	我的箱損壞了。 *ngor gor gip jing laan jor*
Our luggage has not arrived.	我的行李還未到。 *ngor dee hung lay j-owng may do*

你的行李是什麼樣子的？	What does your baggage look like?
你有領行李的標籤嗎？	Do you have the claim check [reclaim tag]?
你的行李 …	Your luggage …
可能運了去 …	may have been sent to …
可能今天稍後到	may arrive later today
請明天再來。	Please come back tomorrow.
請打這個號碼查問你的行李到了沒有。	Call this number to check if your luggage has arrived.

POLICE ➤ 152; COLOR ➤ 143

Train 火車

In Hong Kong, the KCR (Kowloon – Canton Railway) and the MTR (Mass Transit Railway) connect central Hong Kong with the New Territories and Guangdong. The Chinese railway system serves all major cities and tourist centers. Although the average speed is slow, you can get express trains though they are more expensive.

Chinese trains have no classes; instead there are hard seats and sleepers, and soft seats and sleepers. Food and tea are often sold on the trains, and if the train journey takes more than 12 hours, there will usually be a dining car.

硬座 *ngaang jor*

Hard seat car. Usually the seat is padded, but this form of travel is noisy and often very crowded. It might be bearable for a day trip, but it is not recommended for longer journeys.

硬臥 *ngaang ngor*

Hard sleeping car. Generally comfortable as only a set number of people are allowed per car. Sheets and pillows are provided. The best bunk is the middle one since the lower one is used by all and sundry as a seat during the day, and the top one has little headroom and gets very hot and smoky from cigarettes. Lights and speakers go out and off between 9:00 and 10:00 p.m. And if you are at the end of the car in a top bunk where the speakers are located you'll get a rude shock at 6:00 a.m. or thereabout! Note: It is hard to get these sleepers at short notice so reserve a place in advance.

軟座 *yu-een jor*

Soft seat car. Comfortable, and overcrowding is not permitted. Smoking is also prohibited. Soft seats are about the same price as a hard sleeper.

軟臥 *yu-een ngor*

Soft sleeping car. Four comfortable bunks in a closed compartment often with air conditioning. Speakers have a volume control and can even be turned off! Soft sleepers cost nearly as much as flying (on some routes more). Recently the demand for soft sleepers has increased, so once again don't rely on getting a berth at short notice.

Outside of Hong Kong, foreigners pay two and a half times the Chinese price for plane and train tickets. At present on buses there is no double-pricing rule, with the exception of western China. There are no official discounts for tourists other than for foreign students studying in the P.R.C. and certain foreigners authorized to live and work in China (these groups hold "white" and "red" cards which authorize them to pay the local Chinese price).

To the station 去火車站

How do I get to the train station?	火車站怎樣去？ *for che jaam dim yurng hur-ee a*
Do trains to Guangzhou leave from … Station?	去廣州的火車是不是從 … 火車站開出？ *hur-ee gwong jau ge for che, hai mm hai yau … for che jaam hoy a*
How far is it?	火車站有多遠？ *for che jaam yau gay yu-een a*
Can I leave my car there?	我可以把汽車留在那裡嗎？ *ngor hor mm hor yee lau dai ga che hai gor do a*

At the station 在火車站

Where is/are (the) …?	… 在哪裡？ *… hai bin do a*
currency exchange office	外幣兑換處 *ngoy bai dur-ee woon chu-ee*
information desk	詢問處 *sun' mun chu-ee*
baggage check [left-luggage office]	行李寄存處 *hung lay gay chu-een chu-ee*
lost and found [lost property office]	失物認領處 *sut mut ying leng chu-ee*
luggage lockers	行李鎖櫃 *hung lay sor gwai*
platforms	月台（站台）*yu-eet toy (jaam toy)*
snack bar	小食店 *seeu sick dim*
ticket office	售票處 *sau peeu chu-ee*
waiting room	候車室 *hau che sut*

入口	entrance
出口	exit
往月台（站台）	to the platforms
詢問處	information
預訂處	reservations
抵境（到達）	arrivals
離境（出發）	departures

DIRECTIONS ➤ 94

Tickets and reservations 車票和預訂

In mainland China buying a hard-seat ticket at short notice is not normally a problem, but you may not be successful in getting a reserved seat. Buying a ticket for a sleeper can be problematic, even impossible, if you try to do it yourself. If you try and the ticket clerk just says **may-yo**, you need to seek the help of a travel agent at CITS (China International Travel Service), CTS (China Travel Service), CYTS (China Youth Travel Service), or your hotel. You will have to pay a service charge, but this is much better than a long journey in hard-seat class! Remember too that there is usually a three-day advance purchase limit.

I'd like a … ticket to Guangzhou.	我想買一張去廣州的 … 車票。 *ngor surng maai yut jurng hur-ee gwong jau ge … che fay*
one-way [single]	單程 *daan ching*
round-trip [return]	來回 *loy woo-ee*
first/second class	頭等 / 二等 *tau dung/yee dung*
concessionary	優惠 *yau wai*
I'd like to reserve a seat.	我想預訂一個座位。 *ngor surng deng ding gor jor wai*
aisle seat	靠通道的座位 *lo hau wai*
window seat	靠窗口的座位 *ch-urng hau wai*
Is there a sleeping car [sleeper]?	有沒有臥鋪車廂？ *yau mo ngor po che surng a*
I'd like a … berth.	我想要個 … 鋪。 *ngor surng yeeu gor … po*
upper/lower	上 / 下 *surng/ha*

Price 票價

How much is that?	多少錢？ *gay dor chin a*
Is there a discount for …?	… 有沒有折扣？ *… yau mo jit kau a*
children/families	兒童 / 家庭 *sai lo gor/ga ting*
senior citizens	老人 *lo yun*
students	學生 *hock saang*

Queries 詢問

Do I have to change trains?	我需要轉車嗎？ *ngor sai mm sai ju-een che a*
Is it a direct train?	這是直通車嗎？ *nay ga hai mm hai jick t-owng che a*
You have to change at …	你要在 … 轉車。 *nay yeeu hai … ju-een che*
How long is this ticket valid for?	這張車票有效期是多久？ *nay jurng che fay yau hau kay hai gay noy a*
Can I take my bicycle on to the train?	單車可以帶上火車嗎？ *daan che hor mm hor yee daai maai surng for che a*
Can I return on the same ticket?	我可以用同一張車票回來嗎？ *ngor hor mm hor ee y-owng t-owng yut jurng fay faan lay a*
In which car [coach] is my seat?	我的座位在哪個車廂？ *ngor gor jor wai hai bin gor che surng a*
Is there a dining car on the train?	車上有沒有餐車？ *che do yau mo chaan che a*

– *ngor surng maai yut jurng hur-ee fut saan ge che fay.*
– *daan ching yick waak loy woo-ee?*
– *loy woo-ee.*
– *saam baak mun la.*
– *sai mm sai ju-een che a?*
– *yeeu hai gwong jau ju-een che.*
– *mm goy. joy g-in.*

Train times 火車時間

Could I have a timetable, please?	請給我一張時間表。 *mm goy bay jurng see gaan beeu*
When is the … train to Luohu?	… 去羅湖的火車幾點開？ *… hur-ee lor woo ge for che, gay dim hoy a*
first/next/last	第一班 / 下一班 / 最後一班 *dai yut baan/ ha yut baan/ jur-ee hau yut baan*

How frequent are the trains to ...?	去 … 的火車每隔多久一班？ *hur-ee … ge for che gay noy yut baan a*
once/twice a day	每日一班／兩班 *moo-ee yut yut baan/lurng baan*
five times a day	每日五班 *moo-ee yut ng baan*
every hour	每小時一班 *moo-ee gor j-owng tau yut baan*
What time do they leave?	什麼時間開車？ *gay see hoy a*
on the hour	每點正 *moo-ee dim jeng*
20 minutes past the hour	每點二十分 *moo-ee dim yee sup fun*
What time does the train stop at ...?	火車什麼時間在 … 停？ *for che gay see hai … ting a*
What time does the train arrive in ...?	火車什麼時間到 … ？ *for che gay see do …*
How long is the trip [journey]?	路程需要多長時間？ *lo ching yeeu gay noy a*
Is the train on time?	火車準時嗎？ *for che jun' mm jun' see a*

Departures 出發

Which platform does the train to ... leave from?	去 … 的火車從哪個月台（站台）開出？ *hur-ee … ge for che, yau bin gor yu-eet toy (jaam toy) hoy a*
Where is platform 4?	四號月台在哪裡？ *say ho yu-eet toy hai bin do a*
over there	在那邊 *hai gor bin*
on the left/right	在左邊／右邊 *hai jor bin/yau bin*
Where do I change for ...?	去 … 要在哪裡轉車？ *hur-ee … yeeu hai bin do ju-een che*
How long will I have to wait for a connection?	接駁火車要等多長時間？ *bock che yeeu dung gay noy a*

TIME ➤ 221; DIRECTIONS ➤ 94

Boarding 上車

Is this the right platform for the train to …?	去 … 是在這個月台上車嗎？ *hur-ee … hai mm hai nay gor yu-eet toy surng che a*
Is this the train to …?	這是去 … 的火車嗎？ *nay ga for che hai mm hai hur-ee … ga*
Is this seat taken?	這個座位有人嗎？ *nay gor wai yau mo yun a*
I think that's my seat.	這好像是我的座位。 *nay gor jor wai ho chee hai ngor ge*
Here's my reservation.	這是我的預訂證明。 *nay do hai ngor ge deng wai jing ming*
Are there any seats/berths available?	有沒有空的座位 / 床位？ *yau mo h-owng ge jor wai/chong wai*
Do you mind if …?	… 你介意嗎？ *… nay gaai mm gaai yee*
I sit here	我坐這裡 *ngor chor nay do*
I open the window	我開窗 *ngor hoy gor ch-urng*

On the journey 路上

How long are we stopping here for?	我們在這裡停多長時間？ *ngor day hai nay do ting gay noy a*
When do we get to …?	我們什麼時候到 … ? *ngor day gay see do …*
Have we passed …?	我們經過了 … 嗎？ *ngor day ging gwor jor … may a*
Where is the dining/ sleeping car?	餐車 / 臥鋪車廂在哪裡？ *chaan che/ngor po che surng hai bin do a*
Where is my berth?	我的床位在哪裡？ *ngor gor chong wai hai bin do a*
I've lost my ticket.	我丟了車票。 *ngor mm g-in jor che fay*

緊急刹掣	emergency brake	
警鐘	alarm	
自動門	automatic doors	

TIME ➤ 221

Long-distance bus [Coach]
長途汽車

Both Macau and Hong Kong have bus services which connect them with Guangdong. Seats can be reserved in advance with travel agents and tourist offices. In Guangdong, there are government-run and private bus companies, connecting the province with the rest of China.

Where is the bus [coach] station?	長途汽車站在哪裡？ *ch-urng to hay che jaam hai bin do a*
When's the next bus [coach] to …?	下一班去 … 的長途汽車幾點開？ *ha yut baan hur-ee … ge ch-urng to hay che, gay dim hoy a*
Which bay does it leave from?	從個車站開？ *yau bin gor che jaam hoy a*
Does the bus [coach] stop at …?	長途汽車在 … 停嗎？ *churng to hay che hai … ting mm ting a*
How long does the trip [journey] take?	路程需要多長時間？ *lo ching yeeu gay noy a*
Are there … on board?	車上有沒有 …？ *che do yau mo …*
refreshments/toilets	茶點／廁所 *cha dim/chee sor*

Bus/Tram 巴士（公共汽車）／電車

Local bus service networks are extensive, consisting of buses and minibuses. Have plenty of small coins in Hong Kong and Macau as it is not easy to get change. In Guangdong, local buses can be very crowded.

Where can I get a bus/tram to …?	我去 … 到哪裡坐巴士（公共汽車）／電車？ *ngor hur-ee …, hai bin do daap ba see (g-owng g-owng hay che)/din che a*
What time is the … bus to …?	去 … 的巴士（公共汽車）什麼時間開車？ *hur-ee … ge ba see (g-owng g-owng hay che) gay see hoy a*

你需要去那邊。	You need that stop over there
你需要坐 … 號巴士（公共汽車）。	You need bus number …
你需要在 … 轉車。	You must change buses at …

巴士站（公共汽車站）	bus stop
招呼站	request stop
禁止吸煙	no smoking
（緊急）出口	(emergency) exit

Buying tickets 購票

Where can I buy tickets?	到哪裡買車票？ hur-ee bin do maai che fay a
A ... ticket to Zhuhai, please.	買一張去珠海的 ...。 mm goy, yut jurng hur-ee ju-ee hoy ge ...
one-way [single]	單程票 daan ching fay
round-trip [return]	來回票 loy woo-ee fay
multiple journey	多程票 dor ching fay
monthly	月票 yu-eet fay
A booklet of tickets, please.	買一本車票。 mm goy, yut boon che fay
How much is the fare to ...?	去 ... 的車票多少錢？ hur-ee ... ge che fay gay dor chin a

Traveling 乘車

Is this the right bus/tram to ...?	去 ... 是不是坐這輛巴士／電車？ hur-ee ..., hai mm hai chor nay ga ba see/din che a
Could you tell me when to get off?	請問我應該在什麼時候下車？ cheng mun ngor ying goy gay see lock che a
Do I have to change buses?	我需要轉車嗎？ ngor sai mm sai ju-een che a
How many stops are there to ...?	去 ... 要坐多少個站？ hur-ee ... yeeu chor gay dor gor jaam a
Next stop, please!	請下個站停車！ ha gor jaam yau lock, mm goy

◎	不設找贖	exact fare	◎

– cheng mun, hur-ee see jing teng, hai mm hai chor nay ga che a?
– hai, baat ho.
– see jing teng, yut gor.
– ng mun la.
– cheng mun, ngor ying goy gay see lock che a?
– yau nay do say gor jaam.

NUMBERS ➤ 217; DIRECTIONS ➤ 94

Subway [Metro] 地鐵

The MTR (Mass Transit Railway), which is Hong Kong's subway [metro] system, operates from Central across the harbor and up along Kowloon Peninsula. The MTR operates between 6 a.m. and 1 a.m. If you use the MTR frequently it may be worthwhile buying a Common Stored Value Ticket. These are valid for nine months. When using the subway remember that ticket machines do not give change, and that there are no toilets in the MTR stations.

General inquiries 一般查詢

Where's the nearest subway [metro] station?	離這裡最近的地鐵站在哪裡？ *jur-ee kun ge day tit jaam hai bin do a*
Where do I buy a ticket?	到哪裡買車票？ *hur-ee bin do maai che fay a*
Could I have a map of the subway [metro]?	請給我一張地鐵圖。 *mm goy bay jurng day tit to*

Traveling 乘車

Which line should I take for …?	去 … 應該乘哪條線？ *hur-ee … ying goy daap bin teeu sin a*
Is this the right train for …?	去 … 是不是坐這輛列車？ *hur-ee …, hai mm hai chor nay ga che a*
Which stop is it for …?	去 … 要在哪個站下車？ *hur-ee …, yeeu hai bin gor jaam lock che a*
How many stops is it to …?	去 … 要坐多少個站？ *hur-ee … yeeu chor gay dor gor jaam a*
Is the next stop …?	下個站是不是 … ？ *ha gor jaam hai mm hai …*
Where are we?	我們現時在哪裡？ *ngor day yee ga hai bin do a*
Where do I change for …?	去 … 要在哪裡轉車？ *hur-ee …, yeeu hai bin do ju-een che a*
What time is the last train to …?	去 … 的尾班車幾點開？ *hur-ee … ge may baan che gay dim hoy a*

⊖	往其他路線	to other lines	⊕

Ferry 渡輪

Thousands of passengers cross Hong Kong harbor on ferryboats. The most familiar to tourists is the Star Ferry, which connects Kowloon and central Hong Kong. There are also numerous boat services connecting Hong Kong and the outlying islands: Macau, Guangzhou, Shenzhen, Zhuhai, Zhaoqing, and Shantou. Guangzhou is one of the major ports in Southern China and offers boat services to various destinations and leisurely Pearl River cruises. Ask your hotel/travel agent or the respective tourist office – HKTA (in Hong Kong), MGTO (in Macau), or CITS (in mainland China) – about tickets and departure times.

When is the ... car ferry to Zhuhai?	... 去珠海的汽車渡輪幾點開？ ... *hur-ee ju-ee hoy ge hay che do lun' gay dim hoy a*
first/next/last	第一班 / 下一班 / 最後一班 *dai yut baan/ ha yut baan/jur-ee hau yut baan*
hovercraft/ship	飛翔船 / 輪船 *fay churng su-een/ daai su-een*
A round-trip [return] ticket for ...	... 的來回票。 ... *ge loy woo-ee fay*
two adults and three children	兩個成人和三個兒童 *lurng gor daai yun t-owng saam gor sai lo gor*
I want to reserve a ... cabin.	我想訂一個 ... 艙。 *ngor surng deng yut gor ... chong*
single/double	單人 / 雙人 *daan yun/surng yun*

救生圈	life preserver [belt]
救生艇	life boat
召集處	muster station
不能通往載車甲板	no access to car decks

Boat trips 乘船遊覽

Is there a ...?	有沒有 ... ? *yau mo ...*
boat trip	乘船遊覽團 *yau su-een ho ge tu-een*
river cruise	河上遊覽團 *ho surng yau laam tu-een*
What time does it leave/ return?	什麼時間出發 / 回來？ *mut ye see gaan chut' faat/faan lay*
Where can we buy tickets?	到哪裡買票？ *hur-ee bin do maai fay a*

TIME ➤ 221; BUYING TICKETS ➤ 74, 79

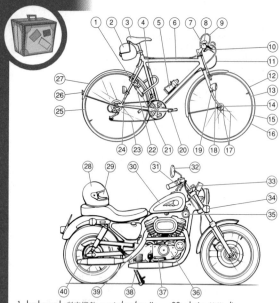

1	brake pad 剎車襯墊 *saat che chun jin*	23	chain 鍊條 *lin*
2	bicycle bag 單車袋 *daan che doy*	24	rear light 尾燈 *may dung*
3	saddle 鞍座 *on jor*	25	rim 輪圈 *lun' hu-een*
4	pump 氣泵 *hay bum*	26	reflector 反射鏡 *faan se geng*
5	water bottle 水瓶 *sur-ee bun'*	27	fender [mudguard] 擋泥板 *dong naai baan*
6	frame 車架 *che ga*	28	helmet 頭盔 *tau kwai*
7	handlebars 車把手 *che ba sau*	29	visor 護目鏡 *woo muk geng*
8	bell 車鈴 *che ling*	30	fuel tank 油箱 *yau surng*
9	brake cable 剎車索 *saat chuk sock*	31	clutch lever 離合器握柄 *lay hup hay uck beng*
10	gear shift [lever] 變速桿 *bin chuk gon*	32	mirror 鏡 *geng*
11	gear/control cable 變速索 *bin chuk sock*	33	ignition switch 發火掣 *faat for jai*
12	inner tube 內胎 *noy taai*	34	turn signal [indicator] 方向指示燈 *fong hurng jee see dung*
13	front/back wheel 前／後輪 *chin/hau lun'*	35	horn 喇叭 *la ba*
14	axle 車軸 *che juk*	36	engine 引擎 *yun king*
15	tire [tyre] 車胎 *che taai*	37	gear shift [lever] 變速桿 *bin chuk gon*
16	wheel 車輪 *che lun'*	38	kick stand [main stand] 主支架 *ju-een jee ga*
17	spokes 輻條 *fuk teeu*	39	exhaust pipe 排氣管；死氣喉 *paai hay goon; say hay hau*
18	bulb 燈泡 *dung daam*	40	chain guard 鍊罩 *lin jaau*
19	headlight 車頭燈 *che tau dung*		
20	pedal 踏板 *daap baan*		
21	lock 車鎖 *che sor*		
22	generator [dynamo] 發電機 *faat din gay*		

Bicycle/Motorbike
單車 (自行車) / 電單車(摩托車)

Major cities like Hong Kong, Macau, and Guangzhou are
very busy and bicycle riding is not recommended. The New
Territories, outlying islands, and smaller towns are better for
bicycle riding, and you can rent a bicycle for a good price if you bargain.

I'd like to rent a …	我想租一輛 … *ngor surng jo yut ga …*
3-/10-speed bicycle	有三個 / 十個檔的單車 (自行車) *yau saam gor/sup gor bor ge daan che (jee hung che)*
moped/motorbike	機動單車(機動自行車) / 電單車(摩托車) *gay d-owng daan che (gay d-owng jee hung che)/din daan che (mor tock che)*
How much does it cost per day/week?	一天 / 一個禮拜要多少錢 ？ *yut yut/yut gor lai baai yeeu gay dor chin a*
Do you require a deposit?	需要付按金嗎 ？ *sai mm sai bay on gum a*
The brakes don't work.	刹掣壞了。 *saat jai waai jor*
There are no lights.	沒有燈。 *mo jor dung*
The front/rear tire [tyre] has a flat [puncture].	前 / 後車胎刺破了。 *chin/hau che taai baau jor*

Hitchhiking 搭順風車

In general, hitchhiking is not officially sanctioned and is not recommended. The same dangers apply as elsewhere in the world. Neither is
hitchhiking free – you will be expected to offer at least a tip.

Where are you heading?	你去哪裡呀 ？ *nay hur-ee bin do a*
I'm heading for …	我去 … *ngor hur-ee …*
Is that on the way to …?	去 … 順路嗎 ？ *hur-ee …, sun' mm sun' lo a*
Could you drop me off …?	可以 … 讓我下車嗎 ？ *hor mm hor yee … bay ngor lock che a*
here/at …	在這裡 / 在 … *hai nay do/hai …*
at the … exit	在 … 出口 *hai … chut' hau*
in the center of town	在市中心 *hai see j-owng sum*
Thanks for giving me a lift.	謝謝你載我到這裡來。 *dor je nay che ngor lay nay do*

DIRECTIONS ➤ 94; NUMBERS ➤ 217

Taxi/Cab 的士（出租汽車）

Major cities have metered taxis or maxicabs/minibuses with set routes where you pay as you get on. It is also possible to hire taxis by the hour/day. Tipping is not obligatory, but in Hong Kong and Macau it is common to round up the fare to the nearest HK$0.50 or dollar. If you use rickshaws, pedicabs, or two-wheeled taxis it is best to negotiate the price in advance. Not many taxi drivers speak English, so it is best to have your destination written out in Chinese or to point it out on a map.

Where can I get a taxi?	在哪裡可以找到的士（出租汽車）？ *hai bin do hor yee wun do dick see (chut' jo hay che) a*
Do you have the number for a taxi?	有沒有叫的士的電話號碼？ *yau mo geeu dick see ge din wa ho ma*
I'd like a taxi ...	我想 ... 要一輛的士。 *ngor surng ... yeeu ga dick see*
now	現在 *yee ga*
in an hour	一小時後 *yut gor j-owng tau hau*
for tomorrow at 9:00	明天九點 *ting yut gau dim*
The address is ...	地址是 ... *day jee hai ...*
I'm going to ...	我要去 ... *ngor yeeu hur-ee ...*

空車 for hire

Please take me to (the) ...	請送我去 ... *mm goy che ngor hur-ee ...*
airport/train station	機場 / 火車站 *gay churng/for che jaam*
this address	這個地址 *nay gor day jee*
How much will it cost?	要多少錢？ *yeeu gay dor chin a*
How much is that?	多少錢？ *gay dor chin a*
You said ... dollars.	你說 ... 元。 *nay wa ... mun*
On the meter it's ...	照咪錶是 ... *jeeu mai beeu hai ...*
Keep the change.	不用找了。 *mm sai jaau la*

> – mm goy che ngor hur-ee che jaam?
> – *ho.*
> – yeeu gay dor chin a?
> – *baat mun. do la.*
> – mm goy. mm sai jaau la.

NUMBERS ➤ 217; DIRECTIONS ➤ 94

Car/Automobile 汽車

In Hong Kong and Macau they drive on the left, in Guangdong on the right. You will find international and local car hire, but driving in big cities is not recommended. To hire a car in Hong Kong, you need to be 25 and have held a driver's license for at least two years.

The speed limit in Hong Kong is 30 m.p.h. (50 k.p.h.) in towns and elsewhere as marked.

In Macau it is illegal to honk your horn.

It is impossible to rent a car in most of mainland China. However, in Beijing, Shanghai, and certain areas such as Hainan Province the idea of drive-away car rental has recently been introduced. Even in these places it is experimental, expensive, and a bureaucratic nightmare. You need an international driver's license but remember that you can only drive within the city limits. Tourists still cannot rent motorbikes or purchase motor vehicles.

If you find it impossible to hire a car, or if you are discouraged by the road signs and the complexity of city traffic, chauffeur-driven cars are an obvious alternative and readily available. The Chinese-made "Shanghai" sedans are being phased out as more comfortable and efficient cars are imported for the tourist market. If you don't want to rent a car for a whole day, it's often possible to arrange for a taxi by the hour plus mileage.

Conversion chart

km	1	10	20	30	40	50	60	70	80	90	100	110	120	130
miles	0.62	6	12	19	25	31	37	44	50	56	62	68	74	81

Fuel 燃油

Gasoline	Premium [Super]/Regular	Diesel
汽油	超級/普通	柴油
hay yau/din yau	cheeu kup/po t-owng	chaai yau

Car rental 租車

It is unlikely that you will be able/want to rent a car during your stay, especially outside of Hong Kong. For further information ➤ 85 or contact a local tourist office.

Where can I rent a car?
在哪裡可以租到汽車？
hai bin do hor yee jo do che a

I'd like to rent a(n) …
我想租一輛 …
ngor surng jo yut ga …

2-/4-door car
兩 / 四門的汽車
lurng/say do moon ge che

an automatic car
有自動波（自動變速）的汽車
yau jee d-owng bor (jee d-owng bin chuk) ge che

car with 4-wheel drive
四驅車
say kur-ee che

car with air conditioning
有空調的汽車
yau h-owng teeu ge che

I'd like it for a day/week.
我想租一天 / 一個禮拜 *ngor surng jo yut yut/yut gor lai baai*

How much does it cost per day/week?
一天 / 一個禮拜多少錢？
yut yut/yut gor lai baai gay dor chin a

Is mileage/insurance included?
包括里數 / 保險在內嗎？
bau mm bau maai lay so/bo him ga

Are there special weekend rates?
週末有沒有特價？
jau moot yau mo duck ga

Can I return the car at …?
我 … 交還汽車，可以嗎？ *ngor … gau faan ga che, duck mm duck a*

What sort of fuel does it take?
這車用哪種燃油？
nay ga che y-owng bin j-owng din yau a

Where is the high [full]/ low [dipped] beam?
高燈 / 低燈在哪裡？
go dung/dai dung hai bin do a

Could I have full insurance?
我可以保全險嗎？
ngor hor mm hor yee bo chu-een him a

DAYS OF THE WEEK ➤ 218; *REPAIRS* ➤ 89

Gas [Petrol] station 加油站

Where's the next gas [petrol] station?	請問下個加油站在哪裡？ *cheng mun ha gor yau jaam hai bin do a*
Is it self-service?	是自助式嗎？ *hai mm hai jee jor sick ga*
Fill it up, please.	請加滿。 *mm goy ga moon kur-ee*
… liters, please.	請加 … 公升汽油。 *mm goy ga … g-owng sing hay yau*
premium [super]/regular	超級 / 普通 *cheeu kup/po t-owng*
lead-free/diesel	無鉛汽油 / 柴油 *mo yu-een hay yau/chaai yau*
I'm at pump number …	加油泵號數是 … *yau bum ho so hai …*
Where is the air pump/water?	氣泵 / 水在哪裡？ *hay bum/sur-ee hai bin do a*

每公升價格	price per liter

Parking 泊車

Parking space is hard to find in Hong Kong, Macau, and large cities in Guangdong.

Is there a parking lot [car park] nearby?	附近有沒有停車場？ *foo gun yau mo ting che churng a*
What's the charge per hour/day?	一小時 / 一天要多少錢？ *yut gor j-owng/ yut yut yeeu gay dor chin a*
Do you have some change for the parking meter?	請問有沒有硬幣可換給我投入停車收費錶？ *cheng mun yau mo saan ngun woon bay ngor, yup ting che mai beeu*
My car has been booted [clamped]. Who do I call?	我的車輪被鎖住了，該找誰？ *ngor ga che bay yun sor jor, yeeu wun bin gor*

NUMBERS ➤ 217; DIRECTIONS ➤ 94

Breakdown 中途壞車

Where is the nearest garage?	離這裡最近的車房在哪裡？ *jur-ee kun ge che fong hai bin do a*
My car broke down.	我的車中途壞了。 *ngor ga che boon lo waai jor*
Can you send a mechanic/ tow [breakdown] truck?	可以派個人／輛拖車來嗎？ *hor mm hor yee paai gor yun/ga tor che lay a*
I belong to … recovery service.	我是 … 拖車服務的會員。 *ngor hai … tor che fuk mo ge woo-ee yu-een*
My registration number is …	我的車牌號碼是 … *ngor gor che paai ho ma hai …*
The car is …	我的車在 … *ngor ga che hai …*
on the highway [motorway]	高速公路上 *go chuk g-owng lo*
2 km from …	離 … 兩公里 *lay hoy … lurng g-owng lay*
How long will you be?	你們多久才能來到？ *nay day gay noy jee lay duck do a*

What is wrong? 出了什麼毛病？

My car won't start.	我的車開不動。 *ngor ga che taat mm jerk*
The battery is dead.	電池沒有電了。 *din chee mo saai din*
I've run out of gas [petrol].	汽油用完了。 *mo saai din yau*
I have a flat [puncture].	我的車胎破了。 *ngor ge che taai baau jor*
There's something wrong with …	… 有毛病。 *… mm tor*
I've locked the keys in the car.	我把車鑰匙鎖在車裡了。 *ngor teeu che see sor jor hai che do*

TELEPHONING ➤ 127; CAR PARTS ➤ 90–91

Repairs 修理

Do you do repairs?	這裡修理汽車嗎？ *nay do jing mm jing che ga*
Can you repair it?	可以替我修理一 下這輛車嗎？ *hor mm hor yee bong ngor jing jing ga che a*
Please make only essential repairs.	請只做必要的修理。 *mm goy jing hai jo bit yeeu ge sau jing*
Can I wait for it?	我在這裡等修理，可以嗎？ *ngor hai do dung sau jing, duck mm duck a*
Can you repair it today?	今天能修好嗎？ *gum yut jing mm jing do a*
When will it be ready?	什麼時候能修好？ *gay see hor yee jing ho a*
How much will it cost?	要多少錢？ *yeeu gay dor chin a*
That's outrageous!	太貴了！ *taai gwai la*
Can I have a receipt for my insurance?	可以開張收條給我報保險嗎？ *hor mm hor yee hoy jurng sau teeu bay ngor bo bo him a*

… 壞了。	The … isn't working.
我沒有必需的零件。	I don't have the necessary parts.
我需要訂購這些零件。	I will have to order the parts.
我只能臨時修理一下。	I can only repair it temporarily.
你的車已徹底損壞了。	Your car is beyond repair.
不能修理了。	It can't be repaired.
… 可以修理好。	It will be ready …
今天稍後	later today
明天	tomorrow
… 天後	in … days

DAYS OF THE WEEK ➤ *218; NUMBERS* ➤ *217*

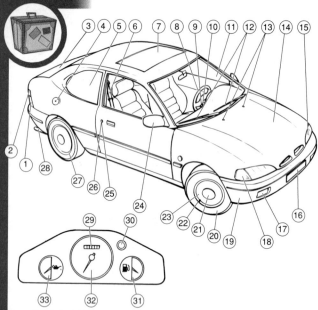

1 taillights [back lights] 尾燈 *may dung*
2 brakelights 刹車燈 *saat che dung*
3 trunk [boot] 行李箱 *hung lay surng*
4 gas tank door [petrol cap] 油箱蓋 *yau surng goy*
5 window 車窗 *che churng*
6 seat belt 座位安全帶 *jor wai on chu-een daai*
7 sunroof 天窗 *tin churng*
8 steering wheel 駕駛盤；軚盤 *ga saai poon; taai poon*
9 ignition 發火器 *faat for hay*
10 ignition key 點火匙 *dim for see*
11 windshield [windscreen] 擋風玻璃 *dong f-owng bor lay*
12 windshield [windscreen] wipers 擋風玻璃水撥 *dong f-owng bor lay sur-ee boot*
13 windshield [windscreen] washer 擋風玻璃洗滌器 *dong f-owng bor lay sai dick hay*
14 hood [bonnet] 車頭蓋 *che tau goy*
15 headlights 車頭燈 *che tau dung*
16 license [number] plate 車牌 *che paai*
17 fog lamp 霧燈 *mo dung*
18 turn signals [indicators] 方向指示燈 *fong hurng jee see dung*
19 bumper 保險桿 *bo him gon*
20 tires [tyres] 車胎 *che taai*
21 hubcap 車輪蓋 *che lun' goy*
22 valve 氣門 *hay moon*
23 wheels 車輪 *che lun'*
24 outside [wing] mirror 車旁倒後鏡 *che pong do hau geng*
25 central locking 中央鎖門裝置 *j-owng yurng sor moon j-owng jee*
26 lock 門鎖 *moon sor*
27 wheel rim 輪圈 *lun' hu-een*
28 exhaust pipe 排氣管；死氣喉 *paai hay goon; say hay hau*
29 odometer [milometer] 里程錶 *lay ching beeu*
30 warning light 警示燈 *ging see dung*
31 fuel gauge 油量錶 *yau lurng beeu*

90

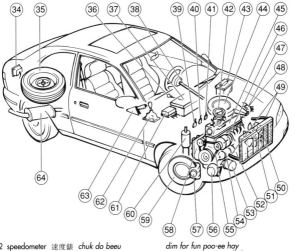

32 speedometer 速度錶 *chuk do beuu*
33 oil gauge 油錶 *yau beeu*
34 backup [reversing] lights 掉頭燈
   deeu tau dung
35 spare wheel 備用車輪 *bay y-owng che taai*
36 choke 阻風門 *jor f-owng moon*
37 heater 加熱器 *ga yit hay*
38 steering column 轉向柱
   ju-een hurng chu-ee
39 accelerator 油門 *yau moon*
40 pedal 踏板 *daap baan*
41 clutch 離合器 *lay hup hay*
42 carburetor 汽化器 *hay fa hay*
43 battery 電池 *din chee*
44 alternator 交流發電機
   gau lau faat din gay
45 camshaft 凸輪軸 *dut lun' juk*
46 air filter 空氣濾清器 *h-owng hay lur-ee ching hay*
47 distributor 點火分配器

dim for fun poo-ee hay
48 points 接觸點 *jip juk dim*
49 radiator hose (top/bottom) 散熱軟管
   (上／下) *saan yit yu-een goon (surng/ha)*
50 radiator 散熱器 *saan yit hay*
51 fan 風扇 *f-owng sin*
52 engine 引擎 *yun king*
53 oil filter 濾油器 *lur-ee yau hay*
54 starter [motor] 起動馬達
   hay d-owng ma daat
55 fan belt 風扇皮帶 *f-owng sin pay daai*
56 horn 喇叭 *la ba*
57 brake pads 刹車襯墊 *saat che chun jin*
58 transmission [gearbox] 變速箱；波箱
   bin chuk surng; bor surng
59 brakes 刹車掣 *saat che jai*
60 shock absorbers 避震器 *bay jun hay*
61 fuses 保險絲；灰士 *bo him see; foo-ee see*
62 gear shift [lever] 變速桿；波棍
   bin chuk gon; bor gwun
63 handbrake 手掣 *sau jai*

Accidents 意外

In Hong Kong and Macau the emergency phone number (ambulance, fire and police) is 999. In Guangdong and the rest of mainland China phone 110 for police assistance.

There has been an accident.	發生了意外。 *faat saang jor yee ngoy*
It's on the highway [motorway].	在高速公路上 *hai go chuk g-owng lo*
It's near …	在 … 附近 *hai … foo gun*
Where's the nearest telephone?	離這裡最近的電話在哪裡？ *jur-ee kun ge din wa hai bin do a*
Call …	叫 … *geeu …*
the police	警察 *ging chaat*
an ambulance	救傷車 *gau surng che*
a doctor	醫生 *yee sung*
the fire department [brigade]	消防局 *seeu fong guk*
Can you help me, please?	你可以幫助我嗎？ *nay hor mm hor yee bong ha ngor*

Injuries 受傷

There are people injured.	有人受傷了。 *yau yun sau jor surng a*
No one is hurt.	無人受傷。 *mo yun sau surng*
He is seriously injured.	他受了重傷。 *kur-ee sau jor ch-owng surng*
She's unconscious.	她不醒人事。 *kur-ee wun jor*
He can't breathe.	他不能呼吸。 *kur-ee tau mm do hay*
He can't move.	他不能動彈。 *kur-ee mm yuk duck*
Don't move him.	別移動他。 *mm ho yuk kur-ee*

ACCIDENT & INJURY ➤ 162; *DIRECTIONS* ➤ 94

Legal matters 法律事宜

What's your insurance company?	你的保險公司叫什麼名字？ *nay gaan bo him g-owng see geeu mut ye meng*
What's your name and address?	你的姓名和地址？ *nay ge sing ming t-owng day jee ne*
That car ran into me.	是那車撞到我的。 *hai gor ga che jong do ngor ga*
That car was going too fast/ driving too close.	她開得太快 / 太近。 *kur-ee ja duck taai faai/taai kun*
I had right of way.	我有優先行駛權。 *ngor yau yau sin hung sai ku-een*
I was (only) driving at … k.p.h.	我當時（只）開每小時 … 公里。 *ngor dong see (jee hai) ja moo-ee seeu see … g-owng lay*
I'd like an interpreter.	我想要一位翻譯。 *ngor surng yeeu gor faan yick*
I didn't see the sign.	我沒看見標誌。 *ngor tai mm do gor beeu jee*
He/She saw it happen.	他 / 她看到當時的情形。 *kur-ee tai do chut' see ge ching ying*
The registration number was …	車牌號碼是 … *che paai ho ma hai …*

可以看看你的 … 嗎？	Can I see your …, please?
駕駛執照	driver's license [licence]
保險單	insurance card
車輛登記文件	vehicle registration document
意外什麼時間發生的？	What time did it happen?
在哪裡發生的？	Where did it happen?
有沒有其他人牽連在內？	Was anyone else involved?
有沒有證人？	Are there any witnesses?
你超速駕駛。	You were speeding.
你的車燈壞了。	Your lights aren't working.
你需要（即時）繳交罰款。	You'll have to pay a fine (on the spot).
你需要去警署 (公安局) 錄口供。	We need you to make a statement at the station.

TIME ➤ 221

Asking directions 問路

Excuse me, please. 請問 *cheng mun*

How do I get to ...? 怎樣去 ... ? *dim yurng hur-ee ... a*

Where is ...? ... 在哪裡 ? *... hai bin do a*

Can you show me on the map where I am? 請在地圖上指出我在哪裡。
mm goy hai day to do, jee chut' ngor yee ga hai bin do

I've lost my way. 我迷路了。 *ngor dong sut jor lo*

Can you repeat that, please? 請再說一遍。 *cheng joy gong yut chee*

More slowly, please. 請說慢點。 *cheng gong maan dee*

Thanks for your help. 謝謝你。 *mm goy saai*

Traveling by car 駕車

Is this the right road for ...? 去 ... 是這條路嗎 ?
hur-ee ..., hai mm hai nay teeu lo a

Is it far from here? 遠不遠 ? *yu-een mm yu-een a*

How far is it to ... from here? ... 離這裡有多遠 ?
... lay nay do yau gay yu-een a

Where does this road lead? 這條路通往哪裡 ?
nay teeu lo t-owng hur-ee bin do a

How do I get onto the highway [motorway]? 怎樣才能上高速公路 ? *dim yurng jee surng do go chuk g-owng lo a*

What's the next town called? 下個市鎮叫什麼名字 ?
ha gor see jun geeu mut ye meng a

How long does it take by car? 開車要多久才到 ?
ja che yeeu gay noy jee do a

It'll take ... minutes. 要 ... 分鐘。 *yeeu ... fun j-owng*

– cheng mun, dim yurng hur-ee for che jaam a?
– *hai dai saam gor lo hau ju-een jor, yin hau jick hur-ee.*
– dai saam gor lo hau ju-een jor. yu-een mm yu-een a?
– *yeeu sup fun j-owng, haang lo.*
– mm goy saai.
– *mm sai mm goy.*

Location 位置

直往前走。	It's straight ahead.
在左邊。	It's on the left.
在右邊。	It's on the right.
在街尾。	It's at the end of the street.
在轉角那裡。	It's on the corner.
轉彎就到。	It's around the corner.
在 ... 的方向。	It's in the direction of ...
在 ... 對面 / 後面。	It's opposite .../behind ...
在 ... 旁邊 / 過了 ... 之後。	It's next to .../after ...
沿著 ... 去。	Go down the ...
橫街 / 大街	side street/main street
穿過廣場。	Cross the square.
過橋。	Cross the bridge.
在第三個路口向右轉。	Take the third turning to the right.
... 向左轉。	Turn left ...
過了第一座交通燈之後	after the first set of traffic lights
在第二個十字路口	at the second intersection [crossroad]

By car 駕車

在這裡的 ...	It's ... of here.
北面 / 南面	north/south
東面 / 西面	east/west
沿著往 ... 的路去。	Take the road for ...
你走錯路了。	You're on the wrong road.
你需回到 ... 去。	You'll have to go back to ...
依著往 ... 的路標去。	Follow the signs for ...

How far? 多遠？

很近 / 很遠	It's close/a long way.
步行需五分鐘	5 minutes on foot
坐車需十分鐘	10 minutes by car
在這條路上大約一百公里以外	about 100 m down the road
離這裡大約十公里	about 10 km away

TIME ➤ 221; NUMBERS ➤ 217

Road signs 道路標誌

禁止通行	access only
替代路線	alternate route
改道	detour [diversion]
選定行車線 (不准換線)	stay in lane
讓路	yield [give way]
低橋	low bridge
單程路	one-way street
道路封閉	road closed
學校	school
請開車頭燈 (大燈)	use headlights

Town plans 城市平面圖

機場	airport
巴士路線 (公共汽車路線)	bus route
巴士站 (公共汽車站)	bus stop
停車場	parking lot [car park]
教堂	church
電影院(戲院)	movie theater [cinema]
大街	main [high] street
詢問處	information office
地鐵站	subway [metro] station
舊區	old town
公園	park
行人斑馬線(人行橫道)	pedestrian crossing
行人專區	pedestrian zone [precinct]
警署 (公安局)	police station
郵局	post office
公眾用途樓宇	public building
運動場	playing field [sports ground]
車站	station
體育館 / 場	stadium
隧道	underpass
的士站 (出租汽車站)	taxi stand [rank]
劇院	theater
你在這裡	You are here.

Sightseeing

Tourist information office
旅遊諮詢中心（旅行社）

The Hong Kong Tourist Association (HKTA) and the Macau Government Tourist Office (MGTO) provide a wealth of information, including free maps, brochures, tour itineraries, and advice on travel. The China Travel Service (CTS) has branches in Hong Kong and Guangdong, where you will also find the China International Travel Service (CITS). In Guangdong, the major hotels will also be able to provide tourist information.

Where's the tourist office?	旅遊諮詢中心（旅行社）在哪裡？ *lur-ee yau jee sun' j-owng sum hai bin do a*
What are the main points of interest?	這裡有些什麼主要名勝？ *nay do yau dee mut ye ju-ee yeeu ge ming sing a*
We're here for …	我們在這裡停留 … *ngor day hai nay do ting lau …*
only a few hours	幾小時 *gay gor j-owng tau*
a day	一天 *yut yut*
a week	一個禮拜 *yut gor lai baai*
Can you recommend …?	你可以介紹 … 嗎？ *nay hor mm hor yee gaai seeu …*
a sightseeing tour	一個遊覽團 *yut gor yau laam tu-een*
an excursion	一個短途旅遊團 *yut gor du-een to lur-ee yau tu-een*
a boat trip	一個乘船遊覽團 *yut gor yau su-een ho*
Do you have any information on …?	你們有沒有 … 的資料？ *nay day yau mo … ge jee leeu*
Are there any trips to …?	有沒有去 … 的旅遊團？ *yau mo hur-ee … ge lur-ee yau tu-een a*

DAYS OF THE WEEK ➤ 218; DIRECTIONS ➤ 94

Excursions 短途旅遊

How much does the tour cost?	遊覽一次要多少錢？ *yau laam yut chee yeeu gay dor chin a*
Is lunch included?	包括午餐嗎？ *bau mm bau maai ng chaan ga*
Where do we leave from?	我們從哪裡出發？ *ngor day yau bin do chut' faat*
What time does the tour start?	遊覽什麼時候開始？ *yau laam gay see hoy chee*
What time do we get back?	我們什麼時候回來？ *ngor day gay see faan lay*
Do we have free time in …?	在 … 有沒有自由活動時間？ *hai … yau mo jee yau woot d-wong see gaan a*
Is there an English-speaking guide?	有沒有說英語的導遊？ *yau mo gong ying mun ge do yau a*

On tour 遊覽

Are we going to see …?	我們會去看 … 嗎？ *ngor day woo-ee mm woo-ee hur-ee tai …*
We'd like to have a look at the …	我們想看看 … *ngor day surng tai ha …*
Can we stop here …?	可以在這裡停一會 … 嗎？ *hor mm hor yee hai nay do ting yut jun …*
to take photographs	拍照 *ying ha surng*
to buy souvenirs	買紀念品 *maai gay nim bun*
for the bathrooms [toilets]	去廁所 *hur-ee chee sor*
Would you take a photo of us, please?	請替我們拍張照好嗎？ *mm goy bong ngor day ying jurng surng, ho ma*
How long do we have here/in …?	我們在這裡 / 在 … 有多長時間？ *ngor day hai nay do/hai … yau gay noy a*
Wait! … isn't back yet.	等一下！… 還未回來。 *dung yut jun, … j-owng may faan lay*

Sights 景點

In Hong Kong and Macau, tourist offices will give you free local maps and plenty of useful tourist information.
In Guangdong, the service varies, depending on which office you visit.

Where is the …	… 在哪裡？ … *hai bin do a*
abbey	大修道院 *daai sau do yu-een*
art gallery	藝術館 *ngaai sut' goon*
battle site	古戰場 *goo jin churng*
botanical garden	植物公園 *jick mut g-owng yu-een*
castle	堡壘 *bo lur-ee*
cathedral	大教堂 *daai gaau tong*
cemetery	墳場 *fun churng*
church	教堂 *gaau tong*
downtown area	市中心 *see j-owng sum*
fountain	噴泉 *pun chu-een*
market	市場 *see churng*
(war) memorial	（戰爭）紀念碑 *(jin jun) gay nim bay*
monastery (Buddhist/Taoist)	佛寺 / 道觀 *fut jee/do goon*
museum	博物館 *bock mut goon*
old town	舊區 *gau kur-ee*
opera house	歌劇院 *gor keck yu-een*
palace	宮殿 *g-owng din*
park	公園 *g-owng yu-een*
parliament building	國會大廈 *gwock woo-ee daai ha*
ruins	遺址 *wai jee*
shopping area	購物區 *kau mut kur-ee*
statue	雕像 *deeu jurng*
theater	劇院 *keck yu-een*
tower	塔 *taap*
town hall	市政廳 *see jing teng*
viewpoint	瞭望處 *leeu mong chu-ee*
Can you show me on the map?	請在地圖上指出來。 *mm goy nay hai day to do jee chut' lay*

DIRECTIONS ➤ 94

Admission 入場

Most museums close on public holidays. In Hong Kong and Macau, the opening hours vary so it's best to check in advance. In mainland China, the usual opening hours are from 9 a.m. to 4 p.m.; museums are often closed on Mondays.

Is the … open to the public?	… 對公眾開放嗎？ … *hoy mm hoy fong bay g-owng j-owng ga*
Can we look around?	我們可以參觀一下嗎？ *ngor day hor mm hor yee chaam goon ha*
What are the opening hours?	什麼時間開放？ *mut ye see gaan hoy fong a*
When does it close?	幾點關門？ *gay dim saan moon a*
Is … open on Sundays?	禮拜日開放嗎？ *lai baai yaat hoy mm hoy a*
When's the next guided tour?	下一趟有導遊的遊覽什麼時候開始？ *ha yut tong yau do yau ge yau laam gay see hoy chee*
Do you have a guide book (in English)?	有沒有（英文）遊覽指南？ *yau mo (ying mun) yau laam jee naam a*
Can I take photos?	可以拍照嗎？ *hor mm hor yee ying surng a*
Is there access for the disabled?	有沒有給傷殘人士用的通道？ *yau mo bay surng chaan yun see y-owng ge t-owng do a*
Is there an audioguide in English?	有沒有英語錄音遊覽指南？ *yau mo ying mun luk yum yau laam jee naam a*

Paying/Tickets 付款／購票

How much is the entrance fee?	入場費是多少？ *yup churng fai gay dor chin a*
Are there any discounts for …?	… 有折扣嗎？ … *yau mo jit kau a*
children	兒童 *sai lo gor*
the disabled	傷殘人士 *surng chaan yun see*
groups	團體 *tu-een tai*
senior citizens	老人 *lo yun*
students	學生 *hock saang*
One adult and two children, please.	一個成人，兩個兒童。 *yut gor daai yun, lurng gor sai lo gor*

– maai ng jurng fay. cheng mun
yau mo jit kau a?
– *yau, sai lo gor t-owng tur-ee yau
yun see sup mun.*
– lurng gor daai yun, saam gor
sai lo gor, mm goy.
– *dor je luk sup mun.*

免費入場	admission free
休息	closed
禮品店	gift shop
最後入場時間下午五時	latest entry at 5 p.m.
下趟遊覽 …	next tour at …
不准進入	no entry
禁止使用閃光燈	no flash photography
開放	open
參觀時間	visiting hours

Impressions 印象

It's …	這眞 …	*jun hai …*
amazing	驚人	*ging yun*
awful	難看	*wut dut*
beautiful	美麗	*ho leng*
bizarre	古怪	*goo gwaai*
boring	乏味	*ho moon*
lots of fun	好玩	*ho waan*
interesting	有趣	*yau chur-ee*
magnificent	雄偉	*h-owng wai*
romantic	浪漫	*long maan*
strange	奇怪	*kay gwaai*
superb	一流	*yut lau*
terrible	很糟	*ho cha*
terrific	出色	*chut' sick*
ugly	難看	*chau gwaai*
It's good value.	這個物有所值。	*nay gor mut yau sor jick*
It's a rip-off.	這等於搶劫。	*gum jick hai churng chin*
I like/don't like it.	我喜歡。 / 我不喜歡。	
	ngor j-owng yee/ngor mm j-owng yee	

Tourist glossary 旅遊詞彙

廟	meeu	temple
墓地	mo day	burial site
宮殿	g-owng din	palace
古跡	goo jick	historical site
海港	hoy gong	harbor
清眞寺	ching jun jee	mosque
紀念堂	gay nim tong	memorial hall
博物館	bock mut goon	museum
紀念碑	gay nim bay	monument
亭	ting	pavillion
塔	taap	pagoda
花園	fa yu-een	garden
教堂	gaau tong	church
寺	jee	monastery
祠堂	chee tong	shrine

陵墓	ling mo	tomb
建築	g-in juk	architecture
藝術	ngaai sut'	art
書法	su-ee faat	calligraphy
陶器	to hay	ceramics/pottery
朝代	cheeu doy	dynasty
玉	yuk	jade
手工藝品	sau g-owng ngaai bun	handicrafts
漆器	chut hay	lacquerware
畫	wa	painting
紙摺品	jee jip bun	papercrafts
雕刻	deeu huck	sculpture
紡織品	fong jick bun	textiles
黃銅製品	wong t-owng jai bun	brassware
木器	muk hay	woodcrafts

Who/What/When?
哪位 / 什麼 / 什麼時候？

What's that building?	那個建築物是什麼？	gor jor hai mut ye
When was it built?	是什麼時候建的？	hai gay see hay ga
Who was the artist/architect?	是哪位藝術家 / 建築師的作品？	hai bin gor ngai sut' ga/g-in juk see ge jock bun
What style is that?	那是什麼款式？	gor gor hai mut ye foon sick

Hong Kong

Accounts of Hong Kong's history often begin when Hong Kong island was given to the British after the first Opium War (1840) and proclaimed a British colony in 1841. The area had, however, been populated by Chinese settlers and pirates for thousands of years before that. After the second Opium War, Britain gained the Kowloon Peninsula in 1860, and in 1898 China leased the New Territories and 235 more islands to Britain for 99 years. In 1984, an agreement was reached which allowed China to take back the entire colony in July 1997, with the promise that Hong Kong could continue its free enterprise economy for another 50 years. Hong Kong is now a Special Administrative Region (SAR) of China.

Macau

The Portuguese explorer Jorge Alvarez arrived in Macau in 1513, and traders soon followed. In 1557, China gave the enclave to the Portuguese, and for centuries it was the only European gateway to China, dominating the East-West trade. The economic rise of Hong Kong diminished the importance of Macau, and it became a gambling haven for the Hong Kongers. Macau is officially a Chinese territory under Portuguese Administration, but it will revert to direct Chinese rule in 1999.

Guangdong

Guangdong's close proximity to Hong Kong has made it a gateway into China and, in recent years, it has enjoyed rapid economic growth as a direct result of this proximity. The capital of Guangdong Province is Guangzhou, also known as Canton. The people of the province are known as Cantonese and so is the language.

Today Guangdong is known more as a business capital than a sightseeing destination. Most foreign visitors to the province are there on business or in transit to other, less developed parts of China. The special economic zones (SEZs) of Shenzhen and Zhuhai, although economic success stories, offer little for the tourist. Likewise Guangzhou is not noted for its beauty, but is a busy, noisy city.

Chinese theater 戲劇

Traditional Chinese opera-theater, including the famous
Beijing opera, provides spectacular performances combining
singing, dance, pantomime, and martial arts. There are over
300 different kinds of opera performed all over China. All have
their own traditions and characteristics in terms of costume, setting, music,
and performance style. Such performances are well worth a visit, and
although you will certainly not understand all of the actors' gestures, let
alone the songs and the words, the rhythm, the colors, the mime, and the
music will guarantee a memorable experience.

Religion 宗教

The Chinese government is officially atheist, yet recently open religious
activity has been permitted again. Many temples, some with their own
monks and novices, have been allowed to reopen. The most widely prac-
ticed religions are Taoism, Buddhism, Islam, Catholicism, and Protestantism. However, only atheists are allowed to become members of the
Chinese Communist Party, which precludes large numbers of people.

Buddhism found its way into China in the first century B.C. and spread
widely, becoming the most influential religion in China. A branch of
Buddhism, Lamaism (also called Tibetan Buddhism), is widespread in
Tibet and Inner Mongolia. Islam was introduced to China in the middle of
the seventh century, and today there are believed to be 14 million
Muslims. Followers of Protestantism and Catholicism are mainly
concentrated in large cities like Beijing and Shanghai.

For many Chinese a mixture of Taoism (combining animism with a system
of maintaining harmony with the universe), Confucianism (concerning the
political and moral aspects of life), and Buddhism (covering the afterlife)
best describes a complicated belief system.

Catholic/Protestant church	天主教 / 基督教教堂	*tin ju-ee gau/gay duk gau gau tong*
mosque	清眞寺	*ching jun jee*
synagogue	猶太教堂	*yau taai gau tong*
What time is …?	幾點做 … ?	*gay dim jor …*
mass	彌撒	*nay saat*
the service	禮拜	*lai baai*

In the countryside 在鄉村

I'd like a map of …	我想要一張 … ngor surng yeeu yut jurng …
this region	這個地區的地圖 nay gor day kur-ee ge day to
walking routes	遠足路線圖 yu-ee juk lo sin to
cycle routes	單車 (自行車) 路線圖 daan che (jee hung che) lo sin to
How far is it to …?	去 … 有多遠? hur-ee … yau gay yu-een a
Is there a right of way?	有沒有通行權? yau mo t-owng hung ku-een a
Is there a trail to … ?	有沒有小徑通往 … ? yau mo lo jai t-owng hur-ee …
Is there a scenic route to … ?	去 … 有沒有風景好的路線? hur-ee … yau mo f-owng ging ho ge lo sin a
Can you show me on the map?	請在地圖上指出來。 mm goy hai day to do jee chut' lay
I'm lost.	我迷路了。 ngor dong sut jor lo

Organized walks 遠足團

When does the guided walk/ hike start?	有嚮導的遠足什麼時候出發? yau hurng do ge yu-een juk gay see chut' faat a
When will we return?	我們什麼時候回來? ngor day gay see faan lay
What is the walk/hike like?	路難走嗎? teeu lo naan mm naan haang a
gentle/medium/tough	不難／普通／很難 mm naan/po t-owng/ho naan
I'm exhausted.	我筋疲力盡了。 ngor mo saai hay lick la
How long are we resting here?	我們在這裡休息多久? ngor day hai nay do yau sick gay noy a
What kind of … is that?	那是什麼 … ? gor j-owng hai mut ye …
animal/bird	動物／鳥 d-owng mut/jerk
flower/tree	花／樹 fa/su-ee

Geographical features 地理名詞

bridge	橋 *keeu*
cave	岩洞 *ngaam d-owng*
cliff	山崖 *saan ngaai*
farm	農場 *n-owng churng*
field	田 *tin*
footpath	小路 *lo jai*
forest	森林 *sum lum*
hill	山崗 *saan gong*
lake	湖 *woo*
mountain	山 *saan*
mountain pass	山口 *saan hau*
mountain range	山脈 *saan muck*
nature reserve	自然護理區 *jee yin woo lay kur-ee*
panorama	全景 *chu-een ging*
park	公園 *g-owng yu-een*
peak	山峰 *saan f-owng*
picnic area	野餐區 *ye chaan kur-ee*
pond	池塘 *chee tong*
rapids	急流 *gup lau*
river	河 *hor*
sea	海 *hoy*
stream	溪 *kai*
valley	山谷 *saan guk*
viewpoint	瞭望處 *leeu mong chu-ee*
village	鄉村 *hurng chu-een*
vineyard/winery	葡萄園 *po to yu-een*
waterfall	瀑布 *buk bo*
wood	樹林 *su-ee lum*

Leisure

Events 娛樂節目

Apart from the English-language dailies, *South China Morning Post*, *Eastern Express*, and *Hong Kong Standard*, there is also the weekly *Hong Kong This Week* and the weekly listings magazine *Hong Kong Diary*, which contain useful information. In Guangdong, the *China Daily* is available in hotels and newsstands in most cities. Your hotel can provide you with information about local events.

Do you have a program of events?	你們有沒有娛樂節目表？ *nay day yau mo yu-ee lock jit muk beeu*
Can you recommend a good …?	你可以介紹一場好的 … 嗎？ *nay hor mm hor yee gaai seeu yut churng ho ge …*
ballet	芭蕾舞 *ba lur-ee mo*
concert	音樂會 *yum ngock woo-ee*
film/movie	電影 *din ying*
opera	歌劇 *gor keck*

Availability 座位查詢

When does it start?	幾點開場？ *gay dim hoy churng a*
When does it end?	幾點散場？ *gay dim saan churng a*
Are there any seats for tonight?	今晚還有座位嗎？ *gum maan j-owng yau mo jor wai a*
Where can I get tickets?	到哪裡買票？ *hur-ee bin do maai fay a*
There are … of us.	我們 … 個人。 *ngor day … gor yun*

Tickets 購票

How much are the seats? *dee*	這些座位多少錢? *nay* *jor wai gay dor chin a*
Do you have anything cheaper?	有便宜些的嗎? *yau mo peng dee ge*
I'd like to reserve ...	我想預訂 ... *ngor surng deng ...*
three tickets for Sunday evening	三張禮拜日晚的票 *saam jurng lai baai yaat maan ge fay*
one ticket for the Friday	一張禮拜五早場的票

你的信用卡 ... ?	What's your credit card ...?
多少號	number
是哪一種	type
什麼時候到期	expiration [expiry] date
請 ... 取票。	Please pick up the tickets ...
下午 ... 前	by ... p.m.
到預售處	at the reservations desk

matinée	*yut jurng lai baai ng jo churng ge fay*
May I have a program, please?	請給我一份節目表。 *mm goy bay yut fun jit muk beeu*
Where's the coatcheck [cloakroom]?	衣帽間在哪裡? *yee mo gaan hai bin do a*

– yau mut ye hor yee bong do nay ga?
– ngor yeeu lurng jurng gum maan ge
  yum ngock woo-ee fay.
– hai.
– hor mm hor yee y-owng sun' y-owng kaat?
– hor yee.
– gum yurng, ngor y-owng Visa kaat la.
– dor je nay ... mm goy hai do chim gor meng.

NUMBERS ➤ 217

Movies [Cinema] 電影

English-language films have Chinese subtitles in Hong Kong; there are also two TV channels in English and two in Chinese. In Guangdong, there are some English-language programs of interest to tourists on radio and TV. You may also find it interesting (despite the language problem) to watch a little state-run television where you will find soap operas, news bulletins, Chinese operas, films, sporting events, and even some advertising.

Is there a multiplex theater [cinema] near here?	這附近有沒有複式電影院？ *nay do foo gun yau mo fuk sick din ying yu-een a*
What's playing at the movies [on at the cinema] tonight?	電影院今晚有什麼電影？ *din ying yu-een gum maan yau mut ye din ying*
Is the film dubbed/subtitled?	這部電影有配音／字幕嗎？ *nay bo din ying yau mo poo-ee yum/jee mock ga*
Is the film in the original English?	這部電影是原裝英語版嗎？ *nay bo din ying hai mm hai yu-een jong ying mun baan a*
A …, please.	要 … mm goy
box [carton] of popcorn	一盒爆谷 *yut hup baau guk*
chocolate ice cream [choc-ice]	一支朱古力雪糕 *yut jee ju-ee goo lick su-eet go*
hot dog	一個熱狗 *yut gor yit gau*
soft drink	一杯汽水 *yut boo-ee hay sur-ee*
small/regular/large	小／中／大 *sai/j-owng/daai*

Theater 戲劇

What's playing at the … theater?	… 劇院現在正上演什麼？ … *keck yu-een yee ga jo gun mut ye hay*
Who's the playwright?	劇作家是誰？ *keck jock ga hai bin gor*
Do you think I'd enjoy it?	你認爲我會喜歡嗎？ *nay goo ngor woo-ee mm woo-ee j-owng yee tai*
I don't know much Cantonese.	我不太會廣東話。 *ngor mm hai gay sick gwong d-owng wa*

Opera/Ballet/Dance
歌劇 / 芭蕾舞 / 舞蹈

Where's the opera house?　　　歌劇院在哪裡？ *gor keck yu-een hai bin do a*

Who is the composer/soloist?　　作曲家 / 獨唱（獨舞）主角是誰？ *jock kuk ga/duk churng (duk mo) ju-ee guk hai bin gor*

Is formal dress expected?　　　要穿禮服嗎？ *yeeu mm yeeu jerk lai fuk a*

Who's dancing?　　　舞蹈員是誰？ *mo do yu-een hai bin gor*

I'm interested in contemporary dance.　　我對現代舞有興趣。 *ngor dur-ee yin doy mo yau hing chur-ee*

Music/Concerts 音樂 / 音樂會

Where's the concert hall?　　音樂廳在哪裡？ *yum ngock teng hai bin do a*

Which orchestra/band is playing?　　由哪個樂團 / 樂隊演奏？ *yau bin gor ngock tu-een/ngock dur-ee yin jau a*

What are they playing?　　他們演奏些什麼？ *kur-ee day yin jau dee mut ye a*

Who is the conductor/soloist?　　指揮 / 歌唱家是誰？ *jee fai/gor churng ga hai bin gor*

Who is the support band?　　由哪個樂隊助陣？ *yau bin gor ngock dur-ee jor jun*

I really like ...　　我很喜歡 ... *ngor ho j-owng yee ...*

folk music/country music　　民間音樂 / 鄉村音樂 *mun gaan yum ngock/hurng chu-een yum ngock*

jazz　　爵士音樂 *jerk see yum ngock*

music of the '60s　　六十年代的音樂 *luk sup nin doy ge yum ngock*

pop/rock music　　流行音樂 / 搖滾樂 *lau hung yum ngock/yeeu gwun ngock*

soul music　　爵士靈歌 *jerk see ling gor*

Have you ever heard of her/him?　　你聽聞過此人嗎？ *nay yau mo teng mun gwor nay gor yun a*

Are they popular?　　他們很受歡迎嗎？ *kur-ee day hai mm hai ho sau foon ying*

Nightlife 夜生活

What is there to do in the evenings?	晚上有些什麼消遣？	*ye maan yau dee mut ye seeu hin a*
Can you recommend a …?	你可以介紹一個 … 嗎？	*nay hor mm hor yee gaai seeu yut gor …*
Is there a … in town?	市內有沒有 …	*see noy yau mo …*
bar/restaurant	酒吧 / 餐廳	*jau ba/chaan teng*
casino	賭場	*do churng*
discotheque	的士高	*dick see go*
gay club	同性戀者俱樂部	*t-owng sing lu-een je kur-ee lock bo*
nightclub	夜總會	*ye j-owng woo-ee*
What type of music do they play?	他們奏哪種音樂？	*kur-ee day jau bin j-owng yum ngock a*
How do I get there?	我怎樣去那裡？	*ngor dim yurng hur-ee gor do a*

Admission 入場

What time does the show start?	表演幾點開始？	*beeu yin gay dim hoy chee a*
Is evening dress required?	需要穿晚裝嗎？	*yeeu mm yeeu jerk maan jong a*
Is there a cover charge?	要付服務費嗎？	*sai mm sai bay fuk mo fai a*
Is a reservation necessary?	需要預訂嗎？	*sai mm sai yu-ee deng*
Do we need to be members?	我們需要是會員嗎？	*ngor day sur-ee mm sur-ee yeeu hai woo-ee yu-een*
Is it customary to dine there?	通常是不是要在那裡進餐？	*t-owng surng hai mm hai yeeu hai gor do sick chaan ga*
How long will we have to stand in line [queue]?	排隊要排多久？	*paai dur-ee yeeu paai gay noy*
I'd like a good table.	我想要一張位置好的桌子。	*ngor surng yeeu yut jurng wai jee ho ge toy*

入場費包括
飲料一份

includes one
complimentary drink

Children 兒童

Can you recommend something for the children?	你可以介紹一些兒童遊玩的地方嗎？ *nay hor mm hor yee gaai seeu yut dee sai lo gor waan ge day fong a*
Are there changing facilities here for babies?	這裡有沒有給嬰兒換尿片的地方？ *nay do yau mo bay B B jai woon leeu pin ge day fong a*
Where are the bathrooms [toilets]?	廁所在哪裡？ *chee sor hai bin do a*
amusement arcade	遊戲機中心 *yau hay gay j-owng sum*
fairground	遊樂場 *yau lock churng*
kiddie [paddling] pool	戲水池 *waan sur-ee chee*
playground	遊樂場 *yau lock churng*
play group	遊戲小組 *yau hay seeu jo*
zoo	動物園 *d-owng mut yu-een*

Baby-sitting 臨時保姆

Can you recommend a reliable baby-sitter?	你可以介紹一位可靠的臨時保姆嗎？ *nay hor mm hor yee gaai seeu yut gor hor kau ge lum see bo mo*
Is there constant supervision?	時刻都有人照看着的嗎？ *hai mm hai see see do yau yun tai ju-ee ga*
Is the staff properly trained?	員工都受過訓練嗎？ *dee yu-een g-owng yau mo sau gwor fun lin ga*
When can I drop them off?	我什麼時候送他們來？ *ngor gay see s-owng kur-ee day lay*
I'll pick them up at ...	我 ... 來接他們。 *ngor ... lay jip kur-ee day*
We'll be back by ...	我們 ... 前回來。 *ngor day ... chin faan lay*
She's 3 and he's 18 months.	她三歲，他十八個月。 *kur-ee saam sur-ee, kur-ee sup baat gor yu-eet*

Sports 體育活動

太極拳 taai gick ku-een

Tai chi chuan or **Taijiquan**. A system of self-defense and well-being based on the **Yin-Yang** (feminine-masculine) theory. It primarily consists of a sequence of body movements in a set routine, incorporating some visualization and breathing exercises. The slow, circular, fluid movements give the impression of shadow boxing. At dawn you may see many older people practising this graceful sport/art in parks.

功夫 g-owng foo

Kung fu. Another Chinese system of self-defense, made famous worldwide by Bruce Lee. **Kung fu** comes in myriad forms, but their common denominator is the clever use of the opponent's force through circular movements and the emphasis on building up internal strength. Hong Kong is well known for its spectacular kung fu movies. Other popular sports in Hong Kong and Macau are horse racing, greyhound racing, cricket, rugby, and dragon boat racing.

American football	美式足球 may sick juk kau
aerobics	健身舞 g-in sun mo
angling	釣魚 deeu yu-ee
archery	射箭 sh-e jin
athletics	田徑 tin ging
badminton	羽毛球 yu-ee mo kau
baseball	壘球 lur-ee kau
basketball	籃球 laam kau
boxing	拳擊 ku-een gick
canoeing	划獨木舟 paai duk muk jau
cycling	單車 (自行車)* daan che (jee hung che)*
gliding	滑翔 waat churng
greyhound racing	賽狗 choy gau
golf	哥爾夫球 gor yee foo kau
hockey	曲棍球 kuk gwun kau

* The term in brackets is used in Cantonese-speaking regions in mainland China.

horse racing	賽馬 *choy ma*
icehockey	冰上曲棍球 *bing surng kuk gwun kau*
judo	柔道 *yau do*
mountaineering	爬山 *paai saan*
rappeling [abseiling]	繞繩下降 *yeeu sing ha gong*
rock climbing	攀崖運動 *paang ngaam wun d-owng*
rowing	划艇 *paai teng*
rugby	欖球 *laam kau*
snooker	桌球 *cherk kau*
soccer [football]	足球 *juk kau*
squash	壁球 *bick kau*
swimming	游泳 *yau wing*
table tennis	乒乓球 *bing bum bor*
tennis	網球 *mong kau*
volleyball	排球 *paai kau*

Spectating 觀看

Is there a soccer [football] game [match] this Saturday?	這個禮拜有沒有足球賽？ *nay gor lai baai yau mo juk kau choy a*
Which teams are playing?	哪兩隊比賽？ *bin lurng dur-ee bay choy*
Can you get me a ticket?	你可以幫我搞張票嗎？ *nay hor mm hor yee bong ngor wun jurng fay a*
What's the admission charge?	入場費是多少？ *yup churng fai gay dor chin a*
Where's the racetrack [racecourse]?	馬場在哪裡？ *ma churng hai bin do a*
Where can I place a bet?	到哪裡投注？ *hur-ee bin do tau ju-ee a*
What are the odds on …?	… 的賠率是多少？ *… ge poo-ee lut' hai gay dor*

115

Playing 參加

Where's the nearest …?	離這裡最近的 … 在哪裡？ *jur-ee kun ge … hai bin do a*
golf course	哥爾夫球場 *gor yee foo kau churng*
sports club	體育會 *tai yuk woo-ee*
Where are the tennis courts?	網球場在哪裡？ *mong kau churng hai bin do a*
What's the charge per …?	… 的收費是多少？ *… sau gay dor chin*
day/round/hour	一天／一場／一小時 *yut yut/yut churng/ yut gor j-owng*
Do I need to be a member?	我需要是會員嗎？ *ngor sur-ee mm sur- ee yeeu hai woo-ee yu-een*
Where can I rent …?	在哪裡可以租到 …？ *hai bin do hor yee jo do …*
boots	球鞋 *kau haai*
clubs	球棒 *kau paang*
equipment	體育器材 *tai yuk hay choy*
a racket	球拍 *kau paak*
Can I get lessons?	我可以請人教導嗎？ *ngor hor mm hor yee cheng yun gaau a*
Do you have a fitness room?	這裡有沒有健身室？ *nay do yau mo g-in sun sut*
Can I join in?	我可以加入嗎？ *ngor hor mm hor yee ga yup a*

對不起，我們的時間約滿了。	I'm sorry, we're booked up.
需付按金 …	There is a deposit of …
你穿幾號？	What size are you?
你需要一張護照相片。	You need a passport-size photo.

更衣室	changing rooms
禁止釣魚	no fishing
只限持有許可證者	permit holders only

116

At the beach 在海灘

The best time for swimming is from April to early November. Both Hong Kong and Macau have official beaches with lifeguards. There are 235 islands in the waters around Hong Kong, but only four are accessible by ferry. The beaches here are often tranquil during the week, but become very crowded on weekends and holidays.

Is the beach pebbly/sandy?	這個海灘是卵石灘 / 沙灘嗎？ *nay gor hoy taan hai mm hai lun' seck taan/sa taan*
Is there a(n) ... here?	這裡有沒有 ... *nay do yau mo ...*
children's pool	兒童泳池 *yee t-owng wing chee*
swimming pool	游泳池 *yau wing chee*
indoor/open-air	室內 / 露天 *sut noy/lo tin*
Is it safe to swim/dive here?	在這裡游泳 / 跳水安全嗎？ *hai nay do yau sur-ee/teeu sur-ee, on mm on chu-een a*
Is it safe for children?	對兒童安全嗎？ *dur-ee sai lo gor on mm on chu-een a*
Is there a lifeguard?	有沒有救生員？ *yau mo gau sung yu-een a*
I want to rent a/some ...	我想租 ... *ngor surng jo ...*
deck chair	一張沙灘椅 *yut jurng sa taan yee*
jet-ski	一架滑水艇 *yut ga waat sur-ee teng*
motorboat	一架汽艇 *yut ga hay teng*
diving equipment	潛水器材 *chim sur-ee hay choy*
umbrella [sunshade]	一把太陽傘 *yut ba taai yurng je*
surfboard	一塊滑浪板 *yut faai waat long baan*
water skis	滑水板 *waat sur-ee baan*
For ... hours.	租 ... 小時 *jo ... gor j-owng tau*

Making Friends

Introductions 介紹

A smile is your best goodwill gesture in China. Try to maintain an oriental degree of patience even if things go wrong. Showing your temper means losing face. Always use formal terms of address (e.g., Mr. Wong) until invited to do otherwise, and take plenty of business cards. Remember that punctuality is very important to the Chinese.

Hello, we haven't met.	你好，我們還未認識。 *nay ho, ngor day j-owng may ying sick*
My name is …	我叫 … *ngor geeu …*
May I introduce …?	我來介紹一下，這是 … *ngor gaai seeu ha, nay wai hai …*
Pleased to meet you.	認識你很高興。 *ho go hing ying sick nay*
What's your name?	你叫什麼名字？ *nay geeu mut ye meng a*
What's your surname? *(polite form)*	你貴姓？ *nay gwai sing a*
How are you?	你好嗎？ *nay ho ma*
Fine, thanks. And you?	很好，謝謝。你呢？ *gay ho, yau sum. nay ne*

– nay ho ma?
– gay ho, yau sum. nay ne?
– gay ho, yau sum.

Where are you from?

你是從哪裡來的？

Where do you come from?	你是從哪裡來的？ *nay hai bin do lay ga*
Where were you born?	你是在哪裡出生的？ *nay hai bin do chut' sai ga*
I'm from ...	我從 ... 來的。 *ngor hai ... lay ge*
Australia	澳洲 *o jau*
Britain	英國 *ying gwock*
Canada	加拿大 *ga na daai*
England	英格蘭 *ying gaak laan*
Ireland	愛爾蘭 *oy yee laan*
Scotland	蘇格蘭 *so gaak laan*
the United States	美國 *may gwock*
Wales	威爾斯 *wai yee see*
Where do you live?	你住在哪裡？ *nay hai bin do ju-ee a*
What part of ... are you from?	你是從 ... 哪個地區來的？ *nay hai ... bin gor day kur-ee lay ga*
Japan	日本 *yut boon*
Korea	韓國 *hon gwock*
China	中國 *j-owng gwock*
We come here every year.	我們每年都來這裡。 *ngor day moo-ee nin do lay nay do*
It's my/our first visit.	這是我／我們第一次來這裡。 *ngor/ngor day hai dai yut chee lay nay do*
Have you ever been to ...?	你去過 ... 嗎？ *nay yau mo hur-ee gwor ...*
the U.K./the U.S.	英國／美國 *ying gwock/may gwock*
Do you like it here?	你喜歡這裡嗎？ *nay j-owng mm j-owng yee nay do a*
What do you think of the ...?	你覺得這裡的 ... 怎麼樣？ *nay gock duck nay do ge ... dim a*
I love the ... here.	我非常喜歡這裡的 ... *ngor ho j-owng yee nay do ge ...*
I don't really like the ... here.	我不太喜歡這裡的 ... *ngor mm hai gay j-owng yee nay do ge ...*
food/people	食物／人 *sick mut/yun*

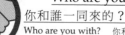

Who are you with?

你和誰一同來的？

Who are you with?	你和誰一同來的？ *nay t-owng bin gor yut chai lay ga*
I'm on my own.	就我一個人。 *jing hai ngor jee gay*
I'm with a friend.	我和朋友一同來的。 *ngor t-owng pung yau yut chai lay ge*
I'm with my ...	我和 ... 一同來的。 *ngor t-owng ... yut chai lay ge*
husband/wife	丈夫 / 太太 *jurng foo/taai taai*
family	家人 *ga yun*
children/parents	孩子 / 父母 *jai nur-ee/foo mo*
boyfriend/girlfriend	男朋友 / 女朋友 *naam pung yau/nur-ee pung yau*
father/son	父親 / 兒子 *foo chun/jai*
mother/daughter	母親 / 女兒 *mo chun/nur-ee*
brother/uncle	兄弟 / 叔父 *hing dai/a suk*
sister/aunt	姊妹 / 叔母 *jee moo-ee/a sum*
What's your son's/wife's name?	你太太叫什麼名字？ *nay taai taai geeu mut ye meng*
Are you married?	你結了婚沒有？ *nay git jor fun may*
I'm ...	我 ... *ngor ...*
married/single	結了婚 / 還未結婚 *jit jor fun/j-owng may git fun*
divorced/separated	離了婚 / 分了居 *lay jor fun/fun jor gur-ee*
engaged	訂了婚 *ding jor fun*
We live together.	我們同居。 *ngor day t-owng gur-ee*
Do you have any children?	你有孩子嗎？ *nay yau mo jai nur-ee*
I have two boys and a girl.	兩個男孩，一個女孩。 *lurng gor jai, yut gor nur-ee*
How old are they?	他們多大了？ *kur-ee day gay daai la*
They're 10 and 12.	十歲和十二歲。 *sup sur-ee t-owng sup yee sur-ee*

What do you do? 你是做什麼工作的？

What do you do?	你是做什麼工作的？ *nay jo mut ye g-owng jock ga*
What are you studying?	你在讀什麼學科？ *nay duk gun mut ye for*
I'm studying ...	我在讀 ... *ngor duk gun ...*
I'm in ...	我是做 ... 的。 *ngor hai jo ... ge*
business	生意 *saang yee*
engineering	工程 *g-owng ching*
retail	零售 *ling sau*
sales	推銷 *tur-ee seeu*
Who do you work for ...?	你在哪家公司工作？ *nay hai bin gaan g-owng see jo ye*
I work for ...	我在 ... 工作。 *ngor hai ... jo ye*
I'm (a/an) ...	我是 ... *ngor hai ...*
accountant	會計師 *woo-ee gaai see*
housewife	家庭主婦 *ga ting ju-ee foo*
student	學生 *hock saang*
retired	退了休 *tur-ee jor yau*
self-employed	個體戶 *gor tai woo*
between jobs	暫時沒有工作 *jaam see mo jo ye*
What are your interests/ hobbies?	你有什麼嗜好？ *nay yau mut ye see ho a*
I like ...	我喜歡 ... *ngor j-owng yee ...*
music	音樂 *yum ngock*
reading	看書 *tai su-ee*
sports	運動 *wun d-owng*
I play ...	我玩 ... *ngor waan ...*
Would you like to play ...?	你想 ... 嗎？ *nay surng mm surng ...*
cards	玩紙牌 *waan jee paai*
chess	下棋 *juk kay*

What weather! 天氣眞 … !

What a lovely day!	天氣眞好！	*tin hay jun hai ho*
What awful weather!	天氣眞壞！	*tin hay jun hai cha*
It's cold/hot today!	今天眞冷／眞熱！ *gum yut ho d-owng/ho yit*	
Is it usually this warm?	通常都這麼熱嗎？ *hai mm hai see see do gum yit ga*	
Do you think it's going to … tomorrow?	你認爲明天會 … 嗎？ *nay goo ting yut woo-ee mm woo-ee …*	
be a nice day	是晴天	*ho tin*
rain	下雨	*lock yu-ee*
snow	下雪	*lock su-eet*
What is the weather forecast for tomorrow?	明天的天氣預報怎麼說？ *tin yut ge tin hay yu-ee bo dim yurng gong a*	
cloudy	多雲	*dor wun*
foggy	大霧	*daai mo*
frosty	有霜	*yau surng*
icy	結冰	*git bing*
stormy	有雷	*yau lur-ee*
windy	大風	*daai f-owng*
It's raining.	下著雨。	*lock gun yu-ee*
It's snowing.	下著雪。	*lock gun su-eet*
It's sunny.	陽光普照。	*ho taai yurng*
Has the weather been like this for long?	這樣的天氣已經多久了？ *gum ge tin hay yee ging gay noy la*	
What's the pollen count?	花粉統計是高還是低？ *fa fun t-owng gaai hai go yick waak dai a*	
high/medium/low	高／中／低 *go/j-owng/dai*	

天氣預報	weather forecast	

122

Enjoying your trip? 旅行愉快嗎？

你是來度假的嗎？	Are you on vacation?
你是坐什麼來的？	How did you get/travel here?
你住在哪裡？	Where are you staying?
你來這裡有多久了？	How long have you been here?
你準備停留多久？	How long are you staying?
你做過些什麼？	What have you done so far?
你接著會去哪裡？	Where are you going next?
這次假期過得愉快嗎？	Are you enjoying your vacation?

I'm here on …	我是 … *ngor hai* …
a business trip	因公事來的 *yun wai g-owng see lay ge*
vacation [holiday]	來度假的 *lay do ga ge*
We came by …	我們是坐 … 來的 *ngor day chor … lay ge*
train/bus/plane	火車 / 巴士 / 飛機 *for che/ ba see/fay gay*
car/ferry	汽車 / 船 *hay che/su-een*
I have a rental car.	我租了一輛汽車。 *ngor jo jor ga che*
We're staying …	我們住在 … *ngor day ju-ee hai* …
in an apartment	一間公寓 *yut gaan g-owng yu-ee*
at a hotel/campsite	酒店 / 營地 *jau dim/ying day*
with friends	朋友家裡 *pung yau uk kay*
Can you suggest …?	你可以提議 … 嗎？ *nay hor mm hor yee tai yee* …
things to do	一些值得做的事 *yut dee jick duck jo ge ye*
places to eat	一些吃飯的地方 *yut dee sick ye ge day fong*
places to visit	一些值得遊覽的地方 *yut dee jick duck yau laam ge day fong*
We're having a great/ terrible time.	我們玩得很開心 / 很不開心。 *ngor day waan duck ho hoy sum/ho mm hoy sum*

Invitations 邀請

Would you like to have dinner with us on …?	… 和我們一起吃晚飯好嗎？ *… t-owng ngor day yut chai sick maan faan, ho ma*
Are you free for lunch?	我可以請你吃午餐嗎？ *ngor hor mm hor yee cheng nay sick ng chaan a*
Can you come for a drink this evening?	你今晚能來喝一杯嗎？ *nay gum maan hor mm hor yee lay yum boo-ee ye*
We are having a party. Can you come?	我們開派對，你能來嗎？ *ngor day hoy party. nay lay mm lay duck a*
May we join you?	我們可以和你們坐在一起嗎？ *ngor day hor mm hor yee chor maai lay a*
Would you like to join us?	和我們坐在一起好嗎？ *t-owng ngor day yut chai la, ho ma*

Going out 約會

What are your plans for …?	你 … 有什麼計劃？ *nay … yau mut ye gai waak a*
today/tonight	今天 / 今晚 *gum yut/gum maan*
tomorrow	明天 *ting yut*
Are you free this evening?	你今晚有空嗎？ *nay gum maan duck mm duck haan a*
Would you like to …?	你想 … 嗎？ *nay surng mm surng …*
go dancing	去跳舞 *hur-ee teeu mo*
go for a drink	去喝一杯 *hur-ee yum boo-ee ye*
go out for a meal	去吃飯 *hur-ee sick faan*
go for a walk	去散步 *hur-ee saan bo*
go shopping	去逛公司 *hur-ee haang g-owng see*
I'd like to go to …	我想去 … *ngor surng hur-ee …*
I'd like to see …	我想看 … *ngor surng tai …*
Do you enjoy …?	你喜歡 … 嗎？ *nay j-owng mm j-owng yee …*

Accepting/Declining 接受 / 推辭

Great. I'd love to.	好哇，我很樂意。 *ho a, ngor ho lock yee*
Thank you, but I'm busy.	謝謝，但我沒空。 *dor je,* *but gwor ngor mm duck haan*
May I bring a friend?	我可以帶個朋友嗎？ *ngor hor mm hor* *yee daai gor pung yau*
Where shall we meet?	我們在哪裡見面？ *ngor day hai bin do g-in min*
I'll meet you ...	我 ... 等你。 *ngor ... dung nay*
in front of your hotel	在你酒店門口 *hai nay jau dim moon hau*
I'll call for you at 8.	我八點來接你。 *ngor baat dim lay jip nay*
Could we make it a bit later/earlier?	可以晚一點 / 早一點嗎？ *hor mm hor* *yee aan dee/ jo dee*
How about another day?	改天好嗎？ *daai yut sin, ho mm ho*
That will be fine.	好吧。 *ho la*

Dining out/in 赴宴

If you are invited to someone's home, bring a gift, but avoid objects considered unlucky such as clocks, anything colored white, black, or blue, or sharp implements.

Let me buy you a drink.	讓我請你喝杯東西。 *dung ngor cheng nay yum boo-ee ye*
Do you like ...?	你喜歡 ... 嗎？ *nay j-owng mm j-owng yee ...*
What are you going to have?	你要點什麼？ *nay yeeu dee mut ye*
That was a lovely meal.	這頓飯很好吃。 *nay chaan faan ho ho sick*

Encounters 相遇

Do you mind if …?	你介意 … 嗎？ *nay gaai mm gaai yee …*
I sit here/I smoke	我坐這裡 / 吸煙 *ngor chor nay do/sick yin*
Can I get you a drink?	我可以請你喝一杯嗎？ *ngor hor mm hor yee cheng nay yum boo-ee ye*
I'd love to have some company.	我很想有人作伴。 *ngor ho surng yau gor poon*
Why are you laughing?	你笑什麼？ *nay seeu mut ye*
Is my Cantonese that bad?	我的廣東話價的那麼糟嗎？ *ngor dee gwong d-owng wa jun hai gum cha*
Shall we go somewhere quieter?	我們找個清靜一點的地方好嗎？ *ngor day wun gor ching jing dee ge day fong, ho mm ho*
Leave me alone, please!	請不要騷擾我！ *cheng nay mm ho so yeeu ngor*
You look great!	你好漂亮！ *nay ho leng*
Would you like to come back with me?	和我一同回去好嗎？ *t-owng ngor yut chai faan hur-ee, ho mm ho*
I'm not ready for that.	我不去了。 *ngor mm hur-ee la*
I'm afraid we have to leave now.	我想我們現在該走了。 *ngor lum ngor day yee ga yeeu jau la*
Thanks for the evening. It was great.	今晚玩得很開心。謝謝。 *gum maan waan duck ho hoy sum. dor je*
Can I see you again tomorrow?	我明天可以再見你嗎？ *ngor ting yut hor mm hor yee joy g-in nay*
See you soon.	再見。 *joy g-in*
Can I have your address?	可以給我的地址嗎？ *hor mm hor yee bay nay gor day jee ngor*

Telephoning 打電話

Hong Kong. The phone system is excellent. Coin-operated phones require a HK$1 coin. However, as local calls are free, most people just pick up any phone – in a bar or shop – and use it even without asking permission. Hotels may charge a handling fee for local calls. Direct dial overseas calls can be made from IDD (International Direct Dialling) public phone booths by dialing 001 followed by the country code, area code, and number. Phone cards come in HK$50, HK$100 and HK$250 denominations. For an English-speaking information service dial 1081.

Macau. Coin-operated phones require M$1; all pay phones allow IDD calls. The international access code is 00, except for Hong Kong, which is just 01 and the number you want.

Guangdong. You can make local calls from your hotel room or from any public telephone – usually without charge. Coin-operated phones are rare and cost 20 fen in coins. International and collect calls can be made from your room and most hotels have direct-dial international services.

Can I have your telephone number?	可以給我你的電話號碼嗎？ *hor mm hor yee bay nay ge din wa ho ma ngor a*
Here's my number.	這是我的號碼。 *nay gor hai ngor ge ho ma*
Please call me.	請給我打電話。 *cheng da din wa bay ngor*
I'll give you a call.	我給你打電話。 *ngor da din wa bay nay*
Where's the nearest telephone booth?	公眾電話亭在哪裡？ *g-owng j-owng din wa ting hai bin do*
May I use your phone?	我可以用你的電話嗎？ *ngor hor mm hor yee je nay gor din wa y-owng*
It's an emergency.	這是急事。 *hai gun gup ge see*
I'd like to call someone in England.	我想打個電話去英國。 *ngor surng da gor din wa hur-ee ying gwock*
What's the area [dialling] code for …?	… 的地區碼幾號？ *… ge day kur-ee ma gay dor ho*
I'd like a phone card, please.	我想買一張電話卡。 *ngor surng maai yut jurng din wa kaat*
What's the number for Information [Directory Enquiries]?	電話號碼查詢要打幾號？ *din wa ho ma cha sun' yeeu da gay dor ho*
I'd like the number for …	我想要 … 的號碼。 *ngor surng yeeu … ge ho ma*
I'd like to call collect [reverse the charges].	我想請對方付費。 *ngor surng cheng dur-ee fong bay chin*

127

Speaking 通話

Hello. This is …	喂，我是 … *wai, ngor hai …*
I'd like to speak to …	我想找 … 聽電話。 *mm goy cheng … teng din wa*
Extension …	內線 … *noy sin …*
Speak louder, please.	請大聲點。 *cheng daai seng dee*
Speak more slowly, please.	請說慢點。 *cheng gong maan dee*
Could you repeat that, please?	請再說一遍。 *cheng joy gong yut chee*
I'm afraid he's/she's not in.	他／她不在。 *kur-ee/kur-ee mm hai do wor*
You have the wrong number.	你打錯了。 *nay da chor la*
Just a moment.	等一下。 *dung yut jun*
Hold on, please.	請等等。 *mm goy dung dung*
When will he/she be back?	他／她什麼時候回來？ *kur-ee/kur-ee gay see faan lay a*
Will you tell him/her that I called?	請告訴他／她我來過電話。 *mm goy wa bay kur-ee/kur-ee teng ngor da gwor din wa lay*
My name is …	我叫 … *ngor geeu …*
Would you ask him/her to phone me?	請叫他／她給我回個電話。 *mm goy geeu kur-ee/kur-ee da faan din wa bay ngor*
I must go now.	我要掛線了。 *ngor yeeu sau sin la*
Nice to speak to you.	和你談話很高興。 *ho go hing t-owng nay gong din wa*
I'll be in touch.	以後再聯絡。 *yee hau joy lu-een lock*
Bye.	再見。 *joy g-in*

Stores & Services

Hong Kong is a shopper's paradise. Visit the street markets for local flavor. In Macau you can find gold, jewelry, and antiques at reasonable prices. Guangdong's capital, Guangzhou, and the Special Economic Zones (SEZs), Shenzhen and Zhuhai, have modern shopping districts which offer an array of Western and Chinese goods. In tourist locations Friendship Stores are good for souvenirs, and the sales people often speak English. Local stores and markets offer a great variety of Chinese handicrafts and souvenirs.

ESSENTIAL

I'd like …	我想要 … *ngor surng yeeu* …
Do you have …?	你們這裡有沒有… ? *nay day nay do yau mo* …
How much is that?	那個多少錢 ? *gor gor gay dor chin a*
Thank you.	謝謝。 *mm goy*

營業	open
休息	closed
大減價	sale

Stores and services 商店及服務
Where is …? … 在哪裡？

Where's the nearest …?	離這裡最近的 … 在哪裡？ *jur-ee kun nay do ge … hai bin do a*
Where's there a good …?	哪裡有好的 … ？ *bin do yau ho ge …*
Where's the main shopping mall [centre]?	最大的購物中心 / 商場在哪裡？ *jur-ee daai ge kau mut j-owng sum/surng churng hai bin do a*
Is it far from here?	離這裡遠嗎？ *yu-een mm yu-een a*
How do I get there?	我怎樣去哪裡？ *ngor dim yurng hur-ee gor do a*

Shops 商店

antique store	古玩店 *goo woon dim*
bakery	麵飽店 *min bau po*
bank	銀行 *ngun hong*
bookstore	書店 *su-ee dim*
butcher	肉店 *yuk po*
camera store	攝影器材公司 *sip ying hay choy g-owng see*
cigarette kiosk [tobacconist]	煙草店 / 香煙檔 *yin cho dim/yin jai dong*
clothing store [clothes shop]	服裝店 *fuk jong dim*
delicatessen	熟食店 *suk sick dim*
department store	百貨公司 *baak for g-owng see*
drugstore	藥房 *yerk fong*
fish store [fishmonger]	魚店 *yu-ee po*
florist	花店 *fa dim*
gift store	禮品店 *lai bun dim*
greengrocer	蔬菜店 *sor choy po*
health food store	健康食品店 *g-in hong sick bun dim*
jeweler	珠寶行 *ju-ee bo hong*
liquor store [off-licence]	酒品店 *jau po*

market	市場 *see churng*
newsstand [newsagent]	報紙檔 *bo jee dong*
pastry store	餅店 *beng dim*
pharmacy	藥房 *yerk fong*
produce store [grocer]	雜貨店 *jaap for po*
record [music] store	唱片店 *churng pin po*
shoe store	鞋店 *haai po*
shopping mall [centre]	購物中心 *kau mut j-owng sum*
souvenir store	禮品店 *lai bun dim*
sporting goods store	體育用品店 *tai yuk y-owng bun dim*
supermarket	超級市場 *cheeu kup see churng*
toy store	玩具店 *woon gur-ee dim*

Services 各類服務

clinic	診所 *chun sor*
dentist	牙醫 *nga yee*
doctor	醫生 *yee sung*
dry cleaner	乾洗店 *gon sai dim*
hairdresser/barber	髮廊 / 理髮店 *faat long/fay faat po*
hospital	醫院 *yee yu-een*
laundromat	自助洗衣場 *jee jor sai yee churng*
optician	眼鏡店 *ngaan geng po*
police station	警署（公安局）* *ging chu-ee (g-owng on guk)* *
post office	郵局 *yau guk*
travel agency	旅行社 *lur-ee hung se*

* The term in brackets is used in Cantonese-speaking regions in mainland China.

131

Opening hours 營業時間

In Hong Kong and Macau local stores are usually open from early in the morning to late at night and do not generally close on the weekends. Department stores are normally open from 10 a.m. to between 6 and 9:30 p.m. seven days a week.

In Guangdong local stores keep equivalent hours to those in Hong Kong and Macau. Department and Friendship stores are open from 9 a.m. to 7 p.m. (8 p.m. in summer) seven days a week.

When does the ... open/shut?	... 幾點開門 / 關門？ ... gay dim hoy moon/saan moon a
Are you open in the evening?	你們這裡晚上營業嗎？ nay day nay do ye maan hoy mm hoy ga
Do you close for lunch?	你們午膳時間休息嗎？ nay day sick aan see gaan yau mm yau ga
Where is the ...	... 在哪裡？ ... hai bin do a
cashier [cash desk]	付款處 foo foon chu-ee
escalator	電動樓梯 din d-owng lau tai
elevator [lift]	電梯 din tai
store directory [guide]	購物指南 kaau mut jee naam
first [ground (Brit.)] floor	地下 day ha
second [first (Brit.)] floor	二樓 yee lau
Where's the ... department?	... 部在哪裡？ ... bo hai bin do a

營業時間	business hours
午膳時間休息	closed for lunch
全日營業	open all day
入口	entrance
電動樓梯	escalator
出口	exit
緊急出口（太平門）	emergency/fire exit
電梯	elevator [lift]
樓梯	stairs

Service 服務

Can you help me?	可以請你幫個忙嗎？ *hor mm hor yee cheng nay* *bong gor mong*
I'm looking for …	我想找 … *ngor surng wun …*
I'm just browsing.	我先看看。 *ngor tai yut tai sin*
It's my turn.	輪到我了。 *lun' do ngor la*
Do you have any …?	你們有沒有 … ? *nay day yau mo …*
I'd like to buy …	我想買 … *ngor surng maai …*
Could you show me …?	請拿 … 給我看看。 *mm goy lor … bay ngor tai tai*
How much is this/that?	這個 / 那個多少錢？ *nay gor/gor gor gay dor chin a*
That's all, thanks.	就這些，謝謝。 *hai gum dor, mm goy*

小姐 / 太太 / 先生早晨 / 你好。	Good morning/afternoon, madam/sir.
有誰在招呼你了嗎？	Are you being helped?
你想要些什麼？	What would you like?
還要些什麼嗎？	Is that everything?
還要別的嗎？	Anything else?

– *surng yeeu dee mut ye ne?*
– *ngor tai yut tai sin, mm goy.*
– *chur-ee bin tai.*
– *mm goy nay!*
– *ngor hor yee dim bong nay?*
– *gor gor gay dor chin a?*
– *mm, ngor tai tai … yee baak mun.*

顧客服務	customer service
自助	self-service
清貨大減價	clearance

Preference 偏好

I want something ...	我要 ... 的。	*ngor yeeu ... ge*
It must be ...	一定要是 ... 的。	*yut ding yeeu ... ge*
big/small	大 / 小	*daai/sai*
cheap/expensive	便宜 / 貴	*peng/gwai*
dark/light (color)	深色 / 淺色	*sum sick/chin sick*
light/heavy	輕 / 重	*heng/ch-owng*
oval/round/square	橢圓形 / 圓形 / 方形	
	tor yu-een ying/yu-een ying/fong ying	
genuine/imitation	眞 / 仿製	*jun/fong jai*
I don't want anything too expensive.	太貴的我不要。	
	taai gwai ge ngor mm yeeu	
In the region of ... HK dollars/ yuan.	... 元左右。	
	... mun jor yau	

你想要什麼 ... 的？	What ... would you like?
顏色 / 形狀	color/shape
品質 / 數量	quality/quantity
你想要哪種？	What sort would you like?
你想要大概什麼價錢的？	What price range are you thinking of?

Do you have anything ...?	有沒有 ... 的？	*yau mo ... ge*
larger/smaller	大些 / 小些	*daai dee/sai dee*
better quality/cheaper	品質好些 / 便宜些	
	jut day ho dee/peng dee	
Can you show me ...?	請拿 ... 給我看看。	
	mm goy lor ... bay ngor tai tai	
that/this one	那個 / 這個	*gor gor/nay gor*
these/those ones	這些 / 那些	*nay dee/gor dee*
the one in the window/ display case	櫥窗 / 玻璃櫃裡的那個	*chu-ee churng/ bor lay gwai lur-ee bin gor gor*
some others	另一些	*ling ngoy yut dee*

COLOR ➤ 143

Conditions of purchase 購買條件

Is there a guarantee?　　　　有沒有保用證？
yau mo bo y-owng jing

Are there any instructions
with it?　　　　　　　　　有沒有說明書？
yau mo su-eet ming su-ee

Out of stock　無存貨

對不起，我們這裡沒有。	I'm sorry, we don't have any.
我們這裡賣完了。	We're out of stock.
我拿另一種給你看看好嗎？	Can I show you something else/ a different sort?
要我們替你訂購嗎？	Shall we order it for you?

Can you order it for me?　　可以替我訂購嗎？
hor mm hor yee bong ngor deng a

How long will it take?　　　要多長時間？　*yeeu gay noy jee yau*

Is there another store
that sells …?　　　　　　　還有沒有其它店賣 …？ *j-owng yau mo*
kay ta dim maai …

Decision　決定

That's not quite what I want.　這個不太合適。
nay gor mm hai gay hup sick

No, I don't like it.　　　　　我不喜歡這個。
ngor mm j-owng yee nay gor

That's too expensive.　　　　太貴了。　*taai gwai la*

I'd like to think about it.　　我要考慮一下。
ngor hau lur-ee ha sin

I'll take it.　　　　　　　　就要這個。　*jau yeeu nay gor*

　　– *jo sun. ngor surng maai yut g-in churng*
　　　jau wun d-owng saam.
　　– *ho. mut ye ngaan sick?*
　– *chaang sick. yeeu s-owng sun ge.*
　– *nay g-in la. yee baak ng sup mun.*
　– *mm, nay g-in mm hai ge hup sick.*

135

Paying 付款

In Guangdong, credit cards are accepted in more and more tourist areas. A 4% commission is charged on credit card purchases. Traveler's checks are accepted at the currency exchange counters of hotels and stores almost everywhere in China.

In Hong Kong and Macau, credit cards are widely accepted. Traveler's checks are widely accepted in stores, though you'll probably get a better exchange rate at a bank.

Where do I pay?	到哪裡付款？	*hur-ee bin do bay chin*
How much is that?	多少錢？	*gay dor chin a*
Could you write it down, please?	請寫下來。	*mm goy se dai*
Do you accept traveler's checks [cheques]?	你們收旅行支票嗎？	*nay day sau mm sau lur-ee hung jee peeu*
I'll pay …	我 …	*ngor*
with cash	付現金	*bay yin gum*
by credit card	用信用卡付	*y-owng sun' y-owng kaat bay*
I don't have any smaller change.	我沒有零錢。	*ngor mo saan jee*
Sorry, I don't have enough money.	對不起，我沒有足夠的錢。	*dur-ee mm ju-ee, ngor mm gau chin*

你用什麼方式付款？	How are you paying?
這宗交易不獲批准 / 接受。	This transaction has not been approved/accepted.
這卡無效。	This card is not valid.
可以看看其他身分證明嗎？	May I have further identification?
你有沒有零錢？	Do you have any smaller change?

Could I have a receipt, please?	請開張收條。	*mm goy hoy jurng sau teeu*
I think you've given me the wrong change.	你找給我的錢好像不對。	*nay jaau bay ngor ge chin ho chee mm ngaam wor*

請在此付款	Please pay here.
嚴禁高買，違者必究。	Shoplifters will be prosecuted.

Complaints 投訴

This doesn't work.	這個壞了。 *nay gor waai jor*
Can you exchange this, please?	請換一個。 *mm goy woon gwor gor*
I'd like a refund.	我要求退款。 *ngor yeeu kau tur-ee foon*
Here's the receipt.	這是收條。 *sau teeu hai nay do*
I don't have the receipt.	我沒有收條。 *ngor mo sau teeu*
I'd like to see the manager.	我要見經理。 *ngor yeeu g-in ging lay*

Repairs/Cleaning 修理 / 洗衣

Most hotels usually have a laundry service. However, in Hong Kong there are many laundromats which may be cheaper.

This is broken. Can you repair it?	這個壞了。能修理嗎？ *nay gor ye waai jor. hor mm hor ye sau jing a*
Do you have ... for this?	你們有沒有適合這個用的 ...？ *nay day yau mo ngaam nay gor y-owng ge ...*
a battery	電池 *din sum*
replacement parts	替換零件 *tai woon ling g-in*
There's something wrong with ...	... 有毛病。 *... mm tor*
Can you ... this?	請把這件衣服 ...。 *mm goy ... nay g-in saam*
clean	洗乾淨 *sai gon jeng*
press	熨好 *tong ho*
patch	縫補一下 *bo faan ho*
Could you alter this?	這件衣服請改一下。 *mm goy goy yut goy nay g-in saam*
When will it be ready?	什麼時候可以改好？ *gay see hor yee goy ho*
This isn't mine.	這不是我的。 *nay g-in mm hai ngor ge*
There's ... missing.	少了 ...。 *seeu jor ...*

TIME ➤ 221; DATES ➤ 219

Bank/Currency exchange
銀行 / 外幣找換店

In Hong Kong and Macau, banks are open from 9 a.m. to 4:30 p.m. and on Saturday mornings.

In Guangdong, banks are open from 8 a.m. to 7 p.m. Monday to Saturday with a break for lunch.

Outside of banking hours, money can be changed in hotels or in money changing offices in Hong Kong and in casinos in Macau. In Guangdong, most tourist hotels and Friendship Stores offer money changing services.

各種外幣	all transactions
外幣找換店	currency exchange
營業 / 休息	open/closed
出納	cashiers

Where's the nearest ...?
離這裡最近的 ... 在哪裡？
jur-ee kun nay do ge ... hai bin do a

bank
銀行 *ngun hong*

currency exchange office
[bureau de change]
外匯兌換處
ngoy woo-ee dur-ee woon chu-ee

Changing money 換錢

Can I exchange foreign
currency here?
我可以在這裡兌換外幣嗎？ *ngor hor mm
hor yee hai nay do dur-ee woon ngoy bai a*

I'd like to change some dollars/
pounds into HK dollars/
renminbi.
我想用美元 / 英鎊兌換港幣 / 人民幣。
*gor surng y-owng may gum/ying bong
woon gong bai/yun mun bai*

I want to cash some
traveler's checks [cheques].
我想兌現旅行支票。 *ngor surng dur-ee
yin lur-ee hung jee peeu*

What's the exchange rate?
匯率是多少？
woo-ee lut' hai gay dor a

How much commission do
you charge?
要付多少手續費
yeeu bay gay dor chin sau juk fai a

Could I have some small
change, please?
請給我一些零錢。
mm goy bay dee saan jee

I've lost my traveler's checks.
These are the numbers.
我丟失了旅行支票。號碼在這裡。
*ngor mm g-in jor lur-ee hung jee peeu.
ho ma hai nay do*

Security　身份查驗

可以看看 … 嗎？	Could I see …?
你的護照	your passport
身分證明	some identification
你的銀行卡	your bank card
你住在哪裡？	What's your address?
你暫時住在哪裡？	Where are you staying?
請填寫這張表。	Fill in this form, please.
請在這裡簽名。	Please sign here.

Cash machines / ATMs　自動提款機

Can I withdraw money on my credit card here?	我可以用信用卡在這裡提款嗎？ *ngor hor mm hor yee y-owng sun' y-owng kaat hai nay do lor chin a*
Where are the ATMs [cash machines]?	提款機在哪裡？ *tai foon gay hai bin do a*
Can I use my … card in the cash machine?	我可以用我的 … 卡從提款機提款嗎？ *ngor hor mm hor yee y-owng ngor ge … kaat hai tai foon gay lor chin a*
The cash machine has eaten my card.	提款機把我的信用卡弄壞了。 *tai foon gay jing laan jor ngor jurng kaat*

自動提款機	automated teller (ATM) [cash machine]

Currency

Hong Kong. The monetary unit is the **Hong Kong dollar (HK$)**, which is divided into 100 **cents**.

> *Coins:* 10, 20, and 50 cents; 1, 2, 5, and 10 dollars
> *Notes:* 10, 20, 50, 100, 500, and 1000 dollars

Macau. The monetary unit is the **pataca (M$)**, which is divided into 100 **avos**. Hong Kong dollars are also used as standard currency, but the pataca is not generally accepted in Hong Kong.

Guangdong. The currency is **renminbi (RMB)** or "People's Money". The monetary unit is the **yuan**, which is divided into 10 **jiao**, and further divided into 10 **fen**.

> *Coins:* 1 yuan; 5 jiao; 1, 2, and 5 fen
> *Notes:* 2, 5, 10, 50, and 100 yuan

Pharmacy 藥房

Hong Kong pharmacies follow both Western and Eastern concepts of health care, displaying familiar pills and bottles along with exotic herbs, roots, etc.

In Guangdong, it is difficult or impossible to find many Western items in pharmacies, so be sure to take any essential medications with you. To avoid problems at customs, make sure all medication is clearly marked and in its original prescription bottle.

Where's the nearest pharmacy?	離這裡最近的藥房在哪裡？*jur-ee kun nay do ge yerk fong hai bin do a*
What time does the pharmacy open/close?	藥房幾點開門／關門？*yerk fong gay dim hoy moon/saan moon a*
Can you make up this prescription for me?	請按這個處方配藥。*mm goy jeeu nay gor yerk fong poo-ee yerk*
Shall I wait?	等一會可以取嗎？*dung yut jun yau mo duck lor*
I'll come back for it.	我回頭來取。*ngor ju-een tau lay lor*

Dosage instructions 劑量說明

How much should I take?	每次服多少？*moo-ee chee sick gay dor*
How often should I take it?	每隔多久服一次？*gaak gay noy sick yut chee*
Is it suitable for children?	適合兒童嗎？*sick mm sick hup yee t-owng a*

每次服 …	Take …
… 片	… tablets
… 茶匙	… teaspoons
飯前／飯後服	before/after meals
用水送服	with water
整片吞下	whole
早上／晚上	in the morning/at night
連續服 … 日	for … days

只可外用	for external use only
非內服藥	not to be taken
	internally

Asking advice 問意見

What would you recommend for ...?	治 ... 什麼藥最好？ *jee ..., mut ye yerk jur-ee ho a*
a cold	傷風 *surng f-owng*
a cough	咳嗽 *kut sau*
diarrhea	肚瀉 *to se*
a hangover	宿醉 *suk jur-ee*
hayfever	花粉過敏症 *fa fun gwor mun jing*
insect bites	蟲咬傷 *ch-owng ngaau surng*
a sore throat	喉嚨痛 *hau l-owng t-owng*
sunburn	晒傷 *saai surng*
motion [travel] sickness	暈浪 *wun long*
an upset stomach	腸胃唔舒服 *churng wai mm su-ee fuk*
Can I get it without a prescription?	沒有處方能買嗎？ *mo yerk fong, maai mm maai duck*

Over-the-counter treatment 無需處方購買的藥品

Can I have ...?	我想買 ... *ngor surng maai ...*
antiseptic cream	消毒膏 *seeu duk go*
(soluble) aspirin	(可溶) 亞士匹靈 *(ho y-owng) a see put ling*
gauze [bandages]	繃帶 *bung daai*
condoms	避孕套 *bay yun to*
cotton [cotton wool]	棉花 *min fa*
insect repellent	蚊怕水 *mun pa sur-ee*
painkillers	止痛藥 *jee t-owng yerk*
vitamin tablets	維他命丸 *wai ta ming yu-een*

141

Toiletries 盥洗用品

I'd like some …	我想買 …	*ngor surng maai …*
after-shave	鬚後水	*so hau sur-ee*
after-sun lotion	晒後水	*saai hau sur-ee*
deodorant	除臭劑	*chur-ee chau jai*
razor blades	剃刀	*tai do*
sanitary napkins [towels]	衛生巾	*wai sung gun*
soap	肥皂	*faan gaan*
sun block	防晒傷膏	*fong saai surng go*
sunscreen	太陽油	*taai yurng yau*
factor …	防護係數 …	*fong woo hai so …*
tampons	內用衛生棉條	*noy y-owng wai sung min teeu*
tissues	紙巾	*jee gun*
toilet paper	廁紙	*chee jee*
toothpaste	牙膏	*nga go*

Haircare 美髮用品

comb	梳	*sor*
conditioner	護髮素	*woo faat so*
hair mousse/gel	髮士 / 定型膠	*moo see/ding ying gau*
hair spray	噴髮膠	*pun faat gaau*
shampoo	洗髮水	*sai tau sur-ee*

For the baby 嬰兒用品

baby food	嬰兒食品	*ying yee sick bun*
baby wipes	嬰兒濕紙巾	*ying yee sup jee gun*
diapers [nappies]	尿片	*neeu pin*
sterilizing solution	消毒水	*seeu duk sur-ee*

Clothing 衣服

You will find all manner of clothing, much very reasonably priced, for sale in the Friendship Stores, street markets (be prepared to bargain), and local department stores. In the chic, expensive boutiques of Hong Kong, and in areas of Guangzhou like Huanshi Donglu, you'll find famous brand-name items from international fashion houses – at a price.

男裝	menswear
童裝	childrenswear
女裝	womenswear

General 一般用語

| I'd like ... | 我想要 ... *ngor surng yeeu* |
| Do you have any ...? | 你們這裡有沒有 ... ?
nay day nay do yau mo ... |

Color 顏色

I'm looking for something in ...	我想找一件 ... 的。 *ngor surng wun g-in ... ge*
beige	米色 *mai sick*
black	黑色 *huck sick*
white	白色 *baak sick*
blue	藍色 *laam sick*
green	綠色 *luk sick*
brown	咖啡色 *fe sick*
gray	灰色 *foo-ee sick*
orange	橙色 *chaang sick*
purple	紫色 *jee sick*
red/pink	紅色 / 粉紅色 *h-owng sick/fun h-owng sick*
yellow	黃色 *wong sick*
light ...	淺 ... *chin ...*
dark ...	深 ... *sum ...*
I want a darker/lighter shade.	我要顏色深些 / 淺些的。 *ngor yeeu sum/chin sick dee ge*
Do you have the same in ...?	這個款式有沒有 ... 的。 *nay gor foon yau mo ... ge*

belt	皮帶	*pay daai*
bikini	三點式泳衣	*saam dim sick wing yee*
blouse	女裝恤衫	*nur-ee j-owng sut' saam*
bra	胸圍	*h-owng wai*
briefs	內褲	*noy foo*
cap	鴨舌帽	*aap jur-ee mo*
coat	大衣	*daai lau*
dress	連衫裙	*lin saam qu-un*
handbag	手袋	*sau doy*
hat	帽	*mo*
jacket	外套	*ngoy to*
jeans	牛仔褲	*ngau jai foo*
leggings	橡筋褲	*jeung gun foo*
pants (U.S.)	褲	*foo*
pantyhose [tights]	襪褲	*mut foo*
raincoat	雨衣	*yu-ee lau*
scarf	頸巾	*geng gun*
shirt	恤衫	*sut' saam*
shorts	短褲	*du-een foo*
skirt	半截裙	*boon jit qu-un*
socks	襪	*mut*
stockings	長襪	*churng mut*
suit	西裝	*sai jong*
sweater	套頭毛衣	*gwor tau lup laang sum*
sweatshirt	長袖運動衫	*churng jau wun d-owng saam*
swimming trunks/swimsuit	游泳褲 / 游泳衣	*yau sur-ee foo/yau wing yee*
T-shirt	T-恤	*T-sut'*
tie	領帶	*leng taai*
tights	襪褲	*mut foo*
trousers	褲	*foo*
underpants	內褲	*noy foo*
with long/short sleeves	長袖 / 短袖	*churng jau/du-een jau*
with a V-/round neck	V 字領 / 圓領	*V jee leng/yu-een leng*

Shoes 鞋

boots	靴	*her*
flip-flops	人字拖鞋	*yun jee tor haai*
running [training] shoes	運動鞋	*wun d-owng haai*
sandals	涼鞋	*lurng haai*
shoes	鞋	*haai*
slippers	拖鞋	*tor haai*

Walking/Hiking gear 遠足用品

knapsack	背囊	*boo-ee nong*
hiking boots	旅行靴	*lur-ee hung her*
waterproof jacket/anorak	防水外套	*fong sur-ee ngoy to*
windbreaker [cagoule]	風衣	*f-owng lau*

Fabric 布料

I want something in …	我要件 … 的。	*ngor yeeu g-in … ge*
cotton	棉布	*min bo*
denim	牛仔布	*ngau jai bo*
lace	厘士 (透花織料)	*lay see (tau fa jick leeu)*
leather	皮	*pay*
linen	亞麻布	*a ma bo*
wool	羊毛	*yurng mo*
Is this …?	這是 … 嗎？	*nay je hai mm hai …*
pure cotton	純棉	*sun' min*
synthetic	人造纖維	*yun jo chim wai*
Is it hand washable/ machine washable?	可以用手洗 / 用洗衣機洗嗎？	*hor mm hor yee y-owng sau sai/y-owng sai yee gay sai a*

只可手洗	handwash only
只可乾洗	dry clean only
不褪色	colorfast
勿熨	do not iron

Does it fit? 合身嗎？

Can I try this on?	我可以試試嗎？ *ngor hor mm hor yee see ha*
Where's the fitting room?	試衣室在哪裡？ *see yee sut hai bin do a*
It fits well. I'll take it.	很合身。就要這件。 *ho ngaam sun. jau yeeu nay g-in*
It doesn't fit.	這件不合身。 *nay g-in mm ngaam sun*
It's too…	太 … *taai …*
short/long	短 / 長 *du-een/churng*
tight/loose	緊 / 鬆 *gun/s-owng*
Do you have this in size …?	這個款式有沒有 … 號？ *nay gor foon yau mo … ho*
What size is this?	這是什麼碼？ *nay gor ha mut ye ma*
Could you measure me, please?	請替我量量。 *mm goy bong ngor dock yut dock*
I don't know Chinese sizes.	我不知道中國尺碼。 *ngor mm jee do j-owng gwock check ma*

Size 尺碼

Outside of Hong Kong you will find that clothing sizes in China are still being standardized and do not correspond to those in the West. In Friendship stores and places where clothes are made for export, you will find sizes given as small, medium, and large. However, you may find these are of a smaller cut than you would find at home.

Chinese measurements combine two factors, one of which is height. For example, a jacket may be sized 165-88, i.e., for a person 1.65 m. tall, who has an 88 cm. chest. When buying shoes the safest way is to try them on, if you can find any large enough – U.S. 7 ½/U.K. 6 is considered large!

加大	extra large (XL)
大	large (L)
中	medium (M)
小	small (S)

1 centimeter (cm.) = 0.39 in.	1 inch = 2.54 cm.
1 meter (m.) = 39.37 in.	1 foot = 30.5 cm.
10 meters = 32.81 ft.	1 yard = 0.91 m.

Health and beauty 健康和美容

I'd like a ...	我想 ... *ngor surng ...*
facial	美容 *may y-owng*
manicure	修甲 *sau gaap*
massage	按摩 *on mor*
waxing	做熱臘脫毛 *jo yit laap tu-eet mo*

Hairdresser/Hairstylist 理髮

Larger hotels usually have barbers/hairdressers – and your treatment may include a head and neck massage. In Guangdong, tipping is not officially permitted. In Hong Kong, a 10–20% tip is normal.

I'd like to make an appointment for ...	我想約個時間 ... *ngor surng yerk gor see gaan ...*
Can you make it a bit earlier/later?	早些 / 晚些可以嗎？ *jo dee/aan dee duck mm duck*
I'd like a ...	我想 ... *ngor surng ...*
cut and blow-dry	剪和吹 *jin t-owng chur-ee*
shampoo and set	洗和捲 *sai t-owng gu-een*
trim	剪髮 *jin faat*
I'd like my hair ...	我想 ... *ngor surng ...*
highlighted	部分頭髮染成淺色 *bo fun tau faat yim chin sick*
permed	電髮 *din faat*
Don't cut it too short.	不要剪得太短。 *mm ho jin duck taai du-een*
A little more off the ...	... 的頭髮還要稍爲短些。 *... dee tau faat j-owng yeeu du-een seeu seeu*
back/front	後邊 / 前邊 *hau bin/chin bin*
neck/sides	頸上 / 兩側 *geng do/lurng bin*
top	頭頂 *tau deng*
That's fine, thanks.	很好, 謝謝。 *gay ho, mm goy*

Household articles 家庭用品

I'd like a(n)/some …	我想要 … ngor surng yeeu …	
adapter	一個多路插座	yut gor dor lo chaap jo
alumin(i)um foil	錫紙	seck jee
bottle opener	一個開瓶器	yut jee hoy jun' goy ge ye
can [tin] opener	罐頭刀	goon tau do
clothes pins [pegs]	晾衣夾	long saam gaap
corkscrew	開瓶鑽	hoy jun' ju-een
light bulb	燈泡	dung daam
matches	火柴	for chaai
paper napkins	紙餐巾	jee chaan gun
plastic wrap [cling film]	保鮮紙	bo sin jee
plug	插頭	chaap tau
scissors	剪刀	gaau jin
screwdriver	螺絲批	lor see pai

Cleaning items 清潔用品

bleach	漂白水	peeu baak sur-ee
detergent [washing powder]	洗衣粉	sai yee fun
dish cloth	碗布	woon bo
dishwashing [washing-up] liquid	洗潔精	sai git jing
garbage [refuse] bags	垃圾袋	laap saap doy
sponge	海綿	hoy min

Crockery/Cutlery 陶瓷 / 刀叉餐具

cups/glasses	杯 / 水杯	boo-ee/sur-ee boo-ee
knives/forks	刀 / 叉	do/cha
spoons	匙羹	chee gung
mugs	大杯	daai boo-ee
plates	碟	dip
bowls	碗	woon
chopsticks	筷子	faai jee

Jeweler 珠寶首飾

Could I see …?	請拿 … 給我看看。 *mm goy lor … bay ngor tai tai*
this/that	這個 / 那個 *nay gor/gor gor*
It's in the window/display cabinet.	在櫥窗 / 玻璃櫃裡。 *hai chu-ee churng/bor lay gwai do*
alarm clock	鬧鐘 *naau j-owng*
battery	電池 *din sum*
bracelet	手鐲 *sau ngaak*
brooch	心口針 *sum hau jum*
chain	鍊 *lin*
clock	鐘 *j-owng*
earrings	耳環 *yee waan*
necklace	頸鍊 *geng lin*
ring	戒指 *gaai jee*
watch	手錶 *sau beeu*

Materials 質料

Is this real silver/gold?	這是真銀 / 金嗎？ *nay je hai mm hai jun ngun/gum a*
Is there a certificate for it?	有證明書嗎？ *yau mo jing ming su-ee a*
Do you have anything in …?	你們有沒有 … 製品？ *nay day yau mo … jai bun*
copper	銅 *t-owng*
crystal	水晶 *sur-ee jing*
cut glass	雕花玻璃 *deeu fa bor lay*
diamond	鑽石 *ju-een seck*
enamel	搪瓷 *tong chee*
gold	金 *gum*
gold-plate	鍍金 *do gum*
pearl	珍珠 *jun ju-ee*
pewter	錫鑞 *seck laap*
platinum	白金 *baak gum*
silver	銀 *ngun*
silver-plate	鍍銀 *do ngun*
stainless steel	不銹鋼 *but sau gong*

Newsstand [Newsagent]/ Tobacconist 報攤/香煙店

News kiosks in major hotels in Guangdong often sell foreign newspapers and magazines. In Hong Kong and Macau, many bookstores and hotels sell international newspapers and magazines.

Do you sell English-language books/newspapers?	你們這裡賣不賣英文書/報紙? *nay day nay do yau mo ying mun su-ee/bo jee maai*
I'd like (a) …	我想買 … *ngor surng maai …*
book	書 *su-ee*
candy [sweets]	糖果 *tong gwor*
chewing gum	香口膠 *hurng hau gaau*
chocolate bar	一排朱古力 *yut paai ju-ee goo lick*
cigarettes (packet of)	一包香煙 *yut bau yin jai*
cigars	雪茄 *su-eet ga*
dictionary	字典 *jee din*
English-Chinese	英漢 *ying hon*
envelopes	信封 *sun' f-owng*
guidebook of …	… 旅遊指南 *… lur-ee yau jee naam*
lighter	打火機 *da for gay*
magazine	雜誌 *jaap jee*
map	地圖 *day to*
map of the town	本市地圖 *boon see day to*
road map of …	… 道路圖 *… do lo to*
matches	火柴 *for chaai*
newspaper	報紙 *bo jee*
American/English	美國/英國 *may gwock/ying gwock*
paper	紙 *jee*
pen	筆 *but*
stamps	郵票 *yau peeu*
tobacco	煙絲 *yin see*

Photography 攝影

I'm looking for a(n) ... camera.

我想找一個 ... 相機。
ngor surng wun yut ga ...
surng gay

automatic 全自動 *chu-een jee d-owng*

compact 袖珍 *jau jun*

disposable 用後即棄的 *y-owng yu-een jau dum ge*

SLR 單鏡頭 *daan geng tau*

I'd like a(n) ... 我要 ... *ngor yeeu ...*

battery 電池 *din sum*

camera case 相機袋 *surng gay doy*

electronic flash 電子閃光燈 *din jee sim gwong dung*

filter 濾色鏡 *lur-ee sick geng*

lens 鏡頭 *geng tau*

lens cap 鏡頭蓋 *geng tau goy*

Film/Processing 菲林 / 沖晒

I'd like a ... film.

我要一筒 ... 菲林。
ngor yeeu yut t-owng ... fay lum

black and white 黑白 *huck baak*

color 彩色 *choy sick*

24/36 exposures

二十四 / 三十六張的
yee sup say/saam sup luk jurng ge

I'd like this film developed,
please.

我想晒這筒菲林。
ngor surng saai nay t-owng fay lum

Would you enlarge this, please?

請放大這張。
mm goy fong daai nay jurng

How much do ... exposures
cost?

... 張要多少錢?
... jurng yeeu gay dor chin a

When will the photos be
ready?

什麼時候可以晒好?
gay see ho yee saai ho

I'd like to collect my photos. 我取相片。 *ngor lor surng*

Here's the receipt. 這是收條。 *sau teeu hai nay do*

Police 警察

The Hong Kong police force is one of the world's best equipped, and deals with crime, traffic, and coastguard duties. Police officers with a red label under their shoulder badges speak English. The emergency phone number is 999 in Hong Kong and Macau. In Guangdong, armed police wear green uniforms and peaked caps, displaying the national insignia of China. They are not to be confused with members of the air force, who wear a red star on their cap. The emergency phone number is 110.

Where's the nearest police station?	離這裡最近的警署（公安局）在哪裡？ *jur-ee kun nay do ge ging chu-ee (g-owng on guk) hai bin do a*
Does anyone here speak English?	這裡有誰會說英語嗎？ *nay do yau mo yun sick gong ying mun a*
I want to report a(n) …	我想報一宗 … *ngor surng bo yut j-owng …*
accident/attack	意外／襲擊案 *yee ngoy/jaap gick on*
mugging/rape	搶劫案／強姦案 *churng gip on/kurng gaan on*
My child is missing.	我的孩子失蹤了。 *ngor gor jai/nur-ee mm g-in jor*
Here's a photo of him/her.	這是他／她的相片。 *nay jurng hai kur-ee/kur-ee ge surng pin*
Someone's following me.	有人跟蹤我。 *yau yun gun j-owng ngor*
I need an English-speaking lawyer.	我需要一位會說英語的律師。 *ngor sur-ee yeeu yut wai sick gong ying mun ge lut' see*
I need to make a phone call.	我需要打個電話。 *ngor yeeu da gor din wa*
I need to contact the … Consulate.	我需要同 … 領事館聯絡。 *ngor yeeu t-owng … ling see goon lu-een lock*
American/British	美國／英國 *may gwock/ying gwock*

你能形容他／她的樣子嗎？	Can you describe him/her?
男／女	male/female
金髮／黑髮／紅髮	blond(e)/dark haired/red-headed
灰白頭髮	gray haired
長髮／短髮／禿頭	long/short hair/balding
身高大約 …	approximate height …
（大約）… 歲	aged (approximately) …
他／她穿 …	He/She was wearing …

 CLOTHES ➤ 144; COLOR ➤ 143

Lost property/Theft 失物／盜竊

I want to report a theft.	我想報一件盜竊案/爆竊案。 *ngor surng bo yut g-in do* *sip on*
My car's been broken into.	我的汽車被人爆竊了。 *ngor ga hay che bay yun baau sip*
I've been robbed/mugged.	我被人打劫。 *ngor bay yun da gip*
I've lost my …	我丟失了 …。 *ngor mm g-in jor …*
My … has been stolen.	我的 … 被人偷了。 *ngor ge … bay yun tau jor*
bicycle	單車 (自行車) *daan che (jee hung che)*
camera	相機 *surng gay*
(rental) car	(租用) 汽車 *(jo y-owng) hay che*
credit cards	信用卡 *sun' y-owng kaat*
handbag	手袋 *sau doy*
money	錢 *chin*
passport	護照 *woo jeeu*
purse/wallet	錢包 *ngun bau*
ticket	票 *fay*
watch	手錶 *sau beeu*
What shall I do?	我該怎樣做？ *ngor ying goy dim jo a*
I need a police report for my insurance claim.	我想要保險公司賠償，需要一份警方報告書。 *ngor surng yeeu bo him g-owng see* *poo-ee surng, sur-ee yeeu yut fun ging* *fong bo go su-ee*

丟失了什麼？	What's missing?
什麼被偷去了？	What's been taken?
什麼時候被偷去的？	When was it stolen?
什麼時候發生的？	When did it happen?
你目前住在哪裡？	Where are you staying?
從哪裡被偷去的？	Where was it taken from?
你當時在哪裡？	Where were you at the time?
我們正在替你找一位翻譯。	We're getting an interpreter for you.
我們會調查這件事。	We'll look into the matter.
請填寫這張表格。	Please fill out this form.

Post office 郵局

In Hong Kong, post offices are open from 8 a.m. to 6 p.m. Monday to Saturday. In Macau, the General Post Office is open from 9 a.m. to 8 p.m. Monday to Saturday. In Macau you'll find red "mini post offices", which are stamp machines.

In Guangdong, hotels have branch post offices or postal service desks open seven days a week, selling stamps, postcards, and writing paper. Hotel branches are open from 8 a.m. to 6 p.m. Monday through Saturday, and on Sunday mornings from 8 a.m. to noon.

General queries 一般查詢

Where is the post office?	郵局在哪裡？ *yau guk hai bin do a*
What time does the post office open/close?	郵局幾點開門／關門？ *yau guk gay dim hoy moon/saan moon a*
Does it close for lunch?	午膳時間休息嗎？ *sick aan see gaan yau mm yau sick ga*
Where's the mailbox [postbox]?	郵筒在哪裡？ *yau t-owng hai bin do a*
Is there any mail for me?	有沒有我的信？ *yau mo ngor ge sun' a*

Buying stamps 買郵票

A stamp for this postcard, please.	要一張寄這明信片的郵票。 *yut gor gay nay jurng ming sun' pin ge yau peeu, mm goy*
A ... dollar/yuan stamp, please.	要一張 ... 元的郵票。 *yut gor ... mun ge yau peeu, mm goy*
What's the postage for a letter to ...?	寄 ... 的信，郵費是多少？ *gay ... ge sun', gay dor chin yau fai*
Is there a stamp machine here?	這裡有沒有郵票出售機？ *nay do yau mo yau peeu chut' sau gay a*

- *nay ho. nay dee ming sun' pin gay hur-ee may gwock.*
- *gay dor jurng?*
- *gau jurng.*
- *ng mun sing gau, yut g-owng say sup ng mun.*

154

Sending packages 寄包裹

I want to send this package [parcel] by …	這個包裹寄 … *nay gor bau gwor gay …*
air mail	空郵 *hong h-owng*
express mail [special delivery]	速遞 (快遞) *chuk dai (faai dai)*
registered mail	掛號 *gwa ho*
It contains …	裡面有 … *lur-ee bin yau …*

請填寫海關申報單。	Please fill out the customs declaration.
價值是多少	What's the value?
裡面有些什麼？	What's inside?

Telecommunications 電訊

Most major hotels have a business center with telephone, fax, and telex services, and probably photocopiers, typewriters, and even computers.

I'd like a phone card, please.	要一張電話卡。 *yut jurng din wa kaat, mm goy*
10/20/50 units.	十 / 二十 / 五十個單位的。 *sup/yee sup/ng sup gor daan wai ge*
Do you have a photocopier?	這裡有影印機嗎？ *nay do yau mo ying yun gay a*
I'd like to send a message …	我想發 … *ngor surng faat …*
by e-mail/fax	一個電子郵件 / 一份傳真 *yut gor din jee yau g-in/yut fun chu-een jun*
What's your e-mail address?	你們的電子郵件地址是什麼？ *nay day ge din jee yau g-in day jee hai mut ye*
Can I access the Internet here?	從這裡能進入國際網絡嗎？ *hai nay do yup mm yup do Internet a*
What are the charges per hour?	一小時收費多少？ *yut gor j-owng sau gay dor chin a*
How do I log on?	怎樣進入網絡？ *dim yurng yup mong lock a*

包裹	packages
下次收信時間 …	next collection …
郵件待領處	general delivery [poste restante]
郵票	stamps
電報	telegrams

Souvenirs 紀念品

You will have no difficulty in finding any number of souvenirs and presents to take home. There is something for everybody and in every price range. The following are just a few suggestions: antiques, bamboo products, carpets and rugs, fans, fabrics, furniture, china, jade, jewelry, kites, tea, ginseng, woks and other Chinese kitchen utensils, and seals (name chops, the traditional Chinese substitute for handwritten signatures).

Favorite buys in Hong Kong fall into two main catergories: the duty-free imported goods – including photographic equipment, electronic goods, and watches – on which you avoid the sales tax you would pay at home; and specialty goods, often handmade, from Hong Kong and China, including traditional items and custom-made garments.

abacus	算盤 *su-een poon*
carpet	地氈 *day jin*
chopsticks	筷子 *faai jee*
electronic goods	電器 *din hay*
fans	扇 *sin*
handicrafts	手工藝品 *sau g-owng ngai bun*
personal seal (name chop)	圖章 *to jurng*
pottery	陶器 *to hay*
porcelain	瓷器 *chee hay*
prints	板畫 *baan wa*
silk	絲綢 *see chau*

Gifts 禮物

bottle of wine	一瓶葡萄酒 *yut jun' po to jau*
box of chocolates	一盒朱古力 *yut hup ju-ee goo lick*
calendar	日曆 *yut lick*
key ring	鑰匙圈 *sor see hu-een*
postcard	明信片 *ming sun' pin*
souvenir guidebook	紀念指南 *gay nim jee naam*
tea towel	茶巾 *cha gun*
T-shirt	T-恤 *T sut'*

Music 音樂

I'd like a …	我要 … *ngor yeeu …*
cassette	一盒卡式錄音帶 *yut hup ka sick luk yum daai*
compact disc	一張激光唱片；CD 細碟 *yut jurng gick gowng churng pin; CD sai dip*
record	一張唱片 *yut jurng churng pin*
videocassette	一盒錄影帶 *yut hup luk ying daai*
Who are the popular native singers/bands?	有哪些受歡迎的本地歌星／樂隊？ *yau bin dee sau foon ying ge boon day gor sing/ngock dur-ee a*

Toys and games 玩具和智力遊戲

I'd like a toy/game …	我想買一個 … 玩具／遊戲。 *ngor surng maai yut gor … woon gur-ee/yau hay*
for a boy	給男孩玩的 *bay naam jai waan ge*
for a 5-year-old girl	給五歲女孩玩的 *bay ng sur-ee nur-ee jai waan ge*
ball	球 *bor*
chess set	象棋 *jurng kay*
doll	玩具娃娃 *g-owng jai*
electronic game	電子遊戲 *din jee yau hay*
pail and shovel [bucket and spade]	沙灘桶和鏟 *sa taan t-owng, t-owng maai chaan*
teddy bear	玩具熊 *woon gur-ee h-owng*

Antiques 古玩

How old is this?	這東西有多長的歷史？ *nay gor ye yau gay churng lick see a*
Do you have anything from the … dynasty?	你們有 … 朝的古玩嗎？ *nay day yau mo … cheeu ge goo woon a*
Can you send it to me?	可以寄給我嗎？ *hor mm hor yee gay bay ngor a*
Will I have problems with customs?	過海關會有問題嗎？ *gwor hoy gwaan woo-ee mm woo-ee yau mun tai a*
Is there a certificate of authenticity?	有沒有真品證明書？ *yau mo jun bun jing ming su-ee a*

Supermarket/Minimart
超級市場 / 小型市場

In Hong Kong and Macau, you will find plenty of department stores and supermarkets which also sell Western foods such as bread, cheese, coffee, jam, etc. In Guangdong, major cities have department stores – for example the Friendship Stores – which sell Western goods.

At the supermarket 在超級市場

Excuse me. Where can I find (a) …?	請問，哪裡有 … ? *cheng mun, bin do yau …*
Do I pay for this here or at the checkout?	在這裡還是到付款台付款？ *hai nay do yick waak hai foo foon toy bay chin a*
Where are the carts [trolleys]/baskets?	推車 / 籃在哪裡？ *tur-ee che/laam hai bin do a*
Is there a … here?	這裡有沒有 … ? *nay do yau mo …*
pharmacy	藥房 *yerk fong*
delicatessen	熟食櫃檯 *suk sick gwai toy*

付現	cash only
清潔用品	cleaning products
奶品	dairy products
鮮魚	fresh fish
鮮肉	fresh meat
新鮮蔬果	fresh produce
急凍食品	frozen foods
家庭用品	household goods
雞鴨類	poultry
罐頭水果 / 蔬菜	canned fruit/vegetables
酒品	wines and spirits
麵飽西餅	bread and cakes

Weights and measures

- **1 kilogram** or **kilo (kg)** = 1000 grams (g); 100 g = 3.5 oz.;
  1 kg = 2.2 lb.; 1 oz. = **28.35 g**; 1 lb. = **453.60 g**

- **1 liter (l)** = 0.88 imp. quart or 1.06 U.S. quart; 1 imp. quart = **1.14 l**
  1 U.S. quart = **0.951 l**; 1 imp. gallon = **4.55 l**; 1 U.S. gallon = **3.8 l**

Food hygiene 食物衛生

開後 … 天內食用	eat within … days of opening
冷藏	keep refrigerated
可用微波爐烹調 / 加熱	microwaveable
食前加熱	reheat before eating
適合素食者	suitable for vegetarians
… 前食用	use by …

At the minimart 在小型市場

I'd like some of that/those.   我要一些那種的。
ngor yeeu yut dee gor j-owng ge

this one/those   這個 / 那個 *nay gor/gor gor*

to the left/right   左邊 / 右邊 *jor bin/yau bin*

over there/here   那邊 / 這裡 *gor bin/nay do*

Which one/ones?   哪個 / 哪些？ *bin gor/bin dee*

I'd like (a) …   我要 …
ngor yeeu …

bag of chips [crisps]   一包薯片 *yut bau su-ee pin*

bottle of wine   一瓶葡萄酒 *yut jun' po to jau*

can [tin] of cola   一罐可樂 *yut goon hor lock*

carton of milk   一盒紙包奶 *yut hup jee bau naai*

jar of jam   一瓶果醬 *jam (yut jun' gwor jurng)*

half-dozen eggs   半打雞蛋 *boon da gai daan*

half-kilo of tomatoes   半公斤番茄 *boon g-owng gun faan ke*

kilo of apples   一公斤蘋果 *yut g-owng gun ping gwor*

liter of milk   一公升牛奶 *yut g-owng sing ngau naai*

piece of cake   一塊蛋糕 *yut faai daan go*

… slices of ham   … 片火腿 *… pin for tur-ee*

100 grams of cheese   一百克芝士 *yut baak huck jee see*

That's all, thanks.   就這些，謝謝。 *hai gum dor, mm goy*

– ngor yeeu boon g-owng gun gor
j-owng tai jee.
– *nay j-owng a?*
– hai, huck tai jee.
– *ho … j-owng yau mo ye yeeu?*
– say gor chaang, mm goy.
– *sum sup mun la.*

Provisions/Picnic 副食 / 野餐

butter	牛油 *ngau yau*
cheese	芝士 *jee see*
cookies [biscuits]	餅乾 *beng gon*
eggs	雞蛋 *gai daan*
grapes	提子 *tai jee*
ice cream	雪糕 *su-eet go*
instant coffee	即溶咖啡 *jick y-owng ga fe*
(loaf of) bread	大麵飽 *daai min bau*
margarine	人造牛油 *yun jo ngau yau*
milk	牛奶 *ngau naai*
potato chips [crisps]	薯片 *su-ee pin*
rolls	餐飽 *chaan bau*
sausages	香腸 *hurng churng*
tea bags	茶包 *cha bau*
beer	啤酒 *be jau*
soft drink	汽水 *hay sur-ee*
wine	葡萄酒 *po to jau*

Try some of the traditional Chinese breads. You will find fried bread rolls
(**ngun see gu-een**) for sale at street stalls and in local restaurants.

饅頭 *maan tau*	steamed buns
燒餅 *seeu beng*	clay-oven bread
銀絲卷 *ngun see gu-een*	steamed or fried bread rolls

Health

Before you leave, make sure your health insurance covers any illness or accident while abroad. If not, ask your insurance representative or travel agent for special health insurance. You do not need any vaccinations to enter China, but check before you leave as the requirements can change. Hong Kong has up-to-date hospitals, and you will have no trouble finding English-speaking staff. For minor ailments, pharmacists can often recommend and supply certain medications. In Macau, the Government Hospital north of San Francisco Garden provides medical treatment. In Guangdong, your interpreter/guide, hotel desk clerk, or CITS office will call a doctor, or arrange for you to be taken to hospital. Foreign tourists treated in a Chinese hospital must pay a registration fee plus the cost of any medication, and there is an additional charge in case of hospitalization. Treatment may involve a combination of modern and traditional Chinese medicine (e.g., accupuncture), but you can decline if you have any objections. **Warning**: Rhesus negative blood is not stored in Chinese blood banks.

Doctor (General) 醫生(一般用語)

Where can I find a doctor/dentist?	在哪裡可以找到醫生／牙醫？ *hai bin do hor yee wun do yee sung/nga yee a*
Where's there a doctor/dentist who speaks English?	哪裡有會說英語的醫生／牙醫？ *bin do yau sick gong ying mun ge yee sung/nga yee a*
Could the doctor come to see me here?	醫生可以來這裡看我嗎？ *yee sung hor mm hor yee lay nay do tai ngor a*
Can I make an appointment for …?	可以約個時間 … 看醫生嗎？ *hor mm hor yee yerk gor see gaan … tai yee sung*
today/tomorrow	今天／明天 *gum yut/ting yut*
as soon as possible	盡快 *jun' faai*
It's urgent.	很緊急。 *ho gun gup*
I have an appointment with Doctor …	我約了時間看 … 醫生。 *ngor yerk jor see gaan tai … yee sung*

– hor mm hor yee yerk gor jun' jo ge
see gaan tai yee sung a
– gum yut ge see gaan yerk moon saai la.
hai mm hai ho gun gup ge
– hai a'
– ho la, nay sup dim sup ng fun lay tai … yee sung la
– sup dim sup ng fun. mm goy saai

Accident and injury 意外和受傷

My … is hurt/injured.	我的 … 受了傷。	*ngor gor … sau jor srng*
husband/wife	丈夫 / 太太	*jung foo/taai taai*
son/daughter	兒子 / 女兒	*jai/nur-ee*
friend	朋友	*pung yau*
baby	小孩	*B B jai*
He/She is …	他 / 她 …	*kur-ee/kur-ee …*
unconscious	不省人事	*wun jor*
(seriously) injured	受了 (重) 傷	*sau jor (ch-owng) srng*
He/She is bleeding (heavily).	他 / 她在流血 (流得很厲害)。 *kur-ee lau gun hu-eet (lau duck ho sai lay)*	
I have a/an …	我 …	*ngor …*
blister	起了個水泡	*hay jor gor sur-ee pock*
boil	生了個瘡	*saang jor gor chong*
bruise	碰傷了	*jong srng jor*
burn	燒傷了	*seeu srng jor*
cut	割破了	*got su-een jor*
graze	擦傷了	*chaat srng jor*
insect bite	被蟲咬傷	*bay ch-owng ngaau srng*
lump	有個腫塊	*hay jor gor lau*
rash	出疹	*chut' chun*
sting	被蜜蜂螫傷	*bay mut f-owng jum srng*
strained muscle	扭傷了肌肉	*nau srng jor gay yuk*
swelling	有個地方腫起	*yau do j-owng jor*
wound	有個傷口	*yau gor srng hau*
My … hurts.	我的 … 很痛。	*ngor ge … ho t-owng*

Symptoms 短期症狀

I've been feeling ill for … days.	我不舒服已有 … 天了。 ngor mm su-ee fuk yee ging yau … yut la
I feel faint.	我覺得虛弱頭暈。 ngor gock duck hur-ee yerk tau wun
I feel feverish.	我發燒。 ngor faat seeu
I've been vomiting.	我嘔吐了很多次 ngor au jor ho dor chee
I have diarrhea.	我肚瀉。 ngor to se
It hurts here.	這裡痛。 nay do t-owng
I have (a/an) …	我 … ngor …
backache	腰痛 yeeu gwut t-owng
cold	傷風 surng f-owng
cramps	抽筋 chau gun
earache	耳痛 yee t-owng
headache	頭痛 tau t-owng
sore throat	喉嚨痛 hau l-owng t-owng
stiff neck	頸部硬直 teeu geng gung jor
stomachache	胃痛 wai t-owng
sunstroke	中暑 j-owng su-ee

Health conditions 健康狀況

I have arthritis.	我有關節炎。 ngor yau gwaan jit yim
I have asthma.	我有哮喘病。 ngor yau hau chu-een beng
I am …	我 … ngor …
deaf	耳聾 yee l-owng
diabetic	有糖尿病 yau tong neeu beng
epileptic	有癲癇症 yau din gaan jing
handicapped	傷殘 surng chaan
(… months) pregnant	懷孕 (有 … 個月了) yau jor sun gay (… gor yu-eet la)
I have a heart condition.	我有心臟病 ngor yau sum jong beng
I have high blood pressure.	我有高血壓。 ngor yau go hu-eet aat
I had a heart attack … years ago.	我 … 年前曾有過一次心臟病發作。 ngor … nin chin see gwo yut chee sum jong beng faat

Doctor's inquiries 醫生叩問

你這麼不舒服有多長時間了？	How long have you been feeling like this?
這是你第一次有這種病症嗎？	Is this the first time you've had this?
你在服其他藥嗎？	Are you taking any other medication?
你對什麼過敏嗎？	Are you allergic to anything?
你打過破傷風預防針嗎？	Have you been vaccinated against tetanus?
你胃口怎麼樣？	Is your appetite okay?

Examination 檢查

我替你測一下體溫／血壓。	I'll take your temperature/blood pressure.
請捲起衣袖。	Roll up your sleeve, please.
請脫掉上身的衣服。	Please undress to the waist.
請躺下。	Please lie down.
張開口。	Open your mouth.
深呼吸。	Breathe deeply.
咳嗽一下。	Cough, please.
哪裡痛？	Where does it hurt?
這裡痛嗎？	Does it hurt here?

Diagnosis 診斷

你需要去照 X-光。	I want you to have an X-ray.
你需要抽血／留大便／尿樣化驗。	I want a specimen of your blood/stools/urine.
你需要看專科醫生。	I want you to see a specialist.
你需要住院。	I want you to go to a hospital.
這裡斷了／扭傷了。	It's broken/sprained.
這裡脫了臼／撕裂了。	It's dislocated/torn.

你有 …	You have (a/an) …
盲腸炎	appendicitis
膀胱炎	cystitis
流行性感冒	flu
食物中毒	food poisoning
骨折	fracture
胃炎	gastritis
痔瘡	hemorrhoids
小腸氣	hernia
… 發炎	inflammation of …
麻疹	measles
肺炎	pneumonia
坐骨神經痛	sciatica
扁桃腺炎	tonsilitis
腫瘤	tumor
性病	venereal disease
這裡發炎。	It's infected.
這病傳染。	It's contagious.

Treatment 治療

我給你 …	I'll give you …
消毒劑	an antiseptic
止痛藥	a painkiller
我給你開 …	I'm going to prescribe …
抗生素	a course of antibiotics
一些栓劑	some suppositories
你對有些藥過敏嗎？	Are you allergic to any medication?
… 服一粒	Take one pill …
每隔 … 小時	every … hours
每日服 … 次	… times a day
飯前 / 飯後服	before/after each meal
痛時服	in case of pain
連續服 … 日	for … days
回家後去看醫生。	Consult a doctor when you get home.

Parts of the body 身體各部名稱

appendix	盲腸	*maang churng*
arm	手臂	*sau bay*
back	背脊	*boo-ee jeck*
bladder	膀胱	*pong gwong*
bone	骨	*gwut*
breast	乳房	*yu-ee fong*
chest	胸部	*h-owng bo*
ear	耳	*yee*
eye	眼	*ngaan*
face	面	*min*
finger	手指	*sau jee*
foot	腳	*gerk*
gland	分泌腺	*fun bay sin*
hand	手	*sau*
head	頭	*tau*
heart	心臟	*sum jong*
jaw	下巴	*ha pa*
joint	關節	*gwaan jit*
kidney	腎	*sun*
knee	膝蓋	*sut tau*
leg	腿	*tur-ee*
lip	口唇	*hau sun'*
liver	肝	*gon*
mouth	口	*hau*
muscle	肌肉	*gay yuk*
neck	頸	*geng*
nose	鼻	*bay*
rib	肋骨	*luck gwut*
shoulder	肩膀	*bock tau*
skin	皮膚	*pay foo*
stomach	胃	*wai*
thigh	大腿	*daai bay*
throat	喉嚨	*hau l-owng*
thumb	拇指	*mo jee*
toe	腳趾	*gerk jee*
tongue	舌頭	*lay*
tonsils	扁桃腺	*bin to sin*
vein	靜脈	*jing muck*

Gynecologist 婦科

I have ... 　　　　　　　　我 ... *ngor* ...

abdominal pains 　　　　　腹部痛 *to t-owng*

period pains 　　　　　　　經期痛 *ging kay t-owng*

a vaginal infection 　　　　陰道發炎 *yum do faat yim*

I haven't had my period 　　我的月經沒來 ... 個月了。 *ngor ge*
for ... months. 　　　　　　*yu-eet ging mo lay ... gor yu-eet la*

I'm on the Pill. 　　　　　　我在服避孕丸
　　　　　　　　　　　　　　ngor sick gun bay yun yu-een

Hospital 醫院

Please notify my family. 　　請通知我的家人。
　　　　　　　　　　　　　　mm goy t-owng jee ngor ge ga yun

I'm in pain. 　　　　　　　　我很痛。 *ngor ho t-owng*

I can't eat/sleep. 　　　　　我吃不下 / 睡不著。
　　　　　　　　　　　　　　ngor sick mm lock ye/fun mm jerk

When will the doctor come? 　醫生什麼時候來？
　　　　　　　　　　　　　　yee sung gay see lay

Which ward is ... in? 　　　... 在哪個病房？
　　　　　　　　　　　　　　... hai bin gor beng fong

I'm visiting ... 　　　　　　我探望 ... *ngor taam* ...

Optician 眼鏡店

I'm near- [short-] sighted/ 　我有近視 / 遠視。
far- [long-] sighted. 　　　　*ngor yau gun see/yu-een see*

I've lost ... 　　　　　　　　我丟失了 ...
　　　　　　　　　　　　　　ngor mm g-in jor ...

one of my contact lenses 　　一塊隱形眼鏡片
　　　　　　　　　　　　　　yut faai yun ying ngaan geng pin

my glasses/a lens 　　　　　眼鏡 / 一塊鏡片
　　　　　　　　　　　　　　ngaan geng/yut faai geng pin

Could you give me a 　　　　可以替我補配嗎？
replacement? 　　　　　　　*hor mm hor yee bong ngor bo poo-ee a*

Dentist 牙醫

I have a toothache.	我牙痛。 *ngor nga t-owng*
This tooth hurts.	這顆牙很痛。 *nay je nga ho t-owng*
I've lost a filling/tooth.	我掉了一顆補牙的填料 / 一顆牙。 *ngor lut jor yut je bo nga ge tin leeu/yut je nga*
Can you repair this denture?	你可以修理這副假牙嗎？ *nay hor mm hor yee sau jing nay foo ga nga*
I don't want it extracted.	我不想拔掉這顆牙。 *ngor mm surng mock nay je nga*

我要給你打針 / 局部麻醉藥。	I'm going to give you an injection/ an anesthetic.
你需要補牙 / 鑲牙冠。	You need a filling/cap (crown).
這顆牙要拔掉。	I'll have to take it out.
我只能臨時修補一下。	I can only fix it temporarily.
… 小時內不能吃東西。	Don't eat anything for … hours.

Payment and insurance 付款及保險

How much do I owe you?	我要付多少錢？ *ngor yeeu bay gay dor chin a*
I have insurance.	我有保險。 *ngor yau bo him*
Can I have a receipt for my insurance?	請開張收條給我報保險。 *mm goy hoy jurng sau teeu bay ngor bo bo him*
Would you fill out this insurance form, please?	請填寫這張保險表格。 *mm goy tin ho nay jurng bo him beeu ga*

Dictionary (A-Z)
English–Cantonese

Most terms in this dictionary are either followed by an example or cross-referenced to pages where the word appears in a phrase. Where there is a difference in usage between Hong Kong and Guangdong Province (mainland China), the latter term is given in brackets.

The notes below provide some basic grammar guidelines.

Nouns and adjectives

There are no articles (a, an, the), singular or plural, in Cantonese. Whether the noun is singular or plural is judged from the context, or by a number modifying the noun.

Adjectives precede the noun and, if they comprise a single character, are generally preceded by the adverb **ho** (*spoken*) and **hun** (*written*) (literal meaning: *very*).

Verbs

Cantonese verbs are even more invariable than English ones, with no differences between singular and plural forms.

ngor hock	I learn
nay hock	you learn (singular)
kur-ee* hock	he/she learns
ngor day hock	we learn
nay day hock	you learn (plural)
kur-ee day hock	they learn

* Although written differently, the characters are both pronounced the same (**kur-ee**).

Past tense

The suffix **jor** is placed after the verb to show that the action has been completed.

Ngor moo-ee yaat <u>sick</u> jo chaan.	I eat breakfast everyday.
Ngor gum yaat <u>sick jor</u> jo chaan.	I ate breakfast today.

The suffix **gwor** after a verb is used to show that an action happened in the past, but without a specific reference to a particular point in time.

Ngor <u>hur-ee gwor</u> j-owng gwock.	I have been to China.

Future tense

The future tense has exactly the same form as the present. To indicate the future nature of an action, an adverb or adverbial phrase is needed.

Ngor hock j-owng mun.	I learn Chinese.
<u>**Ming nin**</u> **ngor woo-ee hock j-owng mun.**	Next year I'm going to learn Chinese.

A

a few 有幾個 yau gay gor 15

a little 少許 seeu seeu 15

a lot 很多 ho dor 15

a.m. 上午 surng ng

abbey 大修道院 daai sau do yu-een 99

about (approximately) ... 左右 ... jor yau 15

abroad 海外 hoy ngoy

accept, to 收 sau 136

access only 禁止通行 gum jee t-owng hung 96

accident (road) 意外 yee ngoy 92, 152

accidentally 不小心 mm seeu sum 28

accompaniments (food) 配菜 poo-ee choy 38

accompany, to 陪 poo-ee 65

acne 暗瘡 um chong

acrylic 丙稀酸類纖維 bing hay su-een chim wai

actor/actress 演員 yin yu-een

adapter 多路插座 dor lo chaap jo 148

address 地址 day jee 84, 126

adjoining room 相連的房間 chee maai ge fong 22

admission charge 入場費 yup churng fai 115

adult (n) 成人 daai yun 81, 100

after 後 hau 165; (time) ...之後 ... jee hau 13

after-shave 鬚後水 so hau sur-ee 142

after-sun lotion 晒後水 saai hau sur-ee 142

afternoon, in the 下午 ha jau 222

aged: to be ~ 歲 ... sur-ee 152

ago 前 chin 222

agree: I don't agree 我不同意 ngor mm t-owng yee

air: ~ conditioning 空調 laang hay 25;
~ mattress (充氣) 床褥 (bum hay) chong yuk 31; **~ pump** 氣泵 hay bum 87; **~ sickness bag** 嘔吐袋 au to doy 70; **~mail** 空郵 h-owng yau 155

airport 機場 gay churng 96

aisle seat 靠通道座位 lo hau wai 69, 74

alarm clock 鬧鐘 naau j-owng 149

alcoholic (drink) 含酒精 yau jau jing

all 全部 chu-een bo

allergic, to be 過敏 gwor mun 164, 165

allergy 過敏症 gwor mun jing

allowance 限額 haang ngaak 67

almost 幾乎 gay foo

alone 單獨 daan duk

already 已經 yee ging 28

also 也 yick do

alter, to 改 goy 137

alternative route 替代路線 tai doy lo sin 96

alumin(i)um foil 錫紙 sek jee 148

always 總是 seng yut 13

a.m. 上午 surng ng; surng jau

am: I am 我是 ngor hai

amazing 驚人 ging yun 101

ambassador 大使 daai see

ambulance 救傷車 gau surng che 92

American (adj) 美國 may gwock 150, 152; (person) 美國人 may gwock yun

amount 數目 so muk 42

amusement arcade 遊戲機廳 yau hay gay teng 113

anaesthetic 麻醉藥 ma jur-ee yerk

and 和 t-owng maai

animal 動物 d-owng mut 106

anorak 風衣 f-owng lau 145

another 其他 kay ta 21

antacid 抗酸藥 kong su-een yerk

antibiotics 抗生素 kong sung so 165

antifreeze 防凍劑 fong d-owng jai

antique 古玩 goo woon 157; **~ store** 古玩店 goo woon dim 130

antiseptic 消毒劑 seeu duk jai 165;
~ cream 消毒膏 seeu duk go 141

any 任何 yum hor

anyone: ~ else 其他人 kay taai yun 93; **does anyone speak English?** 有人會說英語嗎？ yau mo yun sick gong ying mun a

anything else? 還要甚麼？ j-owng yeeu dee mut ye

apartment 公寓 g-owng yu-ee 28, 123

apologize: I apologize 道歉 do hip

appendicitis 盲腸炎 maang churng yim 165

appendix 盲腸 maang churng 166

appetite 胃口 wai hau 164

appointment (to make an ...) 約時間 yerk see gaan 147, 161

approximately 大約 daai yerk 152

April 四月 say yu-eet 219

architect 建築師 g-in juk see 104

are there ...? 有沒有 ...？ yau mo ... 17

arm 手臂 sau bay 166

around (time) **...** 左右 ... jor yau 13

arrive, to 到 do 68, 70, 71, 76

art gallery 藝術館 ngaai sut' goon 99

arthritis, to have 關節炎 gwaan jit yim 163

artificial sweetener 人造糖 yun jo tong 38

artist 藝術家 ngaai sut' ga 104

ashtray 煙灰缸 yin foo-ee gong 39

ask: I asked for ... 我要的是 ... ngor yeeu ge hai ... 41

aspirin (可服) 亞士匹靈 (ho y-owng) a see put ling 141

asthma, to have 哮喘 hau chu-een 163

at (place/time) 在 hai 12, 13

at last! 終於 ... 了 j-owng yu-ee ... la 19

at least 至少 jee seeu 23

athletics 田徑 tin ging 114

ATM/cash machine 自動提款機 jee d-owng tai foon gay 139

attack 襲擊 jaap gick 152

attractive 有吸引力 yau kup yun lick

August 八月 baat yu-eet 219

aunt 叔母 a sum 120

Australia 澳洲 o jau 119

Australian (person) 澳洲人 o jau yun

authentic: is it authentic? 是不是真貨？ hai mm hai jun for

authenticity 真品 jun bun 157

automatic (car) 有自動波 (自動變速) yau jee d-owng bor (jee d-owng bin chuk) 86

automatic camera 全自動相機 chu-een jee d-owng surng gay 151

automobile 汽車 hay che

autumn 秋 (天) chau (tin) 219

avalanche 雪崩 su-eet bung

away (from) 和 ... 相距 t-owng ... surng gaak 12

awful 難看 / 壞 wut dut/cha 101, 122

B **baby** 嬰兒 B B jai 39, 113, 162; **~ food** 嬰兒食品 ying yee sick bun 142; **~ wipes** 嬰兒濕紙巾 ying yee sup jee gun 142; **~-sitter** 臨時保姆 lum see bo mo 113

back (of head) 後邊 hau bin 147; (of body) 背脊 boo-ee jick 166; **~ache** 腰痛 yeeu gwut t-owng 163

back by, to be (return) **...** 前回來 ... chin faan lay 113

backpacking 背包旅行 me boo-ee nong lur-ee hung

bad 不好 mm ho 14

bag 包 bau 159

baggage 行李 hung lay 32, 69, 71; **~ check** 行李寄存處 hung lay gay chu-een chu-ee 71, 73; **~ reclaim** 領回行李處 ling woo-ee hung lay chu-ee 71

bakery 麵飽店 min bau po 130

balcony 露台 lo toy 29

ball 球 bor 157

ballet 芭蕾舞 ba lur-ee mo 108, 111

band (musical group) 樂隊 ngock dur-ee 111, 157

bandage 繃帶 bung daai 141

bank 銀行 ngun hong 130, 138

bar (hotel, etc.) 酒吧 jau ba 26, 112

barber 理髮師 lay faat see

basement 地牢 day lo

basket 籃 laam 158

basketball 籃球 laam kau 114

bath 浴缸 ch-owng lurng gong 21; ~ **towel** 浴巾 ch-owning lurng gun 27

bathroom (toilet) 洗手間 (廁所) sai sau gaan (chee sor) 26; (with bath) 浴室 ch-owng lurng fong 29

battery 電池 din chee (car)/din sum (cell) 88, 137, 149, 151

battle site 古戰場 goo jin churng 99

be, to 是 hai 17

beach 海灘 hoy taan 117

beard 鬍鬚 woo so

beautiful 漂亮/美麗 leng 14, 101

because (of) 因爲 yun wai 14

bed 床 chong 21; ~ **and breakfast** 房間連早餐 fong lin maai jo chaan 24

bedding 床鋪 chong po 29

bedroom 睡房 sur-ee fong 29

beer 啤酒 be jau 40, 160

before 前 chin 165; (time) ... 之前 ... jee chin 13, 222

begin, to 開始 hoy chee

beige 米色 mai sick 143

belong: this belongs to me 這是我的 nay gor hai ngor ge

belt 皮帶 pay daai 144

berth 鋪/床位 po/chong wai 74, 77

best 最好 jur-ee ho

better 好些 ho dee 14, 134

between (time) ... 之間 ... jee gaan 222; ~ **jobs** (unemployed) 暫時沒有工作 jaam see mo jo ye 121

beyond repair (car) 徹底損壞 seng ga waai saai 89

bib 口水兜 hau sur-ee dau

bicycle 單車 (自行車) daan che (jee hung che) 75, 83, 153; ~ **hire** 租單車 (自行車) jo daan che (jee hung che) 83

bidet 坐浴盆 jor yuk poon

big 大 daai 14, 134; **bigger** 大些 daai dee 24

bikini 三點式泳衣 saam dim sick wing yee 144

bill (check) 帳單 daan 32, 42

bin liner 垃圾箱膠袋 laap saap t-owng gaau doy

binoculars 雙筒望遠鏡 surng t-owng mong yu-een geng

bird 鳥 jerk 106

birthday 生日 saang yut 220

biscuits 餅乾 beng gon 160

bite (insect) 蟲咬傷 bay ch-owng ngaau surng

bitten: I've been bitten by a dog 我被狗咬了 ngoy bay gau ngaau chun

bitter 苦 foo 41

bizarre 古怪 goo gwaai 101

black 黑色 huck sick 143; ~ **and white film** (camera) 黑白菲林 huck baak fay lum 151; ~ **coffee** 齋咖啡 jaai fe 40

bladder 膀胱 pong gwong 166

blanket 毛氈 mo jin 27

bleach 漂白水 peeu baak sur-ee 148

bleeding 流血 lau hu-eet 162

blinds 百葉窗 baak yip churng 25

blister 水泡 sur-ee pock 162

blocked, to be 塞了 suck jor 25

blood 血 hu-eet 164; ~ **group** 血型 hu-eet ying; ~ **pressure** (high) (高)血壓 (go) hu-eet aat 163, 164

blouse 女裝恤衫 nur-ee jong sut' saam 144

blue 藍色 laam sick 143

board, on 車上 che do 78

boat 船 su-een 81; ~ **trip** 乘船遊覽 yau su-een ho 81, 97

boil 瘡 chong 162

boiled 滾 gwun

boiler 熱水爐 yit sur-ee lo 29

bone 骨 gwut 166

book 書 su-ee 150; **~store** 書店 su-ee dim 130

book, to 訂 deng

booked up, to be 約滿了 yerk moon saai 116

booklet of tickets 一本車票 yut boon che fay 79

boots 靴 her 145; *(sports)* 球鞋 kau haai 116

boring 乏味 ho moon 101

born: I was born in 我在 ... 出生 ngor hai ... chut' sai

borrow: may I borrow your ...? 你的 ... 可以借給我嗎？ hor mm hor yee je nay ge ... bay ngor

botanical garden 植物公園 jick mut g-owng yu-een 99

bottle 瓶 jun' 37, 159; **~ of wine** 一瓶葡萄酒 yut jun' po to jau 156; **~-opener** 開瓶器 hoy jun' do 148

bottled *(beer)* 啤酒 be jau 40

bowel 大腸 daai churng

bowls 碗 woon 148

box of chocolates 一盒朱古力 yut hup ju-ee goo lick 156

boy 男孩 naam jai/jai (son) 120, 157

boyfriend 男朋友 naam pung yau 120

bra 胸圍 h-owng wai 144

bracelet 手鐲 sau ngaak 149

bread 麵飽 min bau 38

bread: loaf of ~ 一條麵飽 yut teeu min bau 154

break, to 弄壞 jing waai 28

break down: the cooker has broken down 煮食爐壞了 ju-ee sick lo waai jor 28

breakdown 中途壞車 boon lo waai che 88; **~ truck** 拖車 tor che 88; **have a ~** *(of car)* 車中途壞了 ga che boon lo waai jor 88

breakfast 早餐 jo chaan 26, 27

breast 乳房 yu-ee fong 166

breathe, to 呼吸 tau hay/foo kup 92, 164

bridge 橋 keeu 107

briefs 內褲 noy foo 144

bring someone, to 帶 daai 125

Britain 英國 ying gwock 119

British *(adj.)* 英國 ying gwock 152; *(person)* 英國人 ying gwock yun

brochure 介紹冊 gaai seeu su-ee

broken, to be 壞了 waai jor 25, 137; *(bone)* 斷了 tu-een jor 164

bronchitis 支氣管炎 jee hay goon yim

brooch 心口針 sum hau jum 149

brother 兄弟 hing dai 154

brown 啡色 fe sick 143

browse, to 看看 tai tai 133

bruise 碰傷 j-owng surng 162

bucket 桶 t-owng 157

building 建築物 / 樓宇 g-in juk mut/lau yu-ee

built, to be 建 hay 104

bulletin board 佈告板 bo go baan 26

bureau de change 外幣兌換店 (外匯兌換處) ngoy bai jau woon dim 70, 138

burger 漢堡飽 hon bo bau 40; **~ stand** 漢堡飽檔 hon bo bau dong 35

burn 燒傷 seeu surng 162

bus 巴士 (公共汽車) ba see (g-owng g-owng hay che) 70, 78; **~ route** 巴士路線 (公共汽車路線) ba see lo sin (g-owng g-owng hay che lo sin) 96; **~ station** 長途汽車站 churng to hay che jaam 78; **~ stop** 巴士站 (公共汽車站) ba see jaam (g-owng g-owng hay che jaam) 65, 96

business 商業 surng yip 121; **~ class** 商務客位 surng mo haak wai 68; **~ trip** 公務旅行 gong mo lur-ee hung 123; **on ~** 因公事 yun wai g-owng see 66

A-Z

busy *(full up)* 滿座 moon jor 36; *(occupied)* 沒空 mm duck haan 125
butane gas 罐裝煤氣 goon jong moo-ee hay 30, 31
butcher 肉店 yuk po 130
butter 牛油 ngau yau 38, 160
button 鈕扣 nau
buy, to 買 mai 67
by *(near)* 靠 gun 36; *(time)* ... 之前 ... jee chin 13, 222; ~ **bus** 坐巴士 (公共汽車) chor ba see (g-owng g-owng hay che); ~ **car** *(as passenger)* 坐汽車 chor che 17, 123; *(as driver)* 開車 ja che 94; ~ **ferry** 坐船 chor su-een 123; ~ **plane** 坐飛機 chor fay gay 123; ~ **train** 坐火車 chor for che 123; ~ **credit card** 用信用卡 y-owng sun' y-owng kaat 17
bye! 再見！joy g-in

C
cabin 艙 chong 81
cable TV 有線電視 yau sin din see 22
café 咖啡室 ga fe sut 35, 40
cagoule 風衣 f-owng lau 145
cake 西餅 sai beng 40
calendar 日曆 yut lick 156
call, to 叫 geeu 92; *(by telephone)* 打電話給 ... da din wa bay ... 127, 128; ~ **collect** 請對方付費 cheng dur-ee fong bay chin 127; ~ **for someone** 接 ... jip ... 125; ~ **the police!** 叫警察！geeu ging chaat 92
called: to be called 叫 ... geeu ... 94
camera 相機 surng gay 151, 153; ~ **case** 相機袋 surng gay doy 151; ~ **store** 攝影器材公司 sip ying hay choy g-owng see 130
camp, to 露營 lo ying
campbed 摺床 jip chong 31
camping 露營 lo ying 30

campsite 營地 ying day 30, 123
can 罐 goon 159; ~**-opener** 罐頭刀 goon tau do 148
Canada 加拿大 ga na daai 119
Canadian *(person)* 加拿大人 ga na daai yun
cancel, to *(reservation)* 取消 chur-ee seeu 68
cancer *(disease)* 癌症 ngaam jing
candles 蠟燭 laap juk 148
candy 糖果 tong gwor 150
Cantonese *(language)* 廣東話 gwong d-owng wa 110, 126
cap *(hat)* 鴨舌帽 aap jur-ee mo 144; *(dental)* 牙冠 nga goon 168
car *(automobile)* 汽車 hay che 86, 88, 153; ~ **ferry** 汽車渡輪 hay che do lun' 81; ~ **park** 停車場 ting che churng 26, 87, 96; ~ **rental [hire]** 租車 jo che 70; **by** ~ 坐車/開車 chor che/ja che 95
car *(train compartment)* 車廂 che surng 75
carafe 散裝酒瓶 saan jong jau jun' 37
caravan *(trailer)* 旅行拖車 lur-ee hung tor che 30
cards 紙牌 jee paai 121
careful: be careful! 小心！seeu sum
carpet *(rug)* 地毯 day jin
carrier bag 購物袋 kau mut doy
carry-cot 手提嬰兒床 sau tai ying yee chong
cart 推車 tur-ee che 158
carton 盒 hup 159
cases 箱 gip 69
cash 現金 yin gum 17, 136; ~ **machine** 自動提款機 jee d-owng tai foon gay 139
cash, to 兌現 dur-ee yin 138
cashier [cash desk] 付款處 foo foon chu-ee 132
casino 賭場 do churng 112
cassette 卡式錄音帶 ka sick luk yum daai 157

castle 堡壘 bo lur-ee 99

catch, to (bus) 趕（巴士） gong (ba see)

cathedral 大教堂 daai gaau tong 99

Catholic 天主教 tin ju-ee gaau 105

cave 岩洞 ngaam d-owng 107

CD C D 細碟 CD sai dip 157; **~-player** C D 細碟機 CD sai dip gay

cemetery 墳場 fun churng 99

center of town 市中心 see j-owng sum 21

central heating 中央暖氣 j-owng yurng nu-een hay

ceramics 陶瓷 to chee

certificate 證明書 jing ming su-ee 149, 157

chain 鍊 lin 149

change (coins) 硬幣 saan ngun 87; (legal tender of low value) 零錢 saan jee 136; **keep the change** 不用找了 mm sai jaau la 84

change, to 換 woon 39; (bus/train) 轉車 ju-een che 75, 76, 79, 80; (money) 換 woon 138; (reservation) 更改 gung goy 68

changing facilities 換尿片的地方 woon neeu pin ge day fong 113

chapel 小教堂 sai gaau tong 99

charcoal 炭 taan 31

charge(s) 收費 sau fai 30, 87, 116, 155

charter flight 包機航班 bau gay hong baan

cheap 便宜 peng 14, 134; **cheaper** 便宜些 peng dee 21, 24, 109, 134

check [cheque] book 支票簿 jee peeu bo

check in, to (airport) 辦登機手續 baan dung gay sau juk 68; **check-in desk** 登記櫃檯 dung gay gwai toy 69; **checking in** (airport) 辦登機手續 baan dung gay sau juk 69

check out, to (hotel) 退房 tur-ee fong 32; **checkout** (supermarket) 付款台 foo foon toy 158

cheers! 乾杯！ yum boo-ee

cheese 芝士 jee see 160

cheque book 支票簿 jee peeu bo

chess (set) 象棋 jurng kay 121, 157

chest (body) 胸部 h-owng bo 166

chewing gum 香口膠 hurng hau gaau 150

child 孩子 jai (m)/nur-ee (f) 152; **~ seat** (in car) 兒童安全椅 yee t-owng on chu-een yee 86

childminder 臨時保姆 lum see bo mo

children 兒童／孩子們／子女 sai lo gor (colloq.)／yee t-owng (formal)／jai nur-ee (as offspring) 22, 24, 39, 66, 74, 81, 100, 113, 120; **children's meals** 兒童餐 yee t-owng chaan 39

China 中國 j-owng gwock 119

Chinese (cuisine) 中式 j-owng sick jau lau 35; (person) 中國人 j-owng kwock yun

choc-ice 朱古力雪糕條 ju-ee goo lick su-eet go teeu 110

chocolate (flavor) 朱古力 ju-ee goo lick 40; **~ bar** 一排朱古力 yut paai ju-ee goo lick 150; **~ ice cream** 朱古力雪糕條 ju-ee goo lick su-eet go teeu 110

chopsticks 筷子 faai jee 41, 148

Christmas 聖誕（節） sing daan (jit) 220

church 教堂 gaau tong 96, 99, 105

cigarette kiosk 煙草店／香煙檔 yin po/yin jai dong 150

cigarettes, packet of 香煙 yin jai 150

cigars 雪茄 su-eet ga 150

cinema 電影院 din ying yu-een 96, 110

claim check 領回行李標籤 ling woo-ee hung lay beeu chim 71

clean 乾淨 gon jeng 14, 39, 41

clean, to 洗 sai 137

cliff 山岩 saan ngaam 107

cling film 保鮮紙 bo sin jee 148

cotton 棉布 min bo 145; [cotton wool] 棉花 min fa 141

cough 咳嗽 kut sau 141

cough, to 咳嗽 kut sau 164

country (nation) 國家 gwock ga

country music 鄉村音樂 hurng chu-een yum ngock 111

courier (guide) 導遊 do yau

course (meal) 道（菜）do (choy); (of drugs) 療程 leeu ching 165

cousin 堂／表兄弟；堂／表姐妹 tong/beeu hing dai (m); tong/beeu je moo-ee (f)

cover charge 服務費 fuk mo fai 112

craft shop 工藝品店 g-owng ngai bun dim

cramps 抽筋 chau gun 163

creche 托兒所 tock yee sor

credit card 信用卡 sun' y-owng kaat 42, 136, 139, 153; ~ number 信用卡號碼 sun' y-owng kaat ho ma 109

crib (child's) 小床 chong jai 22

crisps 薯片 su-ee pin 160

crockery 碗碟 woon dip 29

cross (crucifix) 十字架 sup jee ga

cross, to (road) 過 gwor 95

crossroad 十字路口 sup jee lo hau 95

crowded 擠逼 jai bick 31

crown (dental) 牙冠 nga goon 168

cruise (n.) 航遊 hong yau

crutches 拐杖 gwaai jurng

crystal 水晶 su-ee jing 149

cuisine (food) 菜式 choy sick 119

cup 杯 boo-ee 39, 148

cupboard 櫥櫃 gwai

currency 貨幣 for bai 67, 138; ~ exchange office 外幣找換店 (外匯兌換處) ngoy bai jau woon dim (ngoy woo-ee dur-ee woon chu-ee) 70, 73, 138

curtains 窗簾 churng lim

customer service 顧客服務 goo haak fuk mo 133

customs 海關 hoy gwaan 67, 157; ~ declaration 海關申報單 bo gwaan daan 155

cut 割破 got su-een 162; ~ and blow-dry 剪和吹 jin t-owng chur-ee 147; ~ glass 雕花玻璃 deeu fa bor lay 149

cutlery 刀叉 do cha 29

cycle route 單車 (自行車) 路線 daan che (jee hung che) lo sin 106

cycling 單車 (自行車) daan che (jee hung che) 114

cystitis 膀胱炎 pong gwong yim 165

每天 moo-ee yut

damaged, to be 損壞了 jing waai jor 28, 71

damp (n./adj.) 潮濕 cheeu sup

dance (performance) 舞蹈 mo do 111

dancing, to go 去跳舞 hur-ee teeu mo 124

dangerous 危險 ngai him

dark (lacking light) 暗 um 24; (color) 深 sum 14, 134, 143; 深些 sum dee 143

daughter 女兒 nur-ee 120, 162

dawn 黎明 ting gwong 222

day 天 yut 97; ~ ticket 當天票 jick yut fay; ~ trip 一日遊 yut yut yau

dead (battery) 沒有電 mo saai din 88

deaf, to be 耳聾 yee l-owng 163

December 十二月 sup yee yu-eet 219

deck chair 沙灘椅 sa taan yee 117

declare, to 申報 sun bo 67

deduct, to (money) 扣除 kau

deep 深 sum; ~ freeze 速凍 gup d-owng

defrost, to 解凍 gaai d-owng

degrees (temperature) 度 do

delay 延遲 yin chee 70

delicatessen (*shop*) 熟食店 suk sick dim 130; (*counter*) 熟食櫃檯 suk sick gwai toy 158

delicious 好吃 ho sick 14

deliver, to 送貨 s-owng for

denim 牛仔布 ngau jai bo 145

dental floss 牙線 nga sin

dentist 牙醫 nga yee 131, 161, 168

dentures 假牙 ga nga 168

deodorant 除臭劑 chur-ee chau jai 142

depart, to (*train, bus*) 開出 hoy chut'

department (*in store*) 部 bo 132; **~ store** 百貨公司 baak for g-owng see 130

departure lounge 候機室 hau gay sut 69

deposit (*security*) 按金 on gum 24, 83, 116

describe, to 形容 ying y-owng 152

destination 目的地 muk dick day

details 詳情 churng sai ching ying

detergent 洗衣粉 sai yee fun 148

develop, to (*photos*) 沖晒 ch-owng saai 151

diabetes 糖尿病 tong leeu beng

diabetic, to be 有糖尿病 yau tong neeu beng 39, 163

diagnosis 診斷 chun du-een 164

dialling (*area*) **code** 地區碼 day kur-ee ma 127

diamond 鑽石 ju-een seck 149

diapers 尿片 neeu pin 142

diarrhea 肚瀉 to se 141, 163; **I have ~** 我肚瀉 ngor to se

dice 骰子 sick jai

dictionary 字典 jee din 150

diesel 柴油 chaai yau 87

diet: I'm on a diet 我在節食 ngor jit sick

difficult 難 naan 14

dining: ~ car 餐車 chaan che 75, 77; **~ room** 餐廳 chaan teng 26, 29

dinner: to have ~ 吃晚飯 sick maan faan 124; **~ jacket** 晚禮服 maan lai fuk

direct 直通 jick t-owng 75

direction, in the... or ... 的方向 hai ... ge fong hurng 95

directions 指路 jee lo 94

director (*of company*) 董事 d-owng see

directory (*telephone*) 電話簿 din wa bo; **Directory Enquiries** 電話號碼查詢 din wa ho ma cha sun' 127

dirty 骯髒 woo jo 14, 28

disabled (*n.*) 傷殘人士 surng chaan yun see 22, 100

discotheque 的士高 dick see go 112

discount (*reduction*) 折扣 jit kau 24, 100

dish (*meal*) 菜 choy/s-owng (*colloq.*) 37; **~ cloth** 碗布 woon bo 148

dishwashing liquid 洗潔精 sai git jing 148

dislocated, to be 脫了臼 tu-eet jor gaau 164

display cabinet/case 玻璃櫃 bor lay gwai 134, 149

disposable camera 用後即棄的相機 y-owng yu-een jau dum ge surng gay 151

distilled water 蒸餾水 jing lau sur-ee

disturb: don't disturb 打擾 da yeeu

dive, to 跳水 teeu sur-ee 117

diversion (*detour*) 改道 goy do 96

diving equipment 潛水器材 chim sur-ee hay choy 117

divorced, to be 離了婚 fun jor gur-ee 120

dizzy: I feel dizzy 我頭暈 ngor tau wun

do: things to ~ 值得做的事 jick duck jo ge ye 123; **what do you do?** (*job*) 你是做什麼工作的? nay jo mut ye g-owng jock ga 121; **do you accept ...?** 你們收 ... 嗎? nay day sau mm sau ... a 136; **do you have ...?** (你們) 有沒有 ...? (nay day) yau mo 37

A-Z

A–Z

English 英語 ying mun 11, 67, 110, 150, 152, 161; (person) 英格蘭人 ying ga laan yun; **~-speaking** 說英語的 gong ying mun ge 98, 152

enjoy, to 喜歡 j-owng yee 110

enlarge, to (photos) 放大 fong daai 151

enough 夠 gau 42, 136; **that's ~** 夠了 gau la 15, 19

ensuite bathroom 私人浴室 see yun yuk sut

entertainment guide 娛樂指南 yu-ee lock jee naam

entrance fee 入場費 yup churng fai 100

entry visa 入境簽證 yup ging chim jing

envelope 信封 sun' f-owng 150

epileptic, to be 有癲癇症 yau din gaan jing 163

equipment (sports) 體育器材 tai yuk hay choy 116

error 錯誤 chor ng

escalator 電動樓梯 din d-owng lau tai 132

essential 必要 bit yeeu 89

E.U. (European Union) 歐洲聯盟 au jau lu-een mung

evening: in the ~ 晚上 ye maan 222; **~ dress** 晚裝 maan jong 112

events 節目 jit muk 108

every: ~ day 每天 moo-ee yut; **~ hour** 每小時 moo-ee gor j-owng tau 76; **~ week** 每星期 moo-ee gor lai baai 13

examination (medical) 檢查 gim cha

example, for 例如 lai yu-ee

except 除了 ... 之外 chur-ee jor ... jee ngoy

excess baggage 超重行李 cheeu ch-owng hung lay 69

exchange, to (goods) 換 woon 137; (currency) 兌換 dur-ee woon 138; **~ rate** 匯率 woo-ee lut' 138

excluding meals 不包括膳食 mm bau sick 24

excursion 短途旅遊 du-een to lur-ee yau 97

excuse me (attention) 請問 cheng mun mm goy 10; **excuse me?** (pardon?) 請再說一遍 cheng joy gong yut chee 11

exit 出口 chut' hau 70, 132

expected, to be (需)要 (sur-ee) yeeu 111

expensive 貴 gwai 14, 134

expiration [expiry] date 到期日 do kay yut 109

exposure (photos) 張 jurng 151

express 速遞 (快遞) chuk daai (faai daai) 155

extension 內線 noy sin 128

extra (additional) 多 dor 23, 27

extracted, to be (tooth) 拔掉 mock 168

eye 眼 ngaan 166

F

fabric 布料 bo leeu 145

face 面 min 166

facial 美容 may y-owng 147

facilities (installations) 設施 chit see 22; (equipment) 設備 chit bay 30

factor ... (sun cream) 防護係數 ... fong woo hai so ... 142

faint, to feel 虛弱頭暈 hur-ee yerk tau wun 163

fall (season) 秋 (天) chau (tin) 219

family (members) 家人 ga yun 66, 167; (unit) 家庭 ga ting 74, 120

famous 著名 chut' ming

fan (cooling) 風扇 f-owng sin 25

far 遠 yu-een 95; **~-sighted** 遠視 yu-een see 167; **how far is it?** 有多遠？ ... yau gay yu-een 73

fare (cost) 車票 che fay 79

farm 農場 n-owng churng 107

fast 快 faai 93; **~ food** 快餐 faai chaan 40; **~ food restaurant** 快餐店 faai chaan dim 35

fast, to be *(clock)* 快 faai 222

fat 脂肪 jee fong 39

father 父親 foo chun 120

faucet 水喉 sur-ee hau 25

faulty: this is faulty 這個壞了 nay gor ye wai jor

favorite 最喜歡的 jur-ee j-owng yee ge

fax machine 傳真機 chu-een jun' gay 155

February 二月 yee yu-eet 219

feed, to 餵 wai 39

feeding bottle 奶瓶 naai jun'

feel ill, to 不舒服 mm su-ee fuk 163

female 女 nur-ee 152

ferry 渡輪 do lun' 81

feverish, to feel 發燒 faat seeu 163

few 很少 ho seeu 15

fiancé(e) 未婚夫（妻）may fun foo (chai)

field 田 tin 107

fifth 第五 daai ng 217

fight *(brawl)* 打架 da gaau

fill out, to *(a form)* 填寫 tin se 155, 168

filling *(dental)* (補牙) 填料 (bo nga) tin leeu 168

film *(movie)* 電影 din ying 108, 110; *(camera)* 菲林 fay lum 151

filter 濾色鏡 lur-ee sick geng 151

find, to 找 wun 18

fine *(penalty)* 罰款 fut foon 93

fine *(well)* 很好 gay ho 19, 118

finger 手指 sau jee 166

fire: ~ alarm 火警警報 for ging ging bo; **~ department [brigade]** 消防局 seeu fong guk 92; **~ escape** 火警通道 for ging t-owng do; **~ extinguisher** 滅火器 mit for t-owng; **there's a fire!** 失火啦！for juk a

firewood 木柴 chaai

first 第一 dai yut 68, 75, 218; **~ class** *(ticket)* 頭等 tau dung 68, 74

fish restaurant 海鮮酒家 hoy sin jau ga 35

fish store [fishmonger] 魚店 yu-ee po 130

fit, to *(of clothes)* 合身 ngaam sun 146

fitting room 試衣室 see yee sut 146

fix, to 修補 sau bo 168

flashlight 電筒 din t-owng 31

flat *(puncture)* (車胎) 刺破了 (che taai) baau jor 83, 88

flavor: what flavors do you have? 你們有哪幾種味道？nay day yau bin gay j-owng may do

flea 跳蚤 teeu sut

flight 班機 (航班) baan gay (hong baan) 68, 70; **~ number** 班機號碼 baan gay ho ma 68

flip-flops 人字拖鞋 yun jee tor haai 145

floor *(level)* 樓 lau 132

florist 花店 fa dim 130

flour 麵粉 min fun 39

flower 花 fa 106

flu 流行性感冒 lau hung sing gum mo 165

flush: the toilet won't flush 廁所抽水失靈了 chee sor ch-owng mm do sur-ee

fly *(insect)* 蒼蠅 woo ying

foggy, to be 大霧 daai mo 122

folk art 民間藝術 mun gaan ngai sut'

folk music 民間音樂 mun gaan yum ngock 111

follow, to *(pursue)* 跟蹤 gun j-owng 152

food 食物 sick mut 39; **~ poisoning** 食物中毒 sick mut j-owng duk 165

foot 腳 gerk 166; **~path** 小徑 lo jai 107

football 足球 juk kau 115

for *(direction to a place)* 去 … hur-ee … 94; **~ a day** 一天 yut yut 86; **~ a week** 一星期 yut gor lai baai 86

forecast 預報 yu-ee bo 122

foreign currency 外幣 ngoy bai 138

forest 森林 sum lum 107

forget, to 忘了 mm gay duck 42

fork 叉 cha 39, 41, 148

form 表 beeu 23; 表格 beeu gaak 153, 168

formal dress 禮服 lai fuk 111

fortnight 兩個星期 lurng gor sing kay

fortunately 幸運地 ho choy 19

fountain 噴泉 pun chu-een 99

four-door car 四門汽車 say do moon ge che 86

four-wheel drive 四輪驅動 say lun' kur-ee d-owng 86

fourth 第四 daai say 217

foyer (hotel, theater) 門廳 / 大堂 daai tong

fracture 骨折 gwut jit 165

frame (glasses) 眼鏡架 ngaan geng ga

free (available) 空 h-owng 36; (not busy) 有空 duck haan 124

freezer 冰櫃 bing gwai 29

French dressing 醋油沙律汁 cho yau sa lut' jup 38

frequent: how frequent? ... 每隔多久一班？ ... gay noy yut baan 76; **frequently** 頻繁 pun mut

fresh 新鮮 sun sin 41

Friday 星期五 lai baai ng 218

fried 炸 ja

friend 朋友 pung yau 162; **friendly** 友善 yau sin

fries 炸薯條 ja su-ee teeu 38, 40

frightened, to be 害怕 hai pa

from (come from) 從 yau 12, 119; **from ... to** (time) 由 ... 至 ... yau ... jee ... 13, 222

front 前邊 chin bin 147; **~ door** 大門 daai moon 26

frosty, to be 有霜 yau surng 122

frying pan 煎鍋 jin wock 29

fuel (gasoline/petrol) 燃油 yin yau 86

full 滿 moon 14; **~ board** (American Plan [A.P.]) 包食宿 bau sick suk 24; **~ insurance** 全險 chu-een him 86

fun, to have 玩得開心 waan duck hoy sum

furniture 傢具 ga see

further (extra) 其他 kay ta 136

fuse 灰士 (保險絲) foo-ee see (bo him see) 28; **~ box** 灰士箱 (保險絲盒) foo-ee see surng (bo him see haap) 28

---

gallon 加侖 ga lun'

game (soccer, etc.) 比賽 bay choy 115

game (toy) 遊戲 yau hay 157

garage 車房 che fong 88

garbage bags 垃圾袋 laap saap doy 148

garden 花園 fa yu-een

gas: I smell gas! 我嗅到煤氣味！ ngor mun do moo-ee hay may; **~ bottle** 煤氣罐 moo-ee hay goon 28

gas station 加油站 (ga) yau jaam 87

gasoline 汽油 din yau 87, 88

gastritis 胃炎 wai yim 165

gate (airport) 閘口 jaap hau 70

gauze 繃帶 bung daai 141

gay club 同性戀者俱樂部 t-owng sing lu-een je kur-ee lock bo 112

genuine 真 jun 134

get, to (find) 搵到 wun do 84; **~ in lane** (stay in lane) 選定行車線 (不准換線) su-een ding hung che sin (mm jun' woon sin) 96; **~ off** 下車 lock che 79; **~ to** (reach) 去 hur-ee 70, 77; **how do I get to ...?** ... 怎樣去？ ... dim yurng hur-ee 73

gift 禮物 lai mut 67, 156; **~ store**
禮品店 lai bun dim 130

girl 女孩 nur-ee (daughter)/nur-ee
jai 120, 157

girlfriend 女朋友 nur-ee pung yau 120

give, to 給 bay

give way (on road) 讓路 yurng
lo 93, 96

gland 分泌腺 fun bay sin 166

glass 杯 boo-ee 37; 水杯 sur-ee
boo-ee 39, 148

glasses (optical) 眼鏡 ngaan geng 167

glossy finish (photos) 光面 gwong min

glove 手套 sau mut

go: to ~ to 去 hur-ee 18; **let's ~!** 我們走
吧！ngor day haang la; **~ away!** 走
開！jau hoy; **where does this bus go?**
這輛巴士去哪裡？nay ga ba see hur-
ee bin do ga; **~ back** (turn around) 回
到 ... 去 faan faan ... hur-ee 95; **~ for
a walk, to** 去散步 hur-ee saan bo
124; **~ on!** 說下去 gong maai lock
hur-ee 19; **~ out** (in evening) 出去玩
chut' hur-ee waan; **~ shopping** 逛公司
haang g-owng see 124

goggles 護目鏡 ngaan jaau

gold 金 gum 149; **~-plate** 鍍金 do
gum 149

golf 哥爾夫球 gor yee foo kau 114; **~
course** 哥爾夫球場 gor yee foo kau
churng 116

good 好 ho 14, 35; (delicious) 好吃 ho
sick 42; **~ morning** 早晨 jo sun 10;
~ afternoon 你好 nay ho 10;
~ evening 你好 nay ho 10; **~ night** 晚
安 jo tau 10; **~ value** 物有所值 mut
yau sor jick 101

good-bye 再見 joy g-in 10

gram 克 huck 159

grandparents 祖父母 jo foo mo

grapes 提子 tai jee 160

grass 草 cho

gray 灰色 foo-ee sick 143

graze (cut) 擦傷 chaat surng 162

great (excellent) 非常
好 fay surng ho 19

great (good idea) 好
ho 125

green 綠色 luk sick 143

greengrocer 雜貨店 jaap for
po 130

grilled 燒烤 seeu

grocer (grocery store) 雜貨店 jaap
for po

ground (earth) 地面 day min 31;
~cloth [~sheet] 鋪地防水布 po day
fong sur-ee bo 31

group 團體 tu-een tai 66, 100

guarantee 保用證 bo y-owng jing 135

guide (tour) 導遊 do yau 98

guidebook 旅遊指南 lur-ee yau jee
naam 150

guided tour 有導遊的遊覽 yau do yau
ge yau daan tai

guided walk/hike 有嚮導的遠足 yau
hurng do ge yu-een juk 106

guitar 吉他 git ta

gum 牙齦 nga yuk

guy rope 支索 laai sing 31

gynecologist 婦科醫生 foo for yee
sung 167

H **hair** 頭髮 tau faat 147;
~ mousse/gel 髮士／定型膠 mo
see/ding ying gaau 142; **~ spray** 噴髮
膠 pun faat gaau 142; **~cut** 剪髮 jin
faat

hairdresser 理髮師 lay faat see 147;
(shop) 髮廊 faat long 131

half, a 一半 yut boon 218; **~ board**
(Modified American Plan [M.A.P.]) 半食
宿 boon sick suk 24; **~ past ...** 點半
... dim boon 221

hammer 鐵鎚 tit chur-ee 31

hand 手 sau 166; **~ luggage**
手提行李 sau tai hung lay 69;
~ washable 可手洗 hor yee sau
sai 145

handbag 手袋 sau doy 144. 153

handicapped, to be 傷殘 surng chaan 163

handicrafts 手工藝品 sau g-owng ngai bun

handkerchief 手絹 sau gun

hanger 衣架 yee ga 27

hangover (n.) 宿醉 suk jur-ee 141

happy: I'm not happy with the service 我對你們的服務不滿意 ngor dur-ee nay day ge fuk mo mm moon yee

harbor 海港 hoy gong

hat 帽 mo 144

have (hold stock of) 有 yau 133; **can I have?** 可不可以給我 ... hor mm hor yee bay ... ngor 18; **~ to** (must) 需要 sur-ee yeeu 79; **~ an appointment** 約了時間 yerk jor see gaan 161

hayfever 花粉過敏症 fa fun gwor mun jing 141

head 頭 tau 166; **~ waiter** 部長 bo jurng 41; **~ache** 頭痛 tau t-owng 163

heading, to be (in a direction) 去 hur-ee 83

health food store 健康食品店 g-in hong sick bun dim 130

hear, to 聽 teng

hearing aid 助聽器 jor ting hay

heart 心臟 sum jong 166; **~ attack** 心臟病發作 sum jong beng faat 163; **~ condition** 心臟病 sum jong beng 163

hearts (cards) 紅心 h-owng sum

heater 暖氣爐 nu-een hay lo

heating 暖氣 nu-een hay 25

heavy 重 ch-owng 14, 69, 134

height 身高 sun go 152

hello 你好 nay ho 10, 118

help: can you help me? 你可以幫助我嗎。 bong: nay hor mm hor yee bong ha ngor 92

hemorrhoids 痔瘡 jee chong 165

her 她的 kur-ee ge 16

here 這裡 nay do 12, 17

hernia 小腸氣 seeu churng hay 165

hers 她的 kur-ee ge 16; **it's hers** 這是她的 hai kur-ee ge

hi! 你好 nay ho 10

high 高 go 122

highlight, to (hair) 部分頭髮染淺色 bo fun tau faat yim chin sick 147

highway 高速公路 go chuk g-owng lo 94

hike (n.) 遠足 yu-een juk 106

hiking 遠足 yu-een juk; **~ boots** 旅行靴 lur-ee hung her 145

hill 山崗 saan gong 107

hire, to 租 jo

his 他的 kur-ee ge 16; **it's his** 這是他的 hai kur-ee ge

hitchhiking 搭順風車 daap sun' f-owng che 83

HIV-positive 染上了愛滋病毒 yim jor oy jee beng duk

hobby (pastime) 嗜好 see ho 121

hold on, to 等一下 dung yut jun 128

hole (in material) 破洞 chu-een l-owng

holiday: on ~ 度假 do ga 66, 123; **~ resort** 度假勝地 do ga sing day

home: we're going home 我們要回去了 ngor day yeeu faan hur-ee la

homosexual 同性戀 t-owng sing lu-een

honeymoon: we're on honeymoon 我們在度蜜月 ngor day do mut yu-eet

hopefully 希望 hay mong 19

horse 馬 ma; **~ racing** 賽馬 choy ma 115

hospital 醫院 yee yu-een 131, 164, 167

hot 熱 yit 14, 122; **~ dog** 熱狗 yit gau 110; **~ spring** 溫泉 wun chu-een; **~ water** 熱水 yit sur-ee 25

hotel 酒店 jau dim 21, 123

hour 小時 j-owng tau 97; **in an ~** 一小時後 yut gor j-owng tau hau 84

house 房屋 uk

housewife 家庭主婦 ga ting ju-ee foo 121

hovercraft 飛翔船 fay churng
su-een 81

how? 怎樣...? dim yurng ... 17;
how are you? 你好嗎 nay ho ma 118;
how far ...? ... 多遠? ... gay yu-een
94, 106; **how long ...?** ... 多長時間？
... gay noy 23, 75, 76, 78, 88, 94,98,
135; **how many ...?** ... 多少個？
... gay dor gor 15, 80; **how much ...?**
(money) ... 多少錢？ ... gay dor chin
15, 21, 65, 84, 100, 109; **how much?**
(quantity) ...多少？ ... gay dor 140;
how often? 每隔多久... 一次？ gaak
gay noy ... yut chee 140; **how old ...?**
多大了？ ... gay daai la 120

hundred 一百 yut baak 217; ~
thousand 十萬 sup maan 217

hungry: I'm hungry 我餓了 ngor to
ngor la

hurry: I'm in a hurry 我趕時間 ngor
gon see gaan

hurt, to 痛 t-owng 164; **my ... hurts**
我的 ... 痛 ngor ge ... t-owng 162;
to be hurt 受傷 sau surng 92, 162

husband 丈夫 jurng foo 120, 162

I

I'd like ... 我想要 ... ngor
surng yeeu 36, 37, 40

I'll have ... 我要 ... ngor yeeu ... 37

ice 冰 bing 38

ice cream 雪糕 su-eet go 40, 160;
~ **parlor** 雪糕店 su-eet go dim 35

icy, to be 結冰 git bing 122

identification 身分證明 sun fun jing
ming 136

ill: I'm ill 我病了 ngor beng jor

illegal: is it illegal? 這是不是非法的？
hai mm hai fay faat ga

imitation 仿製 fong jai 134

immediately 立刻 jick huck 13

in (place) 在 hai 12; (time) ... 後
... hau 13

**included: is ...
included?** ... 包括在內
嗎？ bau mm bau maai
... ga 86, 98

India 印度 yun do

indicate, to 指出 jee chut'

indigestion 消化不良 seeu fa but lurng

Indonesia 印尼 yun nay

indoor pool 室內游泳池 sut noy yau
wing chee 117

inexpensive 價錢不貴的 ga chin mm
gwai ge 35

infected, to be 發炎 faat yim 165

infection 發炎 faat yim 167

inflammation of ... ... 發炎 ... faat
yim 165

informal (dress) 便服 bin fuk

information 資料 jee leeu 97; ~ **desk**
詢問處 sun' mun chu-ee 73; ~ **office**
詢問處 sun' mun chu-ee 96

Information (telephone service) 電話號碼
查詢 din wa ho ma cha sun' 127

injection 打針 da jum 168

injured, to be 受了傷 sau jor
surng 92, 162

innocent 清白的 ching baak ge

insect 蟲 ch-owng 25; ~ **bite** 蟲咬傷
ch-owng ngaau surng 141, 162;
~ **repellent** 蚊怕水 mun pa sur-ee 141

inside 裡面 lur-ee bin 12

insist: I insist 我堅持 ngor g-in chee

insomnia 失眠 sut min

instant coffee 即溶咖啡 jick y-owng
ga fe 160

instead of 而不是 yee mm hai

instructions 說明書 su-eet ming su-ee 135

instructor 教練 gaau lin

insulin 胰島素 yee do so

insurance 保險 bo him 86, 89, 93, 168;
~ **card** 保險單 bo him daan 93;
~ **claim** 要求保險公司賠償 yeeu kau
bo him g-owng see poo-ee surng 153;
~ **claim** 要求保險公司賠償 yeeu kau
bo him g-owng see poo-ee surng

A-Z

interest (hobby) 愛好 oy ho 121

interesting 有趣 yau chur-ee 101

International Student Card 國際學生證 gwock jai hock saang jing 29

Internet 國際網絡 gwock jai mong lock 155

interpreter 翻譯 faan yick 93, 153

intersection 十字路口 sup jee lo hau 95

introduce oneself, to 自我介紹 jee ngor gaai seeu 118

invitation 邀請 yeeu cheng 124

invite, to 請 cheng 124

involved, to be 牽連 hin lin 93

iodine 碘酒 din jau

Ireland 愛爾蘭 oy yee laan 119

Irish (person) 愛爾蘭人 oy yee laan yun

is: is it ...? 是不是 ...? hai mm hai ... 17; **is there ...?** 有沒有 ...? yau mo ... 17; **is this ...?** 這是 ... 嗎? nay je hai mm hai ... 145; **it is ...** 是 ... hai ... 17

Italian (cuisine) 意式 yee sick 35

itch: it itches 這裡癢 nay do hun

itemized bill 收費清單 sau fai ching daan 32

J

jacket 外套 ngoy to 144

jam 果醬 gwor jurng/jam

jammed, to be 打不開 hoy mm do 25

January 一月 yut yu-eet 219

Japan 日本 yut boon 119

Japanese (cuisine) 日式 yut sick 35; (person) 日本人 yut boon yun

jar 瓶 jun' 159

jaw 下巴 ha pa 166

jazz 爵士音樂 jerk see yum ngock 111

jeans 牛仔褲 ngau jai foo 144

jellyfish 海蜇 / 白蚱 hoy jit/baak ja

jet lag: I'm jet lagged 我有時差症狀 ngor yau see cha jing jong

jet-ski 滑水艇 waat sur-ee teng 117

jeweler 珠寶行 ju-ee bo hong 130, 149

job: what's your job? 你是做甚麼工作的? nay jo mut ye g-owng jock ga

join: may we join you? 我們可以和你們坐在一起嗎? ngor day hor mm hor yee chor maai lay a 124

joint 關節 gwaan jit 166; **~ passport** 共同護照 g-owng t-owng woo jeeu 66

joke 玩笑 gong seeu

journalist 記者 gay je

journey 路程 lo ching 75, 76, 78

jug (of water) 瓶 jun'

July 七月 chut yu-eet 219

jump leads 過電纜 gwor din din laam

jumper 套頭毛衣 gwor tau lup laan saam

junction (intersection) 路口 lo hau

June 六月 luk yu-eet 219

K

keep: keep the change! 不用找錢了! mm sai jaau la

kerosene 煤油 for sur-ee; **~ stove** 氣化煤油爐 hay fa for sur-ee lo 31

ketchup 茄汁 ke jup

kettle 水煲 sur-ee bo 29

key 鑰匙 sor see 27, 28; (car) 鑰匙 che see 88; **~ ring** 鑰匙圈 sor see hu-een 156

kiddie pool 戲水池 waan sur-ee chee 113

kidney 腎 sun 166

kilogram 公斤 g-owng gun 159

kilometer 公里 g-owng lay

kind (pleasant) 好心 ho yun

kind: what kind of ... 哪種 ... bin j-owng ...

kiss, to 吻 seck

kitchen 廚房 chu-ee fong 29

knapsack 背囊 boo-ee nong 31, 145

knee 膝蓋 sut tau 166

knickers 女内褲 nur-ee jong noy foo

knife 刀 do 39, 41, 148

know: I don't know 我不知道 ngor mm jee 23

Korea 韓國 hon gwock 119

Korean (person) 韓國人 hon gwock yun

kosher (food) 符合猶太教規的 foo hup yau taai gaau kwai ge

label 標簽 beeu chim

lace 厘士 (透花織料) lay see (tau fa jick leeu) 145

ladder 梯子 tai

lake 湖 woo 107

lamp 燈 dung 25, 29

land, to 降落 gong lock 70

language course 語言課程 yu-ee yin for ching

large 大 daai 69, 110; **larger** 大些 daai dee 134

last (final) 最後 jur-ee hau 68, 75; (week, month, etc.) 上個 surng gor 219; (train) 尾班 may baan 80

last, to 維持 wai chee

late (delayed) 遲 chee 70, 222

later 晚些 aan dee 125, 147

laugh, to 笑 seeu 126

laundromat 自助洗衣場 jee jor sai yee churng 131

laundry: ~ facilities 洗衣設備 sai yee chit bay 30; **~ service** 洗衣服務 sai yee fuk mo 22

lavatory 廁所 chee sor

lawyer 律師 lut' see 152

laxative 輕瀉劑 hing se jai

lead, to (road) 通往 t-owng hur-ee 94; **~-free** (gas/petrol) 無鉛 mo yu-een 87

leader (of group) 領隊 ling dur-ee

leak, to (roof, pipe) 漏水 lau sur-ee

learn, to (language) 學習 hock

leather 皮 pay 145

leave, to (deposit) 留 lau 32, 73; (person) 走 jau 126; (aircraft) 起飛 hay fay 68; (transport) 開出 hoy chut 78; **leave me alone!** 不要騷擾我！ mm ho so yeeu ngor 126

left: on the ~ 在左邊 hai jor bin 76, 95

left-luggage office 行李寄存處 hung lay gay chu-een chu-ee 71, 73

leg 腿 tur-ee 166

legal: is it legal? 這合法嗎？ hup mm hup faat ga

leggings 橡筋褲 jurng gun foo 144

lemon 檸檬 ning m-owng 38

lemonade 檸檬汽水 ning m-owng hay sur-ee

lend: could you lend me ...? 可以借 ... 給我嗎？ hor mm hor yee je ... bay ngor

length (of) 長度 churng do

lens (camera) 鏡頭 geng tau 151; (in glasses) 鏡片 geng pin 167; **~ cap** 鏡頭蓋 geng tau goy 151

lesbian club 女同性戀俱樂部 nur-ee t-owng sing lu-een kur-ee lock bo

less 少些 seeu dee 15

lesson 課 for

let: let me know! 告訴我一下！ wa seng bay ngor jee

letter 信 sun' 154; **~box** 信箱 sun' surng

level (even ground) 平坦 ping 31

library 圖書館 to su-ee goon

lie down, to 躺下 fun dai 164

lifeboat 救生艇 gau sung teng

lifeguard 救生員 gau sung yu-een 117

lifejacket 救生衣 gau sung yee

life preserver [belt] 救生圈 gau sung hu-een

lift (elevator) 電梯 din tai 26, 132

lift (hitchhiking) 載 che 83

light *(color)* 淺色 chin sick 14, 134, 143; **lighter** *(color)* 淺些 chin dee 143; **lighter** *(opp. darker)* 光亮些 gwong maan dee 24

light *(electric)* 電燈 din dung 25; ~ **bulb** 燈泡 dung daam 148

light *(weight)* 輕 heng 14, 134

lighter *(cigarette)* 打火機 da for gay 150

like: ~ **this** *(similar to)* 像這個 ho chee nay gor gum ge

like, to 喜歡 j-owng yee 101, 111, 119, 121; **I like it** 我喜歡這個 ngor j-owng yee nay gor; **I don't like it** 我不喜歡這個 ngor mm j-owng yee nay gor; **I'd like ...** 我想要 ... ngor surng yeeu ... 18, 133

limousine 豪華轎車 ho wa hay che

line *(subway [metro])* 線 sin 80

linen 亞麻布 a ma bo 145

lip 口唇 hau sun 166; ~**stick** 唇膏 sun go

liqueur 甜酒 tim jau/liqueur jau

liquor store 酒品店 jau po 130

liter 公升 g-owng sing 87, 159

little *(small)* 小 sai

live, to 住 ju-ee 119; ~ **together** 同居 t-owng gur-ee 120

liver 肝 gon 166

living room 客廳 haak teng 29

lobby *(theater, hotel)* 大廳 / 大堂 daai tong

local 本地 boon day 35, 37; ~ **anaesthetic** 局部麻醉藥 guk bo ma jur-ee yerk 168

lock, to 鎖 sor 25, 26, 88; ~ **oneself out** 把鑰匙鎖在房間裡 sor see sor jor hai fong do 27

log on, to 進入網絡 yup mong lock 155

long 長 churng 144, 146; ~**-distance bus** 長途汽車 churng to hay che 78; ~**-sighted** 遠視 yu-een see 167; **how long** 多長時間？ gay noy 164

look: I'm just looking 我只是看看 ngor jee hai tai ha; **look like** *(resemble)* 是 ... 樣的 hai ... yurng ge 71; **to be looking for** 想找 surng wun 133

loose 鬆 s-owng 146

lorry *(truck)* 貨車 for che

lose, to 丟失 mm g-in 28, 138, 153; **I've lost ...** 我丟失了 ... ngor mm g-in jor ... 71

lost-and-found office [lost property office] 失物認領處 sut mut ying leng chu-ee 73

lots of fun 好玩 ho waan 101

louder 大聲點 daai seng dee 128

love: I love you 我愛你 ngor oy nay

lovely 好 ho 122

low 低 dai 122; ~ **bridge** 低橋 dai keeu 96; ~**-fat** 低脂肪 dai jee fong

lower berth 下鋪 ha po 74

luck: good luck 祝你好運 juk nay ho wun 220

luggage 行李 hung lay; ~ **cart [trolley]** 行李推車 hung lay che jai 71; ~ **locker** 行李鎖櫃 hung lay sor gwai 71, 73

lump 腫塊 lau 162

lunch 午餐 / 午膳 ng chaan/sick aan 98, 154

lung 肺 fai

M **machine washable** 可機洗 hor yee gay sai 145

madam 女士 nur-ee see

magazine 雜誌 jaap jee 150

magnificent 雄偉 h-owng wai 101

maid 清潔工人 ching git g-owng yun 28

mail *(n.)* 信 sun' 27; **by** ~ 寫信 se sun' 22; ~**box** 郵筒 yau t-owng 154

mail, to 寄 gay

main 主要的 ju-ee yeeu ge 130; ~ **street** 大街 daai gaai 95, 96

make an appointment, to 約時間 yerk see gaan 161

make-up *(cosmetics)* 化妝品 fa jong bun

Malaysia 馬來西亞 ma loy sai a

male 男 naam 152

mallet 木槌 muk chur-ee 31

man *(male)* 男人 naam yun

manager 經理 ging lay 25, 41, 137

manicure 修甲 sau gaap 147

manual *(car)* 手動變速 sau d-owng ju-een bor

map 地圖 day to 94, 106, 150

March 三月 saam yu-eet 219

margarine 人造牛油 yun jo ngau yau 160

market 市場 see churng 99, 131

married, to be 結了婚 git jor fun 120

mascara 睫毛膏 jit mo go

mask *(diving)* 面具 min gur-ee

mass 彌撒 nay saat 105

massage 按摩 on mor 147

match *(soccer, etc.)* 比賽 bay choy 115

matches 火柴 for chaai 31, 148, 150

matinée 早場 jo churng 109

matter: it doesn't matter 不要緊 mm gun yeeu; **what's the matter?** 發生了什麼事？ yau mut ye see a

mattress 床墊 chong yuk

May 五月 ng yu-eet 219

may I ...? (我)可以 ... 嗎？ (ngor) hor mm hor yee ... 37

maybe 也許 waak je

me 我 ngor

meal *(combination of staple and dishes)* 餐 chaan 38; *(with numeral)* 頓飯 chaan faan 42; *(as activity)* (吃)飯 (sick) faan 124, 125, 165

mean, to 意思 yee see 11

measles 麻疹 ma chun 165

measure, to 量 dock 146

measurement 尺寸 check chu-een

meat 肉 yuk 41

medical certificate 醫生證明書 yee sung jing ming su-ee

medication 藥 yerk 164, 165

medium 中 j-owng 122

meet, to 見面 g-in min 125; **pleased to meet you** 認識你很高興 ho go hing ying sick nay 118

meeting place [point] 集合地點 jaap hup day dim 12

member *(of club)* 會員 woo-ee yu-een 112, 116

men *(toilets)* 男廁所 naam chee

mention: don't mention it 不用客氣 mm sai haak hay 10

menu 菜單 choy paai

message 口信 hau sun' 27

metal 金屬 gum suk

meter *(in taxi)* 咪錶 mai beeu 84

metro 地鐵 day tit 80; **~ station** 地鐵站 day tit jaam 80, 96

microwave *(oven)* 微波爐 may bor lo

midday 中午 j-owng ng

midnight 半夜 boon ye 221

migraine 偏頭痛 pin tau t-owng

mileage 里數 mai so (lay so) 86

milk 牛奶 ngau naai 160; **with ~** 要奶 yeeu naai 40

million 一百萬 yut baak maan 217

mind: do you mind if ...? ... 你介意嗎？ ... nay gaai mm gaai yee 77, 126

mine 我的 ngor ge 16; **it's mine!** 這是我的！ hai ngor ge

mineral water 礦泉水 kong chu-een sur-ee

mini-bar 小酒吧 jau ba jai 32

minimart 小型市場 seeu ying see churng 158

minute 分鐘 fun j-owng

mirror 鏡子 geng

missing, to be *(lacking)* 少了 seeu jor 137; *(lost)* 失蹤 mm g-in jor 152

mistake 錯 chor 32, 41, 42

mobile home 活動房屋 woot d-owng fong uk

modern 新款 sun foon 14

moisturizer (cream) 潤膚霜 yun' foo surng

monastery (Buddhist) 佛寺 fut jee 99; (Taoist) 道觀 do goon 99

Monday 星期一 lai baai yut 218

money 錢 chin 42, 136, 139, 153; ~ **order** 匯票 woo-ee peeu

month 月份 yu-eet fun 219; **monthly** (ticket) 月 yu-eet 79

moped 機動單車 (機動自行車) gay d-owng daan che (gay d-owng jee hung che) 83

more 更多 dor dee 15; **I'd like some more ...** 我想要多些 ... ngor surng yeeu dor dee ... 39

morning, in the 上午 surng jau 222

mosque 清眞寺 ching jun jee 105; ~ **bite** 蚊咬 bay mun ngaau

mother 母親 mo chun 120

motion sickness 暈浪 wun long 141

motorbike 電單車 (摩托車) din daan che (mor tock che) 83

motorboat 汽艇 hay teng 117

motorway 高速公路 go chuk g-owng lo 94

mountain 山 saan 107; ~ **bike** 山地單車 saan day daan che; ~ **pass** 山口 saan hau 107; ~ **range** 山脈 saan muck 107

moustache 鬍鬚 woo so

mouth 口 hau 164, 166; ~ **ulcer** 口腔潰瘍 hau hong koo-ee yurng

move, to 換 (房間) woon (fong) 25; **don't move him!** 別移動他！ mm ho yuk kur-ee 92

movie 電影 din ying 108, 110; ~ **theater** 電影院 din ying yu-een 96

Mr. ... 先生 ... sin saang

Mrs. ... 太太 ... taai taai

much 很多 ho dor 15

mugged, to be 被人打劫 bay yun da gip 153

mugging 搶劫 churng gip 152

mugs 大杯 daai boo-ee 148

multiple journey (ticket) 多程 dor ching 79

multiplex cinema 複式電影院 fuk sick din ying yu-een 110

mumps 腮腺炎 soy sin yim

muscle 肌肉 gay yuk 166

museum 博物館 bock mut goon 99

music 音樂 yum ngock 111, 121

musician 音樂家 yum ngock ga

must: I must 我必須 ngor yut ding yeeu

mustard 芥醬 gaai laat 38

my 我的 ngor ge 16

myself: I'll do it myself 我自己來 ngor jee gay lay

N **name** 名字 meng 22, 118, 120; **my name is** 我叫 ... ngor geeu ... 22, 118; **what's your name?** 你叫什麼名字？ nay geeu mut ye meng ci 118; **what's your surname?** 你貴姓？ nay gwai sing a 118

napkin 餐巾 chaan gun 39

nappies 尿片 neeu pin 142

narrow 窄 jaak 14

national 國家的 gwock ga ge

nationality 國籍 gwock jick

nature reserve 自然護理區 jee yin woo lay kur-ee 107

nausea 噁心 jock au

near ... 在 ...附近 hai ... foo gun 12; ~**sighted** 近視 gun see 167; **nearest** 最近 jur-ee kun 80, 88, 92, 130, 140

nearby 附近 foo gun 21, 87

necessary 必需 bit sur-ee 89

neck 頸 geng 147, 166

necklace 頸鍊 geng lin 149

nephew 外甥／姪 ngoy sung/jut

nerve 神經 sun ging

nervous system 神經系統 sun ging hai t-owng

never 從來沒有 ch-owng loy mo 13; **~ mind** 不要緊 mm gun yeeu 10

new 新 sun 14

New Year 新年 sun nin 220

New Zealand 紐西蘭 nau sai laan

New Zealander (person) 紐西蘭人 nau sai laan yun

newspaper 報紙 bo jee 150

newsstand [newsagent] 報紙檔 bo jee dong 131

next 下一 ha yut 68, 75, 78; **next to ...** 在 ... 旁邊 ... jong pin bin 12, 95; **next stop!** 下個站 ha gor jaam 79, 80

nice 很好 ho ho 14

niece 外甥女 / 姪女 ngoy sung nur-ee/jut nur-ee

night: at ~ 晚上 ye maan 222; **~-club** 夜總會 ye j-owng woo-ee 112

noisy 嘈吵 cho 14, 24

non-alcoholic 不含酒精 mo jau jing

non-smoking (adj.) 非吸煙 fay kup yin 36; (area) 非吸煙區 fay kup yin kur-ee 69

none 一個也沒有 yut gor do mo 15, 16

nonsense! 胡說 lu-een gong 19

noon 中午 j-owng ng 221

normal 通常 t-owng surng 67

north 北 buck 95

nose 鼻 bay 166

not: not bad 不錯 mm chor 19; **not good** 不好 mm ho 19; **not yet** 還沒有 j-owng may 13

note 紙幣 jee bai 139

nothing else 沒有其他的了 mo kay ta ye la' 15

notify, to 通知 t-owng jee 167

November 十一月 sup yut yu-eet 219

now 現在 yee ga 13, 84

numbers 號碼 ho ma 138

number plate 車牌 che paai

nurse 護士 woo see

nylon 尼龍 nay l-owng

O

o'clock: it's ... o'clock ... 點 ... dim 221

occasionally 偶爾 / 間中 gaan j-owng

occupied 有人 yau yun 14

October 十月 sup yu-eet 219

odds (betting) 賠率 poo-ee lut' 115

of course 當然 dong yin 19

off licence 酒品店 jau po 130

off-peak 非繁忙時間 fay faan mong see gaan

office 辦公室 se jee lau

often 時常 see surng 13

oil 油 yau

okay (fine) 好 ho 10; (satisfactory) 過 得去 gwor duck hur-ee 19

old (opp. new) 舊 gau 14; (opp. young) 年老 nin lo 14; **~ town** 舊區 gau kur-ee 96, 99; **~-fashioned** 舊款 gau foon 14

olive oil 橄欖油 gaam laam yau

omelet 煎蛋餅 / 奄列 jin daan beng/um lit

on (day, date) 在 hai 13; **~ foot** 步行 haang lo 17, 95; **~ my own** 我一個人 ngor yut gor yun 120; **~ the hour** 每點 正 moo-ee dim jing 76; **~ the left** 在 左邊 hai jor bin 12; **~ the other side** 另一邊 ling ngoy gor bin 95; **~ the right** 在右邊 hai yau bin 12; **~ the spot** 即時 jick see 93

on/off switch 開關 din jai

once 一次 yut chee 217

one: ~-way 單程 daan ching 65, 74; **~-way street** 單程路 daan ching lo 96; **~-way ticket** 單程機票 daan ching gay peeu 68; **~ like that** 像那個一樣的 ho chee gor gor gum yurng ge 16

open 開 hoy 14, 100

open, to *(store)* 開門 / 營業 hoy moon / ying yip 132, 140; *(window)* 開 hoy 77

open-air pool 露天游泳池 lo tin yau wing chee 117

opening hours 開放時間 hoy fong see gaan 132

opera 歌劇 gor keck 108, 111; **~ house** 歌劇院 gor keck yu-een 99, 111

operation *(medical)* 手術 sau sut'

opposite 在 ... 對面 hai ... dur-ee min 12

optician 眼鏡店 ngaan geng po 131

or 或者 waak je

orange 橙色 chaang sick 143

orchestra 樂團 ngock tu-een 111

order, to 叫 geeu 32, 37, 41

organized hike/walk 有嚮導的遠足 yau hurng do ge yu-een juk

our(s) 我們的 ngor day ge 16

outdoor 室外 sut ngoy

outrageous 太貴 taai gwai 89

outside 外面 chut' bin 12, 36

oval 橢圓形 tor yu-een ying 134

oven 烤爐 / 焗爐 guk lo

over there 那邊 gor bin 36, 76

overcharge: I've been overcharged 你多計了價錢 nay gai dor jor ngor chin

overdone *(adj.)* 煮得太老 ju-ee duck taai lo 41

overheat 過熱 yit gwor tau

overnight 一晚 yut maan 23

owe, to 要付 yeeu bay 168; **how much do I owe?** 我要付多少錢？ ngor yeeu bay gay dor chin a

own: on my own 自己一個人 jee gay yut ge yun

owner 主人 ju-ee yun

---

p.m. 下午 ha ng

pacifier *(for baby)* 奶嘴 naai jur-ee

pack, to 收拾 jup 69

package 包裹 bau gwor 155

packed lunch 盒飯 hup faan

packet of cigarettes 一包香煙 yut bau yin jai 150

paddling pool 戲水池 waan sur-ee chee 113

padlock 掛鎖 sor tau

pail 桶 t-owng 157

pain: to be in ~ 痛 t-owng 167; **~killers** 止痛藥 jee t-owng yerk 141, 165

paint, to 畫 waak

painter 畫家 wa ga

painting 畫 wa

pair of, a 一雙 yut surng 218

palace 宮殿 g-owng din 99

palpitations 心悸 sum teeu

panorama 全景 chu-een ging 107

pants *(trousers)* 褲 foo 144

pantyhose 襪褲 mut foo 144

paper 紙 jee 150; **~ napkins** 紙餐巾 jee chaan gun 148

paracetamol 退燒止痛藥 tur-ee seeu jee t-owng yerk

paraffin 煤油 moo-ee yau 31

paralysis 癱瘓 taan jor

parcel 包裹 bau gwor 155

pardon? 請再說一遍 cheng joy gong yut chee 11

parents 父母 foo mo 120

park 公園 g-owng yu-een 96, 99, 107

park, to 泊 paak 30

parking lot 停車場 ting che churng 87, 96

parking meter 停車收費錶 ting che mai beeu 87

parliament building 國會大樓 gwock woo-ee daai lau 99

partner *(boyfriend/girlfriend)* 男 / 女朋友 naam/nur-ee pung yau

parts *(components)* 零件 ling g-in 89

party (social) 派對 paai dur-ee 124

pass through, to (transit) 過境 gwor ging 66

pass, to 經過 ging gwo 77

passport 護照 woo jeeu 66, 69, 153

pastry store 餅店 beng dim 131

patch, to 縫補 f-owng bo 137

patient (n.) 病人 beng yun

pavement, on the 在行人道上 hai hung yun lo

pay, to (money) 支付 bay 42, 67; (bill) 付賬 jau so 42; **~ a fine** 繳交罰款 gau fut foon 93

pay phone 付費電話 yup chin din wa

payment 付款 bay chin

peak 山峰 saan f-owng 107

pearl 珍珠 jun ju-ee 149

pedestrian: ~ crossing 行人過路處 haang yun gwor lo chu-ee 96; **~ zone [precinct]** 行人專區 hung yun ju-een kur-ee 96

pen 筆 but 150

pencil 鉛筆 yu-een but 150

penknife 袖珍摺刀 jau jun jip do 31

people 人 yun 92, 119

pepper 胡椒粉 woo jeeu fun 38

per: ~ day 一天 yut yut 30, 83, 86, 87, 116; **~ hour** 一小時 yut gor j-owng 87, 116, 155; **~ night** 一晚 yut maan 21; **~ week** 一個禮拜 yut gor lai baai 83, 86

perhaps 或許 waak je 19

period (menstrual) 月經 yu-eet ging 167; **~ pains** 經期痛 ging kay t-owng 167

perm, to 電髮 din faat 147

petrol 汽油 din yau 87, 88; **~ station** 加油站 yau jaam 87

pewter 錫鑞 seck laap 149

pharmacy 藥房 yerk fong 131, 140, 158

Philippines 菲律賓 fay lut' bun

phone: ~card 電話卡 din wa kaat 127, 155; **~ call** 電話 din wa 152

phone, to 打電話 da din wa

photo: to take a ~ 拍照 ying surng; **passport-size ~** 護照相片 woo jeeu surng pin 116

photocopier 影印機 ying yun gay 155

photographer 攝影師 sip ying see

phrase 詞句 chee gur-ee 11

phrase book 常用語手冊 surng y-owng yu-ee sau chaak 11

pick someone up, to 接 jip 113

pick up, to (collect) 拿 lor 28

picnic 野餐 ye chaan; **~ area** 野餐區 ye chaan kur-ee 107

piece (of baggage) 件 g-in 69; **a piece of ...** 一塊 ... yut faai ... 40, 159

pill 粒 (藥丸) lup (yerk yu-een) 165

Pill (contraceptive): **to be on the Pill** 在服避孕丸 sick gun bay yun yu-een 167

pillow 枕頭 jum tau 27; **~ case** 枕套 jum tau day

pilot light 火種 for j-owng

pink 粉紅色 fun h-owng sick 143

pipe (smoking) 煙斗 yin dau

pitch (for camping) 露營地 lo ying day

pizzeria 意大利薄餅店 yee daai lay bock beng dim 35

place (space) 位 wai 29

place a bet, to 投注 tau ju-ee 115

plane 飛機 fay gay 68

plans 計劃 gaai waak 124

plant (n.) 植物 jick mut

plastic: ~ bags 塑膠袋 sock gaau doy; **~ wrap** 保鮮紙 bo sin jee 148

plate 碟 dip 39, 148

platform 月台 (站台) yu-eet toy (jaam toy) 73, 76, 77

platinum 白金 baak gum 149

play, to 玩 (music) 演奏 yin jau 111; (of drama) 上演 surng yin 110; **~ group** 遊戲小組 yau hay seeu jo 113; **~ground** 遊樂場 yau lock churng 113

playing field 運動場 wun d-owng churng 96

playwright 劇作家 keck juk ga 110

pleasant 很好 ho ho 14

please 請 cheng mm goy 10

plug 插頭 chaap so 148

p.m. 下午 ha ng/ha jau

pneumonia 肺炎 faai yim 165

point of interest 名勝 ming sing 97

point to, to 指出 jee chut' 11

poison 毒藥 duk yerk

police 警察 (公安) ging chaat (g-owng on) 92, 152; **~ report** 警方報告書 ging fong bo go su-ee 153;
~ station 警署 (公安局) ging chu-ee (g-owng on guk) 96, 131, 152

pollen count 花粉統計 fa fun t-owng gaai 122

polyester 聚酯纖維 jur-ee jee chim wai

pond 池塘 chee tong 107

pop (music) 流行音樂 lau hung yum ngock 111

popcorn 爆谷 baau guk 110

popular 受歡迎 sau foon ying 111, 157

port (harbor) 港口 gong hau

porter 行李員 hung lay yu-een 71

portion 份 fun 39

possible: as soon as possible 盡快 jun' faai

possibly 可能 hor nung 19

post (mail) 信 sun' 27; **~ office** 郵局 yau guk 96, 131, 154; **~box** 郵筒 yau t-owng 154; **~card** 明信片 ming sun' pin 154, 156

post, to 寄 gay

postage 郵費 yau fai 154

potato chips 薯片 su-ee pin 160

potatoes 薯仔 su-ee jai 38

pottery 陶器 to hay

pound (sterling) 英鎊 ying bong 67, 138

power: ~ cut 停電 ting din; **~ points** 電插座 din jaap jor 30

pregnant, to be 懷孕 yau jor sun gay 163

premium (gas/petrol) 高級 go kup 87

prescribe, to 開藥 hoy yerk 165

prescription 處方 yerk fong 140, 141

present (gift) 禮物 lai mut

press, to 熨 tong 137

pretty 漂亮 leng

priest 神父 / 牧師 sun foo/muk see

primus stove 氣化煤油爐 hay fa for sur-ee lo 31

prison 監獄 gaam yuk

probably 很可能 ho hor nung 19

produce store [grocer] 蔬菜店 sor choy po 131

program 節目表 jit muk beeu 109; **~ of events** 娛樂節目表 yu-ee lock jit muk beeu 108

pronounce, to 發音 faat yum

Protestant 基督教 gay duk gaau 105

pub 酒館 / 酒吧 jau goon/jau ba

public building 公眾用途樓宇 g-owng j-owng y-owng to lau yu-ee 96

pump (gas/petrol station) 加油泵 yau bum 87

puncture 車胎破了 baau jor taai 83, 88

puppet show 木偶戲 muk ngau hay

pure: pure cotton 純棉 sun' min 145

purple 紫色 jee sick 143

purse 錢包 ngun bau 153

push-chair 嬰兒車 ying yee che

put: where can I put ...? ... 可以放在哪裡？ ... hor yee baai hai bin do

quality 品質 jut day 134

quantity 數量 so lurng 134

quarter 四分之一 say fun jee yut 217; **~ past** ... 點十五分 ... dim sup ng fun 221; **~ to** ... 點四十五分 ... dim say sup ng fun 221

queue, to 排隊 paai dur-ee 112

quick 快 faai 14

quickest: what's the quickest way? 最快的是哪條路？ bin teeu lo jur-ee faai

quickly 快點 faai dee 17

quiet 清靜 ching jing 14; **quieter** 清靜些 ching jing dee 24, 126

R **rabbi** 拉比 laai bay

race track (racecourse) 馬場 ma churng 115

racket (tennis, squash) 球拍 kau paak 116

railway 鐵路 tit lo

rain, to 下雨 lock yu-ee 122

raincoat 雨衣 yu-ee yee 144

rape 強姦 kurng gaan 152

rapids 急流 gup lau 107

rare (steak) 半熟 boon saan suk; **(unusual)** 罕見 seeu g-in

rash 出疹 chut' chun 162

rather 相當 gay 17

razor 鬚刨 so pau; **~ blades** 剃刀 tai do 142

reading 看書 tai su-ee 121

ready (修) 好 (jing) ho 89, 137, 151

real (genuine) 真 jun 149

really? 真的？ jun ge 19

receipt 收條 sau teeu 32, 89, 136, 137, 151, 168

reception (desk) 接待處 jip doy chu-ee

receptionist 接待員 jip doy yu-een

reclaim tag 領回行李標籤 ling woo-ee hung lai beeu chim 71

recommend, to 介紹 gaai seeu 21, 35; **can you recommend ...?** 你可以介紹 ... 嗎？ nay hor mm hor yee gaai seeu ... 97, 108, 112; **what do you recommend?** 你介紹什麼 (菜式)？ nay yau mut ye ho gaai seeu a 37

record (LP) 唱片 churng pin 157; **~ [music] store** 唱片店 churng pin po 131

red 紅色 h-owng sick 143; **~ wine** 紅酒 h-owng jau 40

reduction (in price) 折扣 jit kau 24, 68, 74

refreshments 茶點 cha dim 78

refrigerator 雪櫃 su-eet gwai 29

refund 退款 tur-ee foon 137

refuse bags 垃圾袋 laap saap doy 148

regards: give my regards to 請替我問候 ... cheng bong ngor mun hau ... 220

region 地區 day kur-ee 106

registered mail 掛號信 gwa ho sun'

registration form 登記表 dung gay beeu 23

registration number (car) 車牌號碼 che paai ho ma 88

regular (size) 中 (的) j-owng (ge) 110; **(gas/petrol)** 普通 po t-owng 87

religion 宗教 j-owng gaau

remember: I don't remember 我不記得 ngor mm gay deuk

renminbi 人民幣 yun mun bai 67

rent, to 租 jo 86, 116, 117; **~ out** 出租 chut' jo 29; **I'd like to rent ...** 我想租 ... ngor surng jo ... 83

repair, to 修理 sau jing 89, 137, 168

repairs 修理 sau jing 89

repeat, to 再說一遍 joy gong yut chee 94, 128; **please repeat that** 請再說一遍 cheng joy gong yut chee 11

replacement 補配 bo poo-ee 167; **~ part** 替換零件 tai woon ling g-in 137

report, to 報 (案) bo (on) 152

require, to 需要 sur-ee yeeu 83

required, to be 需要 sur-ee yeeu 112

reservation 預訂 yu-ee deng 22, 36, 68, 77, 112; **reservations desk** 預售處 yu-ee sau chu-ee 109

reserve, to 訂 deng 21, 28, 36, 74, 81, 109; **I'd like to reserve ...** 我想預訂 ... ngor surng deng ding ... 74

rest, to 休息 yau sick

A-Z

restaurant 餐館/餐廳 chaan goon/chaan teng 35, 112

retail 零售 ling sau 121

retired, to be 退了休 tur-ee jor yau 121

return (adj.) 來回 loy woo-ee 65, 74; **~ ticket** 來回機票 loy woo-ee gay peeu 68

return, to (surrender) 交還 gau faan 86; (travel) 回來 faan lay 75, 81

reverse the charges, to 請對方付費 cheng dur-ee fong bay chin 127

revolting 難吃 nan sick 14

rheumatism 風濕病 f-owng sup beng

rib 肋骨 luck gwut 166

rice 米飯 baak faan 38

right (direction): **on the ~** 在右邊 hai yau bin 76, 95

right (correct) 對 ngaam 14, 106; **that's ~** 對啦 mo chor

right of way (on road) 優先行駛權 yau sin hung sai ku-een 93

ring 戒指 gaai jee 149

rip-off (n.) 敲竹槓 jick hai churng chin 101

river 河 hor 107; **~ cruise** 河上遊覽 ho surng yau laam 81

road 路 lo 94, 95; **~ map** 公路圖 g-owng lo 150; **~ closed** 道路封閉 do lo f-owng bai 96

robbed, to be 被人打劫 bay yun da gip 153

robbery 搶劫 churng gip

rock music 搖滾樂 yeeu gwun ngock 111

rolls 餐飽 chaan bau 160

romantic 浪漫 long maan 101

roof (house, car) 頂 deng; **~-rack** 車頂架 che deng ga

room 房間 fong 21; **~ service** 客房送餐服務 haak fong s-owng chaan fuk mo 26

rope 繩 sing

round (adj.) 圓形 yu-een ying 134; **~ neck** 圓領 yu-een leng 144

round (of golf) 一場 yut churng 116

round-trip (adj.) 來回 loy woo-ee 65, 74; **~ ticket** 來回機票 loy woo-ee gay peeu 68

route 路線 lo sin 106

rubbish 垃圾 laap saap 28

rucksack 背包 boo-ee nong

rude, to be 粗魯 cho lo

ruins 遺址 wai jee 99

run: ~ into (crash) 撞到 jong do 93; **~ out** (fuel) 用完 y-owng saai 88

running shoes 運動鞋 wun d-owng haai 145

rush hour 繁忙時間 faan mong see gaan

Russia 俄國 ngor gwock

 S **safe** (lock-up) 保險箱 bo him surng 27

safe (not dangerous) 安全 on chu-een 117; **to feel ~** 安全 on chu-een 65

safety 安全 on chu-een; **~ pins** 別針/扣針 kau jum

salad 沙律 sa lut'

sales 推銷 tur-ee seeu 121; **~ tax** 增值稅 jun jick sur-ee 24

salt 鹽 yim 38, 39

salty 鹹 haam

same 同一 t-owng yut 75

sand 沙 sa

sandals 涼鞋 lurng haai 145

sandwich 三文治 saam mun jee 40

sandy (beach) 沙 (灘) sa (taan) 117

sanitary napkins [towels] 衛生巾 wai sung gun 142

satellite TV 衛星電視 wai sing din see

satin 緞 du-een

satisfied: I'm not satisfied with this 我不滿意 ngor mm moon yee

196 *ENGLISH ➤ CANTONESE*

shopping: ~ area 購物區 kau mut kur-ee 區; **~ basket** 購物籃 kau mut laam; **~ mall [centre]** 購物中心 kau mut j-owng sum 130, 131; **~ trolley** 購物推車 kau mut tur-ee che; **to go ~** 逛公司 haang g-owng see

short 短 du-een 144, 146, 147; **~sighted** 近視 gun see 167

shorts 短褲 du-een foo 144

shoulder 肩膀 bock tau 166

shovel 鏟 chaan 157

show, to 給 ... 看 bay ... tai 133; **can you show me on ...?** 請在 ... 指出來 mm goy hai ... jee chut' lay 94, 106

shower 花洒 fa sa 21, 26, 30

shut 關 saan 14; **when do you shut?** 你們幾點關門？ nay day gay dim saan moon a

sick: I'm going to be sick 我想吐 ngor surng au

side (of road) 邊 bin 95; **~ street** 橫街 waang gaai 95

side order 另加 ling ga 38

sides (hair) 兩側 lurng bin 147

sights 景點 ging dim

sightseeing: ~ tour 遊覽團 yau laam tu-een 97; **to go ~** 觀光 goon gwong

sign (road sign) 標誌 beeu jee 93

signpost 路標 lo paai

silk 絲綢 see chau

silver 銀 ngun 149; **~-plate** 鍍銀 do ngun 149

Singapore 星加坡 sing ga bor

singer 歌星 gor sing 157

single (ticket) 單程 daan ching 65, 74; (person) 單人 daan yun 81; **~ room** 單人房間 daan yun fong 21; **~ ticket** 單程機票 daan ching gay peeu 68; **to be ~** 單身 daan sun 120

sink 洗臉盆 sai min poon 25

sister 姊妹 jee moo-ee 120

sit, to 坐 chor 36, 77, 126; **sit down, please** 請坐 ching chor

size 尺碼 check ma 146

skin 皮膚 pay foo 166

skirt 半截裙 boon jit kwun 144

sleep, to 睡 fun 167

sleeping: ~ bag 睡袋 sur-ee doy 31; **~ car** 臥鋪車廂 ngor po che surng 74, 77; **~ pill** 安眠藥 on min yerk

sleeve 袖 jau 144

slice 片 pin 159

slippers 拖鞋 tor haai 145

slow 慢 maan 14; **to be ~** (clock) 慢 maan 222; **slow down!** 慢一點！maan dee; **slowly** 慢點 maan dee 11, 17, 94, 128

SLR camera 單鏡頭相機 daan geng tau surng gay 151

small 小 sai 14, 24, 110, 134; **~ change** (coins) 零錢 saan jee 138, 139

smell: there's a bad smell 有股臭味 yau jum chau may

smoke, to 吸煙 sick yin 126

smoking (adj.) 吸煙 kup yin 36; (area) 吸煙區 kup yin kur-ee 69

snack bar 小食店 seeu sick dim 73

snacks 小食 seeu sick

sneakers 運動鞋 wun d-owng haai

snorkel 潛水吸氣管 chim sur-ee kup hay goon

snow, to 下雪 lock su-eet 122

soap 肥皂 faan gaan 142

soap powder 洗衣粉 sai yee fun

soccer 足球 juk kau 115

socket 插座 chaap jor

socks 襪 mut 144

soft drink 汽水 hay sur-ee 110, 160

solarium 日光浴室 yut gwong yuk sut 22

sole (shoes) 鞋底 haai dai

soluble aspirin 可溶阿斯匹靈 hor y-owng a see put ling

some 一些 yut dee

someone 有人 yau yun 16

something 一樣東西 yut yurng ye 16

sometimes 有時 yau see 13

son 兒子 jai 120, 162

soon 很快 ho faai 13

soon: as soon as possible 盡快 jun' jo 161

sore: it's ~ 疼痛 t-owng; **~ throat** 喉嚨痛 hau l-owng t-owng 141, 163

sorry! 對不起！dur-ee mm ju-ee 10

sort 種 j-owng 134

soul music 爵士靈歌 jerk see ling gor 111

sour 酸 su-een 41

south 南 naam 95

South Africa 南非 naam fay

South African (person) 南非人 naam fay yun

souvenir 紀念品 gay nim bun 98, 156; **~ store** 禮品店 lai bun dim 131

soy sauce 醬油 see yau 38

space 空位 h-owng wai 30

spade 鏟 chaan 157

spare (extra) 備用 bay y-owng

speak, to 說 gong 11, 67; **~ to** 同 ... 說話 t-owng ... king ha 18; **do you speak English?** 你會說英語嗎？ nay sick mm sick gong ying mun a 11

special: ~ delivery 速遞 (快遞) chuk daai (faai daai) 155; **~ rate** 特價 duck ga 86

specialist 專科醫生 ju-een for yee sung 164

specimen (medical sample) 抽樣 chau yurng 164

spectacles 眼鏡 ngaan geng

speed, to 超速駕駛 ja faai che 93

spend, to 花費 fa

spicy 辣 laat

sponge 海綿 hoy min 148

spoon 匙羹 chee gung 39, 41, 148

sport 體育 tai yuk 114

sporting goods store 體育用品店 tai yuk y-owng bun dim 131

sports 運動 wun d-owng 121; **~ club** 體育會 tai yuk woo-ee 116; **~ ground** 運動場 wun d-owng churng 96

sprained, to be 扭傷了 nau surng jor 164

spring 春天 chun' tin 219

square (shape) 方形 fong ying 134

stadium 體育館/場 taai yuk goon/churng 96

staff 員工 yu-een g-owng 113

stain 污跡 woo jick

stainless steel 不鏽鋼 but sau gong 149

stairs 樓梯 lau tai 132

stamp 郵票 yau peeu 150, 154; **~ machine** 郵票出售機 yau peeu chut' sau gay 154

stand in line, to 排隊 paai dur-ee 112

standby ticket 剩餘機票 sing yu-ee gay peeu

start, to 開始/開場 hoy chee (activity)/hoy churng (show) 98, 108; (car) 開不動 taat mm jerk 88

statement (legal) 口供 hau g-owng 93

station 車站 che jaam 96

statue 雕像 deeu jurng 99

stay (n.) 住 ju-ee 32

stay, to (in accommodation) 住 ju-ee 63, 123; (remain) 留在 lau hai 65

steak house 牛扒餐廳 ngau pa chaan teng 35

sterilizing solution 消毒水 seeu duk sur-ee 142

stiff neck 頸部僵硬 teeu geng gung jor 163

still: I'm still waiting 我還在等 ngor j-owng dung gun

sting 蜇傷 jum surng 162

stockings 長襪 churng mut 144

stolen, to be 被人偷了 bay yun tau jor 71, 153

stomach 胃 wai 166; **~ache** 胃痛 wai t-owng 163

stools (faeces) 大便 daai bin 164

stop (bus/tram) 停 79; (subway/metro) 站 jaam 80

stop (at), to 停 ting 76, 77, 78, 98

stopcock 水掣 sur-ee jai 28

store (shop) 商店 surng dim 130

stormy, to be 有雷 yau lur-ee 122

stove 煮食爐 ju-ee sick lo 28, 29

straight ahead 直往前走 jick hur-ee 95

strained muscle 扭傷肌肉 nau surng gay yuk 162

strange 奇怪 kay gwaai 101

straw (drinking) 飲管 yum t-owng

strawberry (flavor) 士多啤梨 see dor be lay 40

stream 溪 kai 107

strong (potent) 烈性 lit sing

student 學生 hock saang 74, 100, 121

study, to 讀 duk 121

style 款式 foon sick 104

subtitled, to be 有字幕 yau jee mock 110

subway (metro) 地鐵 day tit 80; **~ station** 地鐵站 day tit jaam 80, 96

sugar 糖 tong 38, 39

suggest, to 提議 tai yee 123

suit 西裝 sai jong 144

suitable for 適合 sick hup

summer 夏(天) ha (tin) 219

sun block 防晒傷膏 fong saai surng go 142

sunbathe, to 晒太陽 saai taai yurng

sunburn 晒傷 saai surng 141

Sunday 星期日 lai baai yut 218

sunglasses 太陽眼鏡 taai yurng ngaan geng

sunscreen 太陽油 taai yurng yau 142

sunshade 太陽傘 taai yurng je 117

sunstroke 中暑 j-owng su-ee 163

super (gas/petrol) 超級 cheeu kup 87

superb 一流 yut lau 101

supermarket 超級市場 cheeu kup see churng 131, 158

supervision 照看 tai ju-ee 113

supplement 附加費 foo ga fai 68, 69

suppositories 栓劑 saan jai 165

sure: are you sure? 你肯定嗎？ nay hung ding a

surfboard 滑浪板 waat long baan 117

surname 姓 sing

sweater 套頭毛衣 gwor tau lup laang saam 144

sweatshirt 長袖運動衫 churng jau wun d-owng saam 144

sweet (taste) 甜 tim

sweets (candy) 糖果 tong gwor 150

swelling 腫起 j-owng jor 162

swim, to 游泳 yau wing 115; **~ pool** 游泳池 yau wing chee 22, 26, 117; **~ trunks** 游泳褲 yau sur-ee foo 144

swimsuit 游泳衣 yau wing yee 144

switch 燈掣 dung jai 25

swollen, to be 腫脹 j-owng jor

symptoms 症狀 jing jong 163

synagogue 猶太教堂 yau taai gaau tong 105

synthetic 人造纖維 yun jo chim wai 145

T

T-shirt T-恤 T sut' 144, 156
table 桌子 toy 36, 112
tablet (藥) 片 (yerk) pin 140
Taiwan 台灣 toy waan
take, to 要 yeeu 24; (carry) 搬 boon 71; (medicine) 服 (藥) sick (yerk) 140, 165; (time) 需要 sur-ee yeeu 78;
I'll take it 就要這個 jau yeeu nay gor 135; **I'll take it** (room) 就要這間 jau yeeu nay gaan 24; **~ out** (extract) 拔掉 mock 168; **~ photographs, to** 拍照 ying surng 98
taken (occupied) 有人 yau yun 77
talk, to 說話 gong ye
tall 高 go 14
tampons 內用衛生棉條 noy y-owng wai sung min teeu 142
tan 晒黑 saai haak
tap 水喉 sur-ee hau 25
taxi 的士 (出租汽車) dick see (chut' jo hay che) 70, 71, 84;
~ stand [rank] 的士站 (出租汽車站) dick see jaam (chut' jo hay che jaam) 96
tea 茶 cha 40; **~ bags** 茶包 cha bau 160; **~ towel** 茶巾 cha gun 156
teacher 教師 gaau see
team 隊 dur-ee 115
teaspoon (measurement) 茶匙 cha gung 140
teddy bear 玩具熊 woon gur-ee h-owng 157
telephone 電話 din wa 22, 92;
~ booth 電話亭 din wa ting 127;
~ call 電話 din wa 32; **~ directory** 電話簿 din wa bo; **~ number** 電話號碼 din wa ho ma 127

telephone, to 打電話 da din wa 127, 128
temperature (body) 體溫 tai wun 164
temporarily 臨時 lum see 89, 168
ten thousand 一萬 yut maan 216
tennis 網球 mong kau 115;
~ court 網球場 mong kau churng 116
tent 帳幕 jurng mock 30, 31;
~ pegs 帳幕釘 jurng mock deng 31;
~ pole 帳幕支柱 jurng mock jee chu-ee 31
terrible 很糟 ho cha 19, 101
terrific 好極了 ho do gick 19
tetanus 破傷風 por surng f-owng 164
Thailand 泰國 taai gwock
thank you 謝謝 dor je mm goy 10
that one 那個 gor gor 16, 134
that's all 就這些 hai gum dor 133
theater 劇院 keck yu-een 96, 99, 110
theft 盜竊 do sip 153
their(s) 他們的 kur-ee day ge 16
theme park 專題樂園 ju-een tai lock yu-een
then (time) 然後 yin hau 13
there 那裡 gor do 12, 17; **there is ...** 有 ... yau ... 17; **there are ...** 有 ... 嗎 yau ... a 17
thermometer 溫度計 / 探熱針 taam yit jum
thermos flask 熱水瓶 nu-een sur-ee woo
these 這些 nay dee 134
they 他／她／它們 kur-ee day
thief 小偷 chaak
thigh 大腿 daai bay 166

thin 瘦 sau

think: ~ **about it** 考慮 hau lur-ee 135; **what do you ~ of ..?** 你覺得 ... 怎麼樣? nay gock duck ... dim 119; **I think** (feel) 我覺得 ngor gock duck 42; **I think** (it seems) 好像 ho chee 77

third 第三 daai saam 217; ~ **party insurance** 第三者責任保險 dai saam je jaak yum bo him

third, a 三分之一 saam fun jee yut 217

thirsty: I am thirsty 我口渴 ngor hau hot

this 這個 nay gor 218; ~ **one** 這個 nay gor 16, 134

those 那些 gor dee 134

thousand 一千 yut chin 216

throat 喉嚨 hau l-owng 166

thrombosis 血栓 hu-eet chu-een

through 通過 t-owng gwor

thumb 拇指 mo jee 166

Thursday 星期四 lai baai say 218

ticket (general) 票 fay 65, 115, 153; (air) 機票 gay peeu 68, 69; (train) 車票 che fay 74, 75; ~ **office** 售票處 sau peeu chu-ee 73

tie 領帶 leng taai 144

tight (vs loose) 緊 gun 146

tights 襪褲 mut foo 144

till receipt 收銀機收條 sau ngun gay sau teeu

time 時間 see gaan 76; **on ~** (punctual) 準時 jun' see 76; **free ~** 自由活動時間 jee yau woot d-owng see gaan 98; ... **times a day** 每日 ... 次 moo-ee yut ... chee 165

timetable 時間表 see gaan beeu 75

tin 罐 goon 159; ~ **opener** 罐頭刀 goon tau do 148

tire (car) 車胎 che taai 83

tired: I'm tired 我累了 ngor ho goo-ee a

tissues 紙巾 jee gun 142

to (place) 到 do 12

tobacco 煙絲 ying see 150

tobacconist 煙草店/ 香煙檔 yin po/yin jai dong 130

today 今天 gum yut 124, 161, 219

toe 腳趾 gerk jee 166

tofu 豆腐 dau foo

together 一起 yut chai 42

toilet 洗手間 (廁所) sai sau gaan (chee sor) 25, 26, 29; ~ **paper** 廁紙 chee jee 25, 29, 142

tomorrow 明天 ting yut 84, 124, 161, 219

tongue 舌頭 lay 166

tonight 今晚 gum maan 108, 110, 124

tonsilitis 扁桃腺炎 bin to sin yim 165

tonsils 扁桃腺 bin to sin 166

too 太 taai 17, 93, 135, 146; ~ **much** 太多 taai dor 15

tooth 牙 nga 168; ~**brush** 牙刷 nga chaat; ~**ache** 牙痛 nga t-owng; ~**paste** 牙膏 nga go 142

top (head) 頭頂 tau deng 147; (of hill) 頂 deng

torch 電筒 din t-owng 31

torn, to be (muscle) 撕裂了 see lit jor 164

torn: this is torn 這個撕破了 nay do see laan jor

tough (food) 靭 ngun 41

tour 遊覽 yau laam 97; **~ guide** 旅行
團導遊 lur-ee hung tu-een do yau 27;
~ operator 旅遊公司 lur-ee yau
g-owng see 26

tourist 遊客 yau haak

tow truck 拖車 tor che 88

towards 向 hurng 12

towel 毛巾 mo gun

tower 塔 taap 99

town (urban area) 市區 see kur-ee 70;
(administrative district) 市鎮 see
jun 94; **~ hall** 市政廳 see jing
teng 99

toy 玩具 woon gur-ee 157; **~ store**
玩具店 woon gur-ee dim 131

traditional 傳統 chu-een t-owng 35

traffic 交通 gau t-owng; **~ jam**
交通堵塞 sut che; **~ violation** [offence]
違反交通規則 wai faan gau t-owng
kwai jug

trail 小徑 lo jai 106

trailer 旅行拖車 lur-ee hung tor
che 30

train 火車 for che 75, 76, 77; **~ station**
火車站 for che jaam 73

training shoes 運動鞋 wun d-owng
haai 145

tram 電車 din che 78

transfer (traveling) 轉機 ju-een gay

transit, in (traveling) 過境 gwor
ging

translate, to 翻譯 faan yick 11

translation 翻譯 faan yick

translator 翻譯 faan yick

trash 垃圾 laap saap 28; **~ cans** 垃圾
桶 laap saap t-owng 30

travel: ~ agency 旅行社 lur-ee
hung se 131; **~ sickness** 暈浪
wun long 141

traveler's check
[cheque]
旅行支票 lur-ee
hung jee peeu 136, 138

tray 托盤 tock poon

tree 樹 su-ee 106

trim 剪髮 jin faat 147

trip (journey) 路程 lo ching 76, 78;
(tour) 旅遊 lur-ee yau 97;
have a good trip 旅途愉快 llur-ee
to yu-ee faai 220

trolley 推車 tur-ee che 158

trouser press 熨褲機 tong foo
gay

trousers 長褲 churng foo 144

truck 貨車 for che

true: that's ~
眞的 jun ga 19;
that's not ~ 那不對 gum gong mm
ngaam

try on, to 試 see 146

Tuesday 星期二 lai baai
yee 218

tumor 腫瘤 j-owng lau 165

tunnel 隧道 sur-ee do

turn, to 轉 ju-een 95; **~ down** (volume,
heat) 關小 saan sai dee; **~ off** 關 saan
25; **~ on** 開 hoy 25; **~ up** (volume,
heat) 開大 hoy daai dee

turning 路口 lo hau 95

TV 電視 din see 22

tweezers 鑷子／毛鉗 sai kim／
mo kim

twice 兩次 lurng chee 217

twin bed 兩張床 lurng jurng
chong 21

twist: I've twisted my ankle 我的腳踝扭
傷了 ngor nau surng jor gerk

two-door car 兩門汽車 lurng do moon
ge che 86

vehicle registration document
車輛登記文件 che lurng dung
gay mun g-in 93

vein 靜脈 jing muck 166

venereal disease 性病 sing
beng 165

ventilator 通風機 t-owng f-owng
gay

very 很 ho 17

video: ~ game 電子遊戲 din jee
yau hay; **~ recorder** 錄影機 luk
ying gay

Vietnam 越南 yu-eet naam

view: with a view of the sea 有海景的
yau hoy ging ge

viewpoint 瞭望處 leeu mong
chu-ee 99, 107

village 鄉村 hurng chu-een 107

vinaigrette 醋油沙律汁 cho yau sa
lut' jup 38

vineyard/winery 葡萄園 po to
yu-een 107

visa 簽證 chim jing

visit (n.) 來訪 loy fong 119

visit, to (in hospital) 探望 taam 167

visiting hours 探訪時間 taam fong
see gaan

vitamin tablets 維他命丸 wai ta ming
yu-een 141

volleyball 排球 paai kau 115

voltage 電壓 din aat

vomit, to 嘔吐 au to 163

W

wait (for), to 等 dung 41, 76,
89, 140

wait! 等一下！ dung yut jun 98

waiter 伙記 for gay 37

waiting room 候車室 hau che
sut 73

waitress 小姐 seeu je 37

wake, to 叫醒 geeu
seng 27, 70

wake-up call 叫醒電話
geeu seng
din wa

Wales 威爾斯 wai yee see 119

walk (n.) 遠足 yu-een juk 106;
~ home 走路回家 haang faan uk
kay 65

walking route 遠足路線 yu-een juk lo
sin 106

wallet 錢包 ngun bau 42, 153

war memorial (戰爭) 紀念碑 (jin jun)
gay nim bay 99

ward (hospital) 病房 beng
fong 167

warm 暖 nu-een 14, 122

washbasin 洗臉盆 sai min
poon

washing: ~ machine 洗衣機 sai yee
gay 29; **~ powder** 洗衣粉 sai yee
fun 148

washing-up liquid 洗潔精 sai git
jing 148

wasp 黃蜂 wong f-owng

watch 手錶 sau beeu 149, 153

water 水 sur-ee 87; **~ bottle** 水瓶
sur-ee jun'; **~ heater** 熱水爐 yit
sur-ee lo 28; **~ skis** 滑水板 waat
sur-ee baan 117

waterfall 瀑布 buk bo 107

waterproof 防水 fong sur-ee; **~ jacket**
防水外套 fong sur-ee ngoy to 145

wave 波浪 bor long

waxing 熱蠟脫毛 yit laap tu-eet mo
147

way (direction) 路 lo 94; **on the ~**
順路 sun' lo 83

we 我們 ngor day

wrong *(faulty)* 毛病
mm tor 88; **to be ~** 有毛病
mm tor 137; **there's something
wrong with ...** ... 有點不妥
... yau dee mm tor

 X-ray X- 光 X gwong 164
yacht 遊艇 yau teng
year 年 nin 219
yellow 黃色 wong sick 143
yes 是 hai 10
yesterday 昨天 kum yut 219
yoghurt 酸奶 su-een naai
you *(formal)* 閣下 gock ha; *(informal)*
你 nay 118
young 年輕 nin heng 14
your(s) *(pl.)* 你們的 nay day ge 16;
(sing.) 你的 nay ge 16
youth hostel 青年宿舍 ching nin
suk se 29
zebra crossing 斑馬線 baan ma sin
zero 零 ling
zip(per) 拉鏈 laai lin

Juern Gah = Expert

Glossary
Cantonese–English

The Cantonese–English glossary covers all the areas where you may need to decode written Cantonese: hotels, public buildings, restaurants, stores, ticket offices, airports, and stations. The Cantonese is written in large type to help you identify the character(s) from the signs you see around you.

General 一般常用語

左	*jor*	LEFT
右	*yau*	RIGHT
入口	*yup hau*	ENTRANCE
出口	*chut' hau*	EXIT
洗手間	*sai sau gaan*	TOILETS (H.K.)
廁所	*chee sor*	TOILETS (China & H.K.)
男	*naam*	MEN (TOILETS)
女	*nur-ee*	WOMEN (TOILETS)
有人	*yau yun*	OCCUPIED
禁止吸煙	*gum jee kup yin*	NO SMOKING
不准進入	*but jun' jun' yup*	NO ENTRY
小心	*seeu sum*	CAUTION
危險	*ngai him*	DANGER
對生命有危險	*dur-ee sung meng yau ngai him*	DANGER OF DEATH
拉 / 推	*laai/tur-ee*	PULL/PUSH

General 一般常用語

失物認領處	*sut mut ying leng chu-ee*	LOST PROPERTY
不准游泳	*but jun' yau wing*	NO SWIMMING
不准入內	*but jun'yup noy*	KEEP OUT
飲用水	*yum yowng sur-ee*	DRINKING WATER
私家重地	*see ga jowng day*	PRIVATE
不准亂拋垃圾	*but jun' lu-een pau laap saap*	NO LITTER
隧道	*sur-ee do*	UNDERPASS [SUBWAY]
小心梯級	*seeu sum tai kup*	MIND THE STEP
油漆未乾	*yau chut may gon*	WET PAINT
頭等	*tau dung*	FIRST CLASS (train)
二等	*yee dung*	SECOND CLASS (train)

CANTONESE ➤ ENGLISH

209

Road signs　道路標誌

停	*ting*	STOP
靠右駛	*kau yau sai*	KEEP RIGHT
靠左駛	*kau jor sai*	KEEP LEFT
單程路	*daan ching lo*	ONE WAY
禁止超車	*gum jee cheeu che*	NO PASSING [OVERTAKING]
禁止停泊	*gum jee ting paak*	NO PARKING
高速公路	*go chuk gowng lo*	HIGHWAY [MOTORWAY]
交通燈	*gau t-owng dung*	TRAFFIC LIGHTS
警告	*ging go*	WARNING
路口	*lo hau*	JUNCTION

詢問處	*sun' mun chu-ee*	INFORMATION
一號月台	*yut ho yu-eet toy*	PLATFORM 1 (H.K.)
一號站台	*yut ho jaam toy*	PLATFORM 1 (China)
一號閘口	*yut ho jaap hau*	GATE 1
海關	*hoy gwaan*	CUSTOMS
入境事務處	*yup g-ing see mo chu-ee*	IMMIGRATION
到境 / 到達	*do ging/do daat*	ARRIVALS
出境 / 出發	*chut' ging/chut' faat*	DEPARTURES
領回行李處	*ling woo-ee hung lay chu-ee*	BAGGAGE RECLAIM
巴士	*ba see*	BUS (H.K.)
公共汽車	*gowng gowng hay che*	BUS (China)
火車	*for che*	TRAIN
租車	*jo che*	CAR RENTAL
延遲	*yin chee*	DELAYED
地鐵	*day tit*	SUBWAY [METRO]

Hotel/Restaurant 酒店 / 餐廳

詢問處	*sun' mun chu-ee*	INFORMATION
接待處	*jip doy chu-ee*	RECEPTION
游泳池	*yau wing chee*	SWIMMING POOL
訂座 / 留座	*deng jor/lau jor*	RESERVED
緊急/火警出口	*gun gup/for ging chut' hau*	EMERGENCY/FIRE EXIT (H.K.)
太平門	*taai ping moon*	EMERGENCY/FIRE EXIT (China)
熱	*yit*	HOT (WATER)
冷	*laang*	COLD (WATER)
職員專用	*jick yu-een ju-een y-owng*	STAFF ONLY
衣帽間	*yee mo gaan*	COATCHECK [CLOAKROOM]
露台 / 花園	*lo toy/fa yu-een*	TERRACE/GARDEN
禁止吸煙	*gum jee kup yin*	NO SMOKING
酒吧	*jau ba*	BAR

Stores 商店

營業	*ying yip*	OPEN
休息	*yau sick*	CLOSED
午膳	*ng sin*	LUNCH
部	*bo*	DEPARTMENT
樓	*lau*	FLOOR
地牢	*day lo*	BASEMENT
電梯	*din tai*	ELEVATOR [LIFT]
電動樓梯	*din d-owng lau tai*	ESCALATOR
付款處 /出納員	*foo foon chu-ee/chut' nup yu-een*	CASHIER
大減價	*daai gaam ga*	SALE
職員專用	*jick yu-een ju-een y-owng*	STAFF ONLY

Sightseeing 遊覽

免費入場	*min fai yup churng*	FREE ADMISSION
成人	*sing yun*	ADULTS
小童	*seeu t-owng*	CHILDREN
優惠	*yau wai*	CONCESSIONS (students/pensioners)
紀念品	*gay nim bun*	SOUVENIRS
茶點	*cha dim*	REFRESHMENTS
請勿觸摸	*ching mut juk mor*	DO NOT TOUCH
禁止攝影	*gum jee sip ying*	NO PHOTOGRAPHY
肅靜	*suk jing*	SILENCE
此路不通	*gum jee t-owng hung*	NO ACCESS

Public buildings 公眾用途樓宇

醫院	*yee yu-een*	HOSPITAL
醫生	*yee sung*	DOCTOR
牙醫	*nga yee*	DENTIST
警署	*ging chu-ee*	POLICE (H.K.)
公安局	*gowng on guk*	POLICE (China)
銀行	*ngun hong*	BANK
郵局	*yau guk*	POST OFFICE
市政廳	*see jing teng*	TOWN HALL
的士站	*dick see jaam*	TAXI STAND [RANK] (H.K.)
出租汽車站	*chut' jo hay che jaam*	TAXI STAND [RANK] (China)
藥房	*yerk fong*	PHARMACY
游泳池	*yau wing chee*	SWIMMING POOL
公共游泳池	*gowng gowng yau wing chee*	PUBLIC SWIMMING POOL
博物館	*bock mut goon*	MUSEUM

GRAMMAR

In Cantonese, there are general numbers (listed opposite) used for talking about sums of money, telephone numbers, etc., and there is a system for combining a number with an object-specific *counter*. This system groups objects into types according to shape and size. Thus there are specific ways of counting flat objects, machines, animals, people, etc. When you are not sure of the correct counter, you can always try using the general numbers (**yut**, **yee**, **saam**, etc.) or better, the "all-purpose" counters listed below.

"All-purpose" counters

When you don't know the specific counter use:

1	yut gor	2	lurng gor*
3	saam gor	4	say gor
5	ng gor	6	luk gor
7	chut gor	8	baat gor
9	gau gor	10	sup gor

* When the number 2 is used with any counter the word **lurng** is used rather than **yee**, which is only used for general, arthimetical numbers.

If you don't know the specific counter for a bottle, use the "all-purpose" system, for example:

I'd like two bottles of beer.	I'd like two bottles of beer.
Yeeu lurng gor be jau.	**Yeeu lurng jun'** (or **jee**) **be jau.**
("all-purpose" counter)	(counter for bottles)

Note that the counter usually precedes the word it qualifies.

Other counters

Thin, flat objects (stamps, paper, etc.)		Small objects (indeterminate shape		Packets (any size)	
yut jurng	1	yut lup	1	yut bau	1
lurng jurng	2	lurng lup	2	lurng bau	2
saam jurng	3	saam lup	3	saam bau	3
say jurng	4	say lup	4	say bau	4
ng jurng	5	ng lup	5	ng bau	5

Numbers

Alongside the traditional system of numerals, the Chinese are also familiar with the written form of Western numerals, and you will find these used for telephone numbers, room numbers, and some prices.

0	零 *ling*	26	二十六	*yee sup luk*
1	一 *yut*	27	二十七	*yee sup chut*
2	二 *yee*	28	二十八	*yee sup baat*
3	三 *saam*	29	二十九	*yee sup gau*
4	四 *say*	30	三十	*saam sup*
5	五 *ng*	31	三十一	*saam sup yut*
6	六 *luk*	32	三十二	*saam sup yee*
7	七 *chut*	40	四十	*say sup*
8	八 *baat*	50	五十	*ng sup*
9	九 *gau*	60	六十	*luk sup*
10	十 *sup*	70	七十	*chut sup*
11	十一 *sup yut*	80	八十	*baat sup*
12	十二 *sup yee*	90	九十	*gau sup*
13	十三 *sup saam*	100	一百	*yut baak*
14	十四 *sup say*	101	一百零一	*yut baak ling yut*
15	十五 *sup ng*	102	一百零二	*yut baak ling yee*
16	十六 *sup luk*	200	二百	*yee baak*
17	十七 *sup chut*	500	五百	*ng baak*
18	十八 *sup baat*	1,000	一千	*yut chin*
19	十九 *sup gau*	10,000	一萬	*yut maan*
20	二十 *yee sup*	35,750	三萬五千七百五十	*saam maan ng chin chut baak ng sup*
21	二十一 *yee sup yut*			
22	二十二 *yee sup yee*	100,000	十萬	*sup maan*
23	二十三 *yee sup saam*	1,000,000	一百萬	*yut baak maan*
24	二十四 *yee sup say*			
25	二十五 *yee sup ng*			

Numerical expressions

first	第一	*daai yut*
second	第二	*daai yee*
third	第三	*daai saam*
fourth	第四	*daai say*
fifth	第五	*daai ng*
once	一次	*yut chee*
twice	兩次	*lurng chee*
three times	三次	*saam chee*
a half	一半	*yut boon*
half an hour	半小時	*boon seeu see*
half a tank	半個油箱	*boon gor yau surng*
half eaten	吃了一半	*sick jor yut boon*
a quarter	四分之一	*say fun jee yut*
a third	三分之一	*saam fun jee yut*
a pair of ...	一雙 ...	*yut dur-ee ...*
a dozen ...	一打 ...	*yut da ...*
1998	一九九八年	*yut gau gau baat nin*
2001	二零零一年	*yee ling ling yut nin*
the 1990s	九十年代	*gau sup nin doy*

Days 星期幾

Monday	禮拜一	*lai baai yut*
Tuesday	禮拜二	*lai baai yee*
Wednesday	禮拜三	*lai baai saam*
Thursday	禮拜四	*lai baai say*
Friday	禮拜五	*lai baai ng*
Saturday	禮拜六	*lai baai luk*
Sunday	禮拜日	*lai baai yaat*

Months 月份

January	一月 *yut yu-eet*
February	二月 *yee yu-eet*
March	三月 *saam yu-eet*
April	四月 *say yu-eet*
May	五月 *ng yu-eet*
June	六月 *luk yu-eet*
July	七月 *chut yu-eet*
August	八月 *baat yu-eet*
September	九月 *gau yu-eet*
October	十月 *sup yu-eet*
November	十一月 *sup yut yu-eet*
December	十二月 *sup yee yu-eet*

Dates 日期

It's ...	今天是 ... *gum yut hai ...*
July 10	七月十號 *chut yu-eet sup ho*
Tuesday, March 1	三月一號星期二 *saam yu-eet yut ho sing kay yee*
yesterday	昨天 *kum yut*
today	今天 *gum yut*
tomorrow	明天 *ting yut*
this .../last ...	這個 ... / 上個 ... *nay gor .../surng gor ...*
next week	下個星期 *ha gor sing kay*
every month/year	每月 / 年 *moo-ee yu-eet/nin*
on [at] the weekend	週末 *jau moot*

Seasons 季節

spring	春 *chun'*
summer	夏 *ha*
fall [autumn]	秋 *chau*
winter	冬 *d-owng*
in spring	在春天 *hai chun' tin*
during the summer	在夏天的時候 *hai ha tin ge see hau*

Greetings 祝賀

Happy birthday!	生日快樂！ *saang yut faai lock*
Merry Christmas!	聖誕快樂！ *sing daan faai lock*
Happy New Year!	新年快樂！ *sun nin faai lock*
Happy Easter!	復活節快樂！ *fuk woot jit faai lock*
Best wishes!	祝你一切順利！ *juk nay yut chai sun' lay*
Congratulations!	恭喜！ *g-owng hay*
Good luck!/All the best!	祝你好運／一切順利！ *juk nay ho wun/yut chai sun' lay*
Have a good trip!	旅途愉快！ *lur-ee to yu-ee faai*
Give my regards to …	請替我問候 … *cheng bong ngor mun hau …*

Public holidays 公眾假期

Hong Kong

January 1	New Year's Day
January/February	Lunar New Year *
April	Ching Ming Festival (Tomb Sweep Day)
May/June	Tuen Ng Festival
July 1	Hong Kong's return to China
October 1	National Day
October 6	Chinese Mid-Autumn Festival
October 28	Chung Yeung Festival
December 25 – 26	Christmas

Guangdong

There are seven official holidays for all Chinese people:

January 1	New Year's Day
Spring Festival *	Lunar New Year
May 1	International Labor Day
October 1 – 2	National Day

* 3 days in January or February, according to the lunar calendar

Macau

Macau celebrates New Year's Day and the lunar New Year as do Hong Kong and Guangdong. Other major holidays are:

April	Ching Ming Festival (Tomb Sweep Day)
March/April	Easter (4 days)
May/June	Dragon Boat Festival
September	Chinese Mid-Autumn Festival
October 28	Chung Yeung Festival
December 24 – 25	Christmas

Time 時間

In ordinary conversation time is expressed as shown above. For airline and train timetables, however, the 24-hour clock is used.

Despite the size of China, there is only one time zone. China is eight hours ahead of GMT all year round: it does not change its clocks to reflect winter and summer time.

Excuse me, can you tell me the time?	請問現在幾點了？	*cheng mun yee ga gay dim la*
It's …	現在是 …	*yee ga hai …*
five past one	一點零五分	*yut dim ling ng fun*
ten past two	兩點十分	*lurng dim sup fun*
a quarter past three	三點十五分	*saam dim sup ng fun*
twenty past four	四點二十分	*say dim yee sup fun*
twenty-five past five	五點二十五分	*ng dim yee sup ng fun*
half past six	六點半	*luk dim boon*
twenty-five to seven	六點三十五分	*luk dim saam sup ng fun*
twenty to eight	七點四十分	*chut dim say sup fun*
a quarter to nine	八點四十五分	*baat dim say sup ng fun*
ten to ten	九點五十分	*gau dim ng sup fun*
five to eleven	十點五十五分	*sup dim ng sup ng fun*
twelve o'clock (noon/midnight)	（正午／半夜）十二點	*(jing ng/boon ye) sup yee dim*

at dawn	黎明	*tin gwong*
in the morning	上午	*surng jau*
during the day	白天	*yut tau*
before lunch	午飯前	*sick aan chin*
after lunch	午飯後	*sick aan hau*
in the afternoon	下午	*ha jau*
in the evening	晚上	*ye maan*
at night	晚上	*ye maan*

I'll be ready in five minutes.	我五分鐘後會準備好。	*ngor ng fun j-owng hau duck*
He'll be back in a quarter of an hour.	他十五分鐘後回來。	*kur-ee sup ng fun j-owng hau faan lay*
She arrived half an hour ago.	她半小時前來到。	*kur-ee boon gor j-owng tau chin lay do*
The train leaves at …	火車將於 … 開出	*for che jurng yu-ee … hoy chut'*
13:04	十三時零四分	*sup saam see ling say fun*
0:40	零時四十分	*ling see say sup fun*
The train is 10 minutes late/early.	火車遲了 / 早了十分鐘	*for che chee jor/jo jor sup fun j-owng*
It's five minutes fast/slow.	快 / 慢五分鐘	*faai/maan ng fun j-wong*
from 9:00 to 5:00	由九點至五點	*yau gau dim jee ng dim*
between 8:00 and 2:00	八點至兩點之間	*baat dim jee lurng dim jee gaan*
I'll be leaving by …	我 … 之前走。	*ngor … jee chin jau*
Will you be back before …?	你 … 之前能回來嗎？	*nay … jee chin faan mm faan duck do lay*
We'll be here until …	我們會留在這裡直到 …	*ngor day woo-ee hai do lau do …*

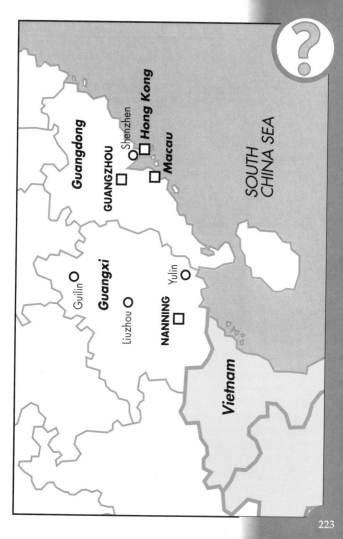

Guangdong

Guangxi

GUANGZHOU

Shenzhen

Hong Kong

Macau

NANNING

Guilin

Liuzhou

Yulin

Vietnam

SOUTH
CHINA SEA

Quick reference 快速參照

Good·morning.	早晨。	*jo sun*
Good afternoon/ evening.	你好。	*nay ho*
Hello./Good-bye.	你好。/再見。	*nay ho/joy g-in*
Excuse me. (getting attention)	請問。	*cheng mun/mm goy*
Excuse me? [Pardon?]	請再說一遍。	*cheng joy gong yut chee*
Sorry!	對不起！	*dur-ee mm ju-ee*
Please.	請	*cheng/mm goy*
Thank you.	謝謝	*dor je/mm goy*
Do you speak English?	你會說英語嗎？	*nay sick mm sick gong ying mun a*
I don't understand	我不明白。	*ngor mm ming*
Where is …?	… 在哪裡？	*… hai bin do a*
Where are the bathrooms [toilets]?	洗手間（廁所）在哪裡？	*sai sau gaan (chee sor) hai bin do a*

Emergency 緊急情況

Help!	救命啊！	*gau meng a*
Go away!	走開！	*jau hoy*
Leave me alone!	不要騷擾我！	*mm ho so yeeu ngor*
Call the police!	叫警察！	*geeu ging chaat (g-owng on)*
Stop thief!	捉賊呀！	*juk chaak a*
Get a doctor!	叫醫生！	*geeu yee sung*
Fire!	失火啦！	*for juk a*
I'm ill.	我不舒服。	*ngor mm su-ee fuk*
I'm lost.	我迷路了。	*ngor dong sut jor lo*
Can you help me?	你可以幫助我嗎？	*nay hor mm hor yee bong ha ngor*

Emergency ☎

Hong Kong/Macau **999**   Guandgong   (fire) **119**   (police) **110**

Embassies/Consulates (Hong Kong)

Australia: 2827 8881	Eire: 2826 2798
Canada: 2810 4321	U.K.: 2901 3000
New Zealand: 2877 4488	U.S.: 2530 1190

There are also consulates for Australia (331 2738) and the U.S. (888 8911) in Guangzhou.